CONFESSIONS
OF A
SHE-FAN

CONFESSIONS OF A SHE-FAN

THE COURSE OF TRUE LOVE
WITH THE NEW YORK YANKEES

JANE HELLER

RODALE

Rodale books may be purchased for business or promotional use or for special sales. For information, please write to:
Special Markets Department, Rodale Inc., 733 Third Avenue, New York, NY 10017

Printed in the United States of America
Rodale Inc. makes every effort to use acid-free ♾, recycled paper ♻.

Book design by Joanna Williams

Library of Congress Cataloging-in-Publication Data

Heller, Jane.
    Confessions of a she-fan : the course of true love with the New York Yankees / Jane Heller.
        p.   cm.
    Includes index.
    ISBN-13 978–1–59486–898–6 hardcover
    ISBN-10 1–59486–898–0 hardcover
    1. New York Yankees (Baseball team)   2. Heller, Jane.   3. Baseball fans—United States. I. Title.
GV875.N4H44 2009
796.357'64097471—dc22   2008028360

Distributed to the trade by Macmillan

2   4   6   8   10   9   7   5   3   1   hardcover

We inspire and enable people to improve their lives and the world around them
For more of our products visit **rodalestore.com** or call 800-848-4735

For Bruce Gelfand, My Friend and Coach

Acknowledgments

This book wouldn't have happened if not for the constant nudging of my friend Marty Bell, who said I should either write about my baseball addiction or get over it already.

It also wouldn't have happened if not for my enablers in the sports section at the *New York Times*. Columnist Harvey Araton was kind enough to pass along my "divorce essay" to his editor, Tom Jolly, who published the essay and unwittingly set the book in motion.

It wouldn't have happened without the efforts of my longtime literary agent, Ellen Levine, who champions me no matter what cockamamie subject I'm writing about.

Leigh Haber, my editor at Rodale, skillfully and diplomatically helped me cut 600 pages of ramblings down to size. She encouraged me at every turn, and I am extremely grateful for her enthusiasm. Thanks, too, to her competent and always upbeat assistant, Meredith Quinn.

Supportive friends Larry Brooks, Gary Paul Gates, Sandy and Doug McCartney, Kathy Sulkes, and Susan Tofias aided and abetted me in this venture, as did my sister, Susan Alexander, and my mother, Jocelyn Reznick.

Thanks to Matt Silverman and Cass Halpin of the Tampa Bay Rays for their generosity and to the Players Association's Gene Orza, who proved that chivalry is not dead.

My loudest cheers go to the members of the Yankees media corps who took time out from their hectic schedules to share their thoughts about the team:

Peter Abraham (the *Journal News*/LoHud.com), Mark Feinsand (*New York Daily News*), Tyler Kepner (the *New York Times*), George King (*New York Post*), Sweeny Murti (WFAN Radio), Kat O'Brien (*Newsday*), Jen Royle (MLB.com/YESNetwork.com), Charles Wenzelberg (*New York Post*), and especially John Sterling (WCBS Radio). Another round of cheers for Moss Klein (*Newark Star-Ledger*), who regaled me with tales from the *Bronx is Burning* years.

I interviewed several baseball "She-Fans" for this book, and I regret that the final draft of my manuscript didn't permit their inclusion. Thanks to Terry Lee Bilsky, Brenda Friend Brandt, Yvette Filce, Melodie Johnson Howe, and Kate Lagana for their insights.

My husband, Michael Forester, came along on my journey to Yankeeville. For that and for many other heroic gestures, I thank him.

CONFESSIONS
OF A
SHE-FAN

Prologue
August 6, 2007

A-Rod's eyes are the color of pistachio. I know this because I am staring straight into them right now. He and I are sharing a moment. Time is standing still. It feels as if there is nobody in the packed restaurant but the two of us, and I am dizzy, light-headed.

I try to steady myself, but he is larger than life in his blue jeans and green-striped polo shirt—not one of those 'roid guys with their cartoon muscles and huge, pimply heads, but "cut," as they say at the gym. Ripped. Sculpted. And the skin on his face is so smooth, without even the slightest stubble. I wonder if he gets it waxed.

I sip my Pinot Noir, set my glass down on the table, and moisten my lips before speaking his name.

His name. Oops. Which one should I use? A-Rod? Alex? Al? (Well, that is what his old high school buddy and current teammate Doug Mientkiewicz calls him.)

I will go with Al. I like the sound of it. It is charmingly blue-collar for a man with a $252 million contract.

On this August evening, we are in Toronto—the same city where he was photographed in May with that busty but rather butch-looking blonde . . . the same city where he nearly incited a brawl when he shouted "Hah!" or "Mine!" or "I got it!" as he was heading to third base and caused the Blue Jays' Howie Clark to drop the ball. So much history here, but tonight it is all about us, about our being together at Spuntini, a favorite ristorante of Joe Torre's that is only minutes from our hotel. Al and I are staying at the Park Hyatt in the trendy Yorkville neighborhood, as are all the Yankees, and we—

Okay.

He and I are not *together* together in Toronto. He is here because the Yankees are playing a three-game series against the Jays, and I am here because I am writing a book about whether or not I am a loyal Yankee fan. We have never met, let alone shared any "moments." It is my less-than-cut husband Michael who is sitting across the table from me, winding his Capellini Funghi around his fork, oblivious to the fact that we are in the presence of greatness. A-Rod, having stepped out from the private room where Torre is hosting a dinner, is merely walking past us on his way to the men's room.

"Can you follow him in there?" I whisper to Michael, to whom I have been married for 15 years. He claims to be a Yankee fan, but he was born and raised in Connecticut, a state that harbors Red Sox fans, so I am never 100 percent sure. Still, he came along with me on this 2-month odyssey, during which I am following the Yankees to every city and every game, and he seems to be enjoying himself. At least, he was.

He looks up from his pasta. "Run that by me again?"

I nod in the direction of the men's room. "That was A-Rod. He's taking a leak. Can you go in there and—"

"And what?" he says, fully engaged now and not in a good way.

"Just go in there after him and play it by ear."

"Play what by ear?"

"You know."

"Forget about it."

"Why?"

"You want me to check out how big it is and you're asking me why?"

"Maybe it's not big. Maybe it's really tiny. Maybe that's why he's so insecure."

Michael shakes his head as if I am insane and resumes eating.

"Look," I say, leaning in closer, "it's not like I'm asking you to give him a blow job. I just want you to follow him in there and strike up a conversation, tell him it's fantastic that he's leading the majors in homers and RBIs. Or act like you don't recognize him and talk about the weather or whatever it is men talk about in there."

"Men don't talk about anything in there."

"Ever?"

"No."

"Can't you make an exception? I need material for my book—a funny anecdote, a little story, something. I promised the publisher."

"I'm not going in there."

"*Come on!* Where's your sense of fun? Of adventure?"

"Not in that bathroom." Michael stabs his fork at a stray strand of pasta. "If you want to talk to him so badly, go in there yourself."

"You're so passive." This is the worst thing I can say to him.

"Oh, calm down." This is the worst thing he can say to me.

"I can't believe we're in the middle of a foreign country and you won't help me."

"We're in Canada, not Afghanistan."

"The point is I could lose this book contract if I don't get access to the players. We'll be homeless."

"Stop it."

"One simple favor. Please. If you really love me, you'll—"

A-Rod passes our table on his way back to dinner with Joe and the boys. I smile sweetly when it appears that he will look in my direction, but he does not. He faces forward without so much as a glance during his second lap through the restaurant. In an instant, he is gone.

"Great." I sink into my chair. "Another missed opportunity to meet a Yankee and write about it."

"You can write about how you had a fight with your husband."

"I didn't need to leave home for that."

Book One

you
broke
my
heart

Week 1
April 2, 2007

The Yankees always start slow. Offense takes a while to come around, especially ours. It's cold out there. The ball doesn't travel very well. You can't really say that to the media because it sounds like an excuse, but it's true. This team will score a ton of runs, and by the end of the year, we'll be right where we need to be.

A MEMBER OF THE 2007 YANKEES

It is Monday, Opening Day. I am beyond excited that the baseball season is finally here, that the Yankees are finally here. They are the love of my life.

I missed them so much during the long, cold, winter months. Okay, I live in Santa Barbara, California, so the winter months are not that cold. Still, I am always aching for news of them during the off-season, never mind actual video images of their pinstripes, and April can't come soon enough. Opening Day is about Possibility and Hope and Maybe This Year. It is better than Christmas. Better than birthdays. Better than sex. I will get to my husband in a second.

And yet even as I can't wait for the first pitch, I am dreading it, too. My Yankees have been picked by many sportswriters to win it all in 2007, but what if we don't make it past the ALDS like last year? What if we don't get to the postseason? What if we can't even beat the pathetic Devil Rays today? Open your heart to a baseball team and you're liable to get it broken.

Before you say I am working myself up for no good reason, I will give you a good reason: Joe Torre is sending Carl Pavano to the mound as our Opening

Day starter. Carl Fucking Pavano. The same guy who has not pitched in 643 days following a string of injuries that included a sore butt. The same guy who cracked up his Porsche and his ribs and neglected to tell anybody in the Yankees organization. The same guy who is so despised by his teammates that they papered his locker with the back covers of the New York tabloids that pictured him with the headline "Crash Test Dummy."

Apparently, there is no one else to send to the mound today. Pettitte and Moose are not lined up to pitch, and Wang is on the DL with a strained hamstring. The rotation is not just thin; it is anorexic.

And to add to my sense of foreboding on this otherwise joyous occasion, I will not be able to watch the game on TV. Major League Baseball made an exclusive deal with DirecTV for the Extra Innings package that broadcasts out-of-market games, and since I have cable, not a satellite dish, I am shut out.

"I should boycott the whole season," I announce to my husband as he is eating his Rice Krispies at 9:45 a.m. He is piling the cereal so high in the bowl that little Krispies are bouncing all over the floor. It is one of the many things he does that drive me nuts.

"We could get a dish," he says. His name is Michael Forester. He has a silvery-gray mustache and beard with wispy head-hair to match, although there is not much head-hair to speak of anymore. I honestly think he gets balder every time I look. He wears glasses and is 6 feet tall and has the craggy appearance of a sailor or a photographer, both of which he is. He also has a soft, whispery voice that reminds everyone of Clint Eastwood's, and he is very quiet and even-tempered—the opposite of me. He once accused me of loving the Yankees more than I love him, and I scoffed at the notion. It is simply that he is the old ball and chain whose laundry I do, and the Yankees are, well, the Yankees.

"We can't get a dish," I remind him. We live way up in the hills. We get not only the big-time Santa Anas but also Sundowner winds that whip through the canyons at night, especially in the spring and summer. A dish would not have a chance up here.

I disappear into my office and follow the game on my computer. Who am I kidding? I could never boycott baseball. Most of my women friends think it is peculiar—freakish, even—that I am such a fan. They cannot fathom how I can get manicures and color my hair but would much rather talk about Johnny Damon than Jimmy Choo. They are still amazed that I declined an invitation to a baby shower because the Yankees were playing the Red Sox and the game was on Fox. "Why can't you just TiVo it?" my friend Renee suggested. There was no way to explain, except to say that I would never attend a baby shower during a Yankees–Red Sox game, not even if the baby in question was my own.

Why baseball and not football or basketball? I love that there is a slow pace; the games are so leisurely, I can read a book or clean the house or check my e-mail and not miss much. I love that there is no time clock; a game lasts as long as it lasts. I love that there is a matchup between a pitcher and batter; it is a contest within a contest. I love that I can see the players' faces; they are not hidden behind protective equipment. I love that the game is multifaceted; there is hitting and pitching and running and fielding. I love that the athletes are such a mixed bag of characters; they are wily veterans and unripe kids and everything in between. And I love that I can understand it; I don't have to be a math genius to figure out the rules. Come to think of it, there is nothing I don't love about baseball, except that it ends every fall.

Today's game starts at 10:00 a.m. here on the West Coast. I am a writer of novels—13 romantic comedies that have sold to Hollywood and provided me with a healthy income but have yet to be made into movies. I am supposed to be working on a new novel, but instead I procrastinate. I sit in front of my computer and "watch" the game as well as post entries on a Yankees blog. I have a macho screen name on the blog—I am known as Bronx Bad Ass—because I noticed that women who call themselves things like Yankee Princess are either disparaged or dismissed. Everybody on the blog assumes I am a guy, and I get a kick out of it when they answer my posts with "Listen, dude." Today, we are all trying to outdo each other with our insulting remarks about Pavano, the general consensus being that he has "shit the bed."

Carl only goes 4½ innings, allowing five runs (four earned), but the Yanks beat the Devil Rays 9–5, thanks in part to A-Rod's two-run homer.

I feel much better with our first victory under my belt. I allow myself to relax, to smile, to look forward to the rest of the day. When the Yankees win, I have a sense that all is right with the world. I have never been good at losing, although as a tennis player I was not very good at winning. I had a killer forehand but was not a killer myself. I would make it to the finals of tournaments, only to fold. As a Yankee fan, I never fold.

The second game of the series against Tampa Bay on the 4th is rained out, but the third on the 5th results in a 7–6 loss in what is supposed to be Pettitte's triumphant return to the Bronx. The Yankees commit three errors, three wild pitches, and a passed ball. I tell myself it takes a few days to iron out the kinks, that there is no cause for concern. I am just glad I am able to watch the games on TV now. Major League Baseball and the cable companies made a deal after all. I am not being shut out.

The Yankees open a weekend series against the Orioles, and it turns out that there may be cause for concern. Mussina is a dud in Friday night's loss, and Damon sits out the game with a strained right calf.

Igawa gives up seven runs in his major league debut on Saturday, and Matsui goes on the DL with a strained hamstring. A pattern is emerging already—every starter will pitch badly and every position player will get injured—and I don't like it. A-Rod hits two more homers, including a grand slam in the bottom of the ninth that wins the game. I can only hope his homer thing is a pattern, too.

He goes deep again in Sunday's game, but our rookie starter, Darrell Rasner, is so shaky that Pettitte has to pitch in relief, and the Yankees lose the game and the series to the Orioles. *The Orioles.* Come on.

I know, I know. It is only the end of the first week of the season. But I am slightly uneasy, skittish. I am yelling derogatory things at the TV when Michael and I watch the games together, forcing him to withdraw into his sailing magazines. He used to get a kick out of how "spirited" a fan I was. Now he looks at me with bewilderment.

"I thought you couldn't wait for the season to start," he says as the O's congratulate each other on the field.

"I couldn't," I say, giving Kevin Millar the finger.

"Then why do you seem so miserable?"

I suppose this is where I should just flat-out admit that the quality of my days and nights is significantly influenced by whether the Yankees win or lose. Which is another way of saying that I can't bear it when they lose. Which is another way of saying that I want them to win every game—and not in tight pitchers' duels; I prefer blowouts.

But I didn't always have such nutty expectations. I used to view baseball as a simple, innocent pleasure. My father died of a brain tumor when I was 6, so our house was not a cheery place for a child—except when my two grandpas came over on Sunday afternoons to pick up the paternal slack. They would settle into their chairs in the den, light up their La Primadora cigars, watch Yankee games on our black-and-white Zenith TV, and teach my older sister Susan and me how to keep score with our pencils and pads. Mickey Mantle would hit a home run and everybody would clap, and suddenly the atmosphere was festive instead of funereal. For those few hours I could forget that I was the only kid in first grade whose daddy was absent on Parents' Day. For those few hours I could block out all the grownups' scary, mysterious whispers about hospitals and seizures and cancer. For those few hours I could parrot the funny words I heard on TV—*bunt* and *chin music* and *safety squeeze*—and be pals with Grandpa Lou and Grandpa Max. Who cared that I had absolutely no idea what the words meant? Baseball made me happy. The Yankees made me happy. They were something to hang on to, to believe in.

I know people hate the "Evil Empire" because they always win and always spend money and always grab headlines. To me they are not evil; they are royalty. They continue to provide a kind of No-Sadness Zone where the skies are bluer and the grass is greener—an escape—but the pinstripes also symbolize excellence and achievement and brilliance. When the Yankees win, I have this notion that their brilliance somehow rubs off on me.

AL EAST STANDINGS/APRIL 8

TEAM	W	L	PCT	GB
TORONTO	3	2	.600	—
BOSTON	3	3	.500	0.5
NEW YORK	2	3	.400	1.0
TAMPA BAY	2	3	.400	1.0
BALTIMORE	2	4	.333	1.5

Week 2
April 9, 2007

Players never panic. The fans panic. Especially Yankee fans. They're so used to having the most amazing talent that they don't understand how hard it is to hit .300 from April 1 to September 30. You can't do it. I don't care who you are.

He is right. I am panicking. The Yankees are not off to a good start. There is no consistency. We cannot get any momentum going. And we are riddled with injuries to the point where Cashman fires the team's fitness coach. Things just feel—I don't know—wrong somehow.

Here is an example. We beat the Twins on the 9th and 10th, thanks to A-Rod, who hits a homer in both games. I definitely brighten whenever he comes to the plate now instead of hiding my eyes like I did last year. But then we lose the finale on the 11th. Mussina departs early with a strained hamstring, and Farnsworth gives up four runs in a third of an inning, causing me to hurl abuses at him. I don't love his geeky glasses or his titanium necklace that is supposed to promote positive energy flow. Please. He doesn't get batters out, and he sulks while he's at it.

The A's arrive at the Stadium on Friday, and we lose to them in 11 innings. Igawa is unimpressive again, but it is Farnsworth who serves up the homer in the seventh to tie the game at 4–4. We have to ship this guy back to wherever he came from and get someone else. We beat Oakland on Saturday—yes, A-Rod hits another bomb—but lose to the A's on Sunday in a heartbreaking and disturbing way: Mo gives up a three-run homer with two outs in the bottom of the ninth to Marco Scutaro. He tells the media he is fine, but I will tell you who is not fine: Pavano and Mussina. They both go on the 15-day DL. This is why I am panicking. I have developed intermittent headaches and am ready to go on the 15-day DL myself.

AL EAST STANDINGS/APRIL 15

TEAM	W	L	PCT	GB
BOSTON	6	4	.600	—
TORONTO	7	5	.583	—
BALTIMORE	6	6	.500	1.0
NEW YORK	5	6	.455	1.5
TAMPA BAY	5	7	.417	2.0

Week 3
April 16, 2007

*I don't know if they're superstitions or habits, but yeah, I have them.
Like if we won last night, I'll take the exact same way to the park the
next day, whether there's traffic or not. And if we're really rolling, I'll
eat the same thing until we lose. I'm not the only one, either. Joe holds
Derek's bat during every game. And every time Joe goes to the mound,
Derek taps him on the N-Y. We all have our stuff.*

Cleveland comes into town for three games, and we finally
have a punching bag. We sweep them. Chase Wright, the rookie pitcher
du jour, wins his major league debut, but the series is all about A-Rod. He hits
a homer in each game, and I am starting to fall for him in that way women fall
for men who come to their rescue. He is coming to my rescue right now. He is
a big, strong, good-looking hero who is giving me a reason to think that the
Yankees will pull out of this funk. My only bone to pick with him is that he
uses too much gloss. A hero who comes to your rescue should not have lips that
are shinier and plumper than yours.

Like many fans, I am superstitious, and it is this weekend against the Red Sox
at Fenway that this personality quirk of mine pops out like a rash. I remind
myself that it is only April and the division title is not at stake, plus all the other
bullshit things you say in an attempt not to descend into the madness that is
this rivalry. Nothing works.

I can't decide what to wear for the game or where to sit.

I have lucky clothes. If I am wearing my Bernie Williams T-shirt and the Yankees win, I will wear the Bernie Williams T-shirt until they lose. Only then does it go into the hamper, and only then do I pull out the Derek Jeter T-shirt.

I have lucky food. If I eat pasta for dinner and the Yankees win, I will eat pasta for dinner until they lose, then switch to, say, turkey burgers.

I have lucky sitting/standing positions. The living room's sitting options are the white sofa directly across from the TV or one of the two club chairs, which are slipcovered in a nubby green fabric, have ottomans, and are sort of like chic Barcaloungers. If I am sitting on the sofa when the Yankees win, I will sit on the sofa—on the same cushion—until they lose, then either move to one of the chairs for the next game or watch it standing directly in front of the TV. And speaking of TVs, we have two in our house. If I am watching the one in the living room and the Yankees lose, I will move to the one in the bedroom the next time.

I never invite friends over to watch a game, not since Laurie and Peter Grad came for dinner during game seven of the 2001 World Series. It was not Mo's fault that the Diamondbacks scored off him in the ninth. It was *my* fault for turning my head away from the TV to offer Laurie and Peter some chocolate mousse cake with crème fraîche. I will not make that mistake again.

And I pray for the Yankees in actual churches. I am a nice Jewish girl from Scarsdale, but my nonbeliever mother sent me to Camp Birchmere, a quasi-Christian sleepaway camp where I sang the doxology before every Sunday dinner for eight summers. I have been drawn to churches ever since—not to their dogma but to their rituals, their majesty, their beauty. In fact, Michael and I went to the Easter vigil at the Santa Barbara Mission on Saturday night. A historic landmark in California, the Old Mission is also a thriving Catholic parish, and the place was overflowing with worshippers. During the candlelight service, I made sure to throw in an appeal for the Yanks. "At the very least, please don't let them embarrass me in Boston" is how I put it.

These maneuvers are simply my attempt to feel that I am in control over baseball situations when, in fact, I have no control over them whatsoever. I hate that.

The opener at Fenway on the 20th is a matchup between Schilling and Pettitte, and neither gets the decision. A-Rod hits not one but two homers, passing Willie Stargell and Stan Musial on the all-time list with 476. We are ahead 6–2 until the eighth, when Joe goes to Mo for a five-out save. I like Joe. I do. But

I disapprove of his use of Mo in the eighth. To prove my point, Mo gives up a single to Varitek, a triple to Crisp, and a single to Cora, and we lose 7–6. I despise Red Sox fans for many reasons, one of which is that they cannot seem to let go of their bitterness toward the Yankees, even though *they* were the ones who won the damn World Series in 2004. Get over your sad and pathetic history, people, and move on! But what really galls me is how they brag that their players have "figured Mo out" and that their closer, Jonathan "Pap Smear" Papelbon, is better. Come back to me when he has over 400 saves.

We lose the Saturday game, too. This time it is by the score of 7–5. It is remarkable that we almost win, given that our starter is a kid named Jeff Karstens and their starter is their ace, Josh Beckett, and that David Ortiz—"Big Sloppy"—drives in four runs. There is nothing more sickening than watching that guy hang all over the plate and never having our pussy pitchers knock him on his ass.

We lose the finale on Sunday 7–6. The Red Sox sweep. Chase Wright, the rookie pitcher from the other night, gives up four consecutive home runs in the third inning, equaling a major league record. I gnash my teeth as I watch Manny, Drew, Lowell, and Varitek round the bases. Maybe God has a different idea than I do regarding what constitutes embarrassment. Or maybe He didn't hear me at the Easter vigil because Easter is His peak season and He was overbooked.

After the game on Sunday night, Michael and I argue about Brian Cashman, of all people. I say the Yankees keep losing because of the crappy pitchers he is putting on the mound, and Michael says it is not Cashman's fault that Wang and Mussina are on the DL.

"He's using the rookies because he has no choice," he says.

"What about Igawa and Pavano?" I counter. "He must have been delusional to think the Yankees could win with them in the rotation."

"Winning." He shakes his head in disapproval. "You're supposed to appreciate the journey, not just the destination."

"Money doesn't grow on trees, a watched pot never boils, and two wrongs don't make a right. Got it."

"My point is that you should enjoy watching the games. Why are they such torture for you?"

When did I become the sort of fan who takes baseball so seriously? When did the simple pleasure of watching my team evolve into an all-consuming lust for victory?

Not in my teenage years, although lust of another sort figured prominently. I was in high school when I developed major crushes on ballplayers. I loved Mickey, of course, and had pictures of him taped to the walls of my bedroom right next to my Beatles posters. But in 11th and 12th grades, I branched out and started focusing on other, lesser players like Steve Whitaker, who wore number nine, played right field, and was very, very cute. My fantasy was to date a Yankee and marry a Yankee and have lots of Yankee children. Never mind that most of the Yankees were already married; I was oblivious to their real lives. And never mind that I was a virgin with no clue how to be anything else; in my imagination, my special Yankee and I would flirt and hold hands and maybe even make out, but that was the extent of it. I wanted to know how to meet my Yankee, go on dates with him, and still get my homework done.

Susan, my older sister, was engaged to Bob, a lawyer who lived in the city in an apartment next door to three girls—three girls who happened to be baseball groupies. He introduced me, and they were kind enough to coach me in the art. All I had to do was swap my teenybopper, suburban look for an older, more provocative one, show up at the ballpark for batting practice, and hang out near the railing acting "approachable." This was before Yankee Stadium was policed by security people who eject you for even thinking about acting approachable. "If a player likes you, he'll send an usher to get your phone number," said Barb, the ringleader.

I was a senior at Scarsdale High when the '68 season began. I was ready to head to Yankee Stadium to snag myself a player. There was just one problem: I didn't have a car. I needed an accomplice. And it couldn't be one of the boys with whom I often went to games. I didn't troll for players when I was at the Stadium with my buddies Bubba, Jimmy, Christy, and Steve; I actually watched baseball with them. Besides, I would look unavailable if I were sitting with a *guy*.

Lee Eisner was my friend from Camp Birchmere. She had no interest in baseball, but she had a bronze Mustang. I convinced her that it would be fun to go out with a Yankee or at least try to.

We hatched a plan. Each time we ventured to the Bronx, we told our parents we were going to the library or someplace equally benign-sounding. We would hop on the Major Deegan and change into our slutty clothes once we got to the ballpark. We would tease our hair and go heavy-handed on the makeup and put on very short skirts and tight tops. Neither of us had a boyfriend nor a clue what to do with one; we were baffled by the mechanics of actual sex. Lee once used the shift of her car to demonstrate to me how to give a guy a hand job, but questions remained about how fast, how slow, when to stop.

We would arrive 2 hours before the game, buy tickets, strut down to the front row of the field boxes, and hover. There were no guards in those days, so nobody chased us away.

"Hey, Pepitone!" I would shout. "That was some shot you hit yesterday!"

"Thanks," he would say and come over to talk to us.

It was thrilling. When the players went into the dugout after BP, we would maintain our position and wait for an usher to show up to secure our names and numbers. It didn't happen. Not at first.

But then one of the players did call us. Well, he called me. Lee and I had gone to batting practice the day before, decked out like hookers, and I was chatting up Ruben Amaro, who was probably old enough to be my father. He asked for my number and I gave it to him, never imagining that he would use it.

I was getting ready for school in the morning when the phone rang. My mother answered it. She knocked on my bedroom door looking suspicious.

"A man named Ruben is asking for Juanita," she said, tightening the sash around her bathrobe.

I felt my heart lurch. "He's my Spanish teacher."

Before my mother could remember that I took French that year, I ran downstairs to the phone in the kitchen. It had a long cord so I could stretch it out and talk in the hallway.

"Hello?" I whispered. "This is Juanita. I mean, Jane."

"This is Ruben," he said. "Did I wake you up?"

"I had to get up for school. I have a calculus test this morning."

"How about you and your pretty friend meet me and a friend tonight at Stella D'oro?"

Stella D'oro? Wasn't that a breadstick?

"The restaurant," he clarified. "Off the Deegan in the Bronx."

"Sounds like fun," I said, wondering what excuse I would give my parents this time.

"See you later," said Ruben.

Oh my God! Lee and I were going on a date! With two Yankees! That very night!

I was not interested in marrying Ruben Amaro, but he was the Yankee who called, not Mickey Mantle or even Steve Whitaker, so we went. Lee's date was a player neither of us can remember now. What we do remember is that the four of us sat at a table at Stella D'oro, had something to eat and drink, and flirted. But when the two Yankees reached for us and tried to kiss us on the lips, we would not let them. They were very sweet about it—they did not call us cock teases or throw drinks on us—but they realized we were not groupies after all, just a couple of chaste princesses from Westchester.

The incident emboldened us. We'd had a brush with sex and survived, so we kept going to batting practice to get picked up by Yankees.

Eventually word spread that we were not worth the trouble. Undaunted, I asked the girls who lived next door to my now brother-in-law for introductions to players on other teams, just for kicks. For example, I had drinks with two relief pitchers from the California Angels when they were in New York to play the Yanks: a journeyman named George Brunet and the infamous spitballer Jack Hamilton. I met them at a bar on Manhattan's Upper East Side and got drunk on screwdrivers, the only alcoholic beverage I could think of to order. George and Jack were very large men who seemed amused by how much I knew about baseball and treated me like their kid sister.

In the summer of '68, Lee and I took our act to France. We spent 2 months on the Riviera meeting cute French boys and then refusing to have sex with them, too. Lee just said no to them, but I was more creative. I carried a picture of Mickey Mantle in my wallet and when a boy got a little too friendly, I whipped out Mickey's picture, pointed to it, and said, "*Mon fiancé. Je l'aime.*"

AL EAST STANDINGS/APRIL 22

TEAM	W	L	PCT	GB
BOSTON	12	5	.706	—
BALTIMORE	11	7	.611	1.5
NEW YORK	8	9	.471	4.0
TORONTO	8	10	.444	4.5
TAMPA BAY	7	11	.389	5.5

Week 4
April 23, 2007

Everything's contagious in baseball. How many times do you see a guy make a good play and then somebody else makes a good play? Then there's a game where the ball hits off a guy's glove, and then another ball doesn't get run down in the gap. Winning is contagious. Unfortunately, so is losing.

After the sweep at Fenway, I start watching the games with a new wariness—an increased sense that this team, with its undeveloped rookies and its creaky vets, does not have it.

Here is why: On the 23rd and 24th, we lose two to the Devil Rays at Tropicana Field. If that is not the depths of misery, I don't know what is. Igawa stinks up the first game, allowing seven runs. And Wang, fresh off the DL, starts the second game, only to have Myers serve up a grand slam to Carl Crawford.

Joe Torre says it is too early to panic, but the Yankees are officially panicking. They announce that Phil Hughes, the pitching prospect whose golden arm was supposed to get a full year of seasoning down on the farm, will make his major league debut versus Toronto on the 25th. It feels like a desperation move instead of a promotion.

It is on this night that the insomnia starts. I don't sleep well when the Yankees lose, but I don't sleep at all when they are in the cellar.

The first of the two-game home stand against Toronto is rained out on the 25th, so Hughes makes his debut on the 26th. He is not the phenom I was hoping for. We lose 6–0. Now the bats are cold, too. According to

Michael Kay on the YES Network, the Yankees are off to their worst 20-game start since 1991.

I picture the Yankees team from 1991. They were a sad, sad group that year except for Mattingly, but—come to think of it—I didn't get upset about losing in those days. I was still the sort of fan who enjoyed watching them no matter how badly they played. No rants about whether they were trying hard enough. No superstitious behavior in an effort to nudge them to victory. No gnashing of teeth. No insomnia. I just loved them and that was that, to honor and to cherish, for better or worse.

That is also the year I starting dating Michael. I was separated from my second husband and renting a house in Connecticut and figuring I would be off men for the rest of my life. I was 0-for-2, after all. But then I was set up with Michael at a friend's dinner party, and he called a few days later, asking if he could stop by.

"Thanks, but I'm really busy right now," I said.

"With what? It's Sunday afternoon."

"I'm watching a Yankees game. They're getting killed, but they could always come back."

"I'm a Yankee fan," said Michael. "I'll watch the game with you."

"If you want."

Even then I put baseball first. I don't know why he didn't run like hell in the other direction, but instead he drove right over.

I fell in love with him for many reasons. He is a guy's guy who knows about race cars and can fix household gadgets and thinks being on a sailboat during a storm is fun. He is also a sensitive soul who is not afraid to tear up when something moves him. It didn't hurt that he had a bearded-photographer, *Bridges of Madison County* hero look that I found rather appealing.

But I also fell in love with him because we shared a passion for the Yankees.

"When I was 13, I broke my ankle playing football with my friends," he told me that Sunday afternoon. "My father wanted to take me to the hospital, but I just knew Roger Maris would hit his 60th home run that day. I refused to go until the game was over."

I almost said "I love you" right then and there. But we continued to watch the Yankees get creamed, and I kept my emotional outbursts focused on my team.

"I like how you're not all about winning," he said when he saw how hard I cheered.

Poor guy. As all too often happens with couples, he thought he was marrying one person and ended up with someone else.

⚜

On Friday the 27th, the Yankees host the Red Sox for the first of three games at the Stadium. Having barely recovered from the last series against them, I am not looking forward to this one.

"I'll die if we get swept again," I tell Michael as the game starts.

"Stop being so negative," he says before going outside to fire up the grill. We are having barbecued chicken for dinner. The spaghetti and the turkey burgers did not help us beat Boston last time, so I insisted on a change in the menu.

The barbecued chicken is a bust. We lose ugly—11–4—with Pettitte allowing five runs. Proctor, Vizcaino, and Mo are awful, too. Yes, Mo. The only bright spot is Jeter's 15-game hitting streak.

We actually win the Saturday game 3–1, although there is more bad news. Karstens gets smacked in the knee in the first inning by a line drive off the bat of Lugo. A cracked fibula. I am not making this up!

The rubber match on Sunday is a horror show—a 7–4 loss thanks to Wang and the split fingernail that is inhibiting him from throwing his good sinker. I know pitchers are fragile creatures, but am I supposed to believe that the Yankees can't find a medical professional to deal with a fingernail? At the very least, Mrs. Wang must have a good manicurist and/or a tube of Krazy Glue.

The New York papers are fueling speculation that Joe could be out of a job if the team continues its free fall.

"Hopefully, we can catch a good streak here real soon," Damon is quoted as saying.

I have come to like Johnny Damon. I loathed him as a Red Sock, of course, but he is always upbeat and cheerful and usually makes contact at the plate. Abreu, on the other hand, is high on my shit list. He is in the worst offensive slump of his career, and he plays right field as if he is terrified of getting his uniform dirty. Just once I would like to see him dive for a ball.

"They need someone to motivate them," I tell Michael as he turns off the TV. "I wish I could talk to them."

"And say what?"

"That there is behavior I will not tolerate."

He rolls his eyes, lifts the cordless phone off its cradle, and hands it to me. "Call the dugout. Maybe they're still there."

He is joking, but I am not. I grab the phone. "What's the area code for Tampa? I'm calling Steinbrenner."

"You've turned into a female George."

"There are worse things," I say. "He's a great owner."

"A great owner?"

"All those championships wouldn't have happened without him," I say. "He spoiled me. I'm used to winning now."

There. I said it. I am used to winning. If there were a 12-step program for Yankee fans whose innocent passions became hardcore addictions in '96 when we began our run under Torre, I would be chairing the meetings.

"My name is Jane, and I am a Yankeeholic."

AL EAST STANDINGS/APRIL 29

TEAM	W	L	PCT	GB
BOSTON	16	8	.667	—
TORONTO	12	12	.500	4.0
BALTIMORE	12	13	.480	4.5
TAMPA BAY	11	14	.440	5.5
NEW YORK	9	14	.391	6.5

Week 5
April 30, 2007

Joe was getting 100 percent from everybody. We had a guy we respected—as a manager, as a man, as a friend, almost as a father. Everybody who walked through that tunnel gave everything they had every single night. Sometimes you don't get that. Sometimes you hear "I'm tired today." But I never heard that from any of the guys.

Yesterday the Boss issued a statement through Howard Rubenstein saying he supports the manager and the team. Like all Steinbrenner Statements, this one carries a not-so-veiled threat: The Yankees had better start winning or else. I could not agree more.

But it is a new month and a fresh start for the Yanks. They open a three-game series against the Rangers in Arlington. On May 1, we kick Texas around 10–1. Phil Hughes throws a no-hitter going into the seventh for his first major league victory but leaves the game with a hamstring injury. Can you catch hammies the way you catch herpes? And Damon is out with a back problem. The guy is going all Carl Pavano on us.

May 2 is my birthday, and the game is rained out, which means I am forced to actually celebrate my big day by leaving the house. Michael takes me to the Plow & Angel at the posh San Ysidro Ranch in Montecito. The waiters bring out a dessert with a candle on top and sing "Happy Birthday" to me. I am mortified because I am not the type who enjoys being sung to by waiters and because I am at that age where it is not a huge thrill to be another year older. Forget what all those rah-rah baby boomer women say about how great it is to have wisdom and experience and disposable income. I would rather have fewer wrinkles and perkier tits.

We play a doubleheader on May 3 to make up for the rained-out game, and we win both contests. Pettitte gets the victory in the opener, and Mussina, just activated from the DL, allows only one run over five innings. I take back the nasty things I said about him, but I wish I could warm to him. He is serious whenever he is on TV, kind of sourpussy. I wonder if he bows from the waist during sex, the way he bows out of the stretch.

We are home for a four-game set against Seattle this weekend, and the results are mixed. The Friday-night game on May 4 is an abomination. We lose 15–11, and the Mariners have 20 fucking hits. I boo the TV. Michael boos, too, and he hardly ever boos the TV. We rebound with an 8–1 victory on Saturday, with Wang missing a perfect game by only five outs. Sunday's game involves a near-brawl after the Mariners bean Josh Phelps for his hard slide into Johjima, their catcher, and Proctor returns the favor by throwing behind Betancourt. Darrell Rasner and four relievers combine for a four-hit shutout, and the Yankees win. But the big event is the announcement during the seventh-inning stretch that Roger Clemens, who speaks to the masses from George's private box like the pope, will return to the Yankees in late May/early June.

I am conflicted about the Rocket's return. I don't blame the Yanks for wanting reinforcements. But why bring back a guy with a history of groin problems and hammy problems and God knows what else? He is old in pitcher years. Besides, we threw him a farewell tour when he was retiring 2 years ago, only to have him unretire and play for the Astros. What kind of scumbag does that to the Yankees? What kind of slimy, ungrateful worm leaves and then comes crawling back?

AL EAST STANDINGS/MAY 6

TEAM	W	L	PCT	GB
BOSTON	20	10	.667	—
NEW YORK	14	15	.483	5.5
BALTIMORE	14	17	.452	6.5
TAMPA BAY	14	17	.452	6.5
TORONTO	13	18	.419	7.5

Week 6
May 7, 2007

I hated Roger Clemens from playing against him. Couldn't stand the guy. But he made us better. He made us believe in ourselves. He gave little pep talks to individual players. Like to Bobby, he said, "When I faced you in Philly, you were the toughest out in the league. Where is that guy?" He would challenge you, but he would be behind you.

While I wait for Clemens to take his spot in the rotation, I am saddled with more rookies. The latest is Matt DeSalvo, no relation to Albert DeSalvo, the Boston Strangler, as far as I know. He only allows a run in the May 7 finale against the Mariners, but Mo serves up a homer to Beltre in the ninth and takes the loss. I love Mo and can't imagine my Yankee fan life without him, but I love him more when he strikes batters out with his rising cutter. At least Igawa is out of the picture now. He is sent down to Class A Tampa to learn how to pitch here in America. He is in danger of becoming the next Hideki Irabu. George will not call him a fat pussy toad because Howard Rubenstein is speaking for him these days, but I am thinking that a putdown involving the word *pussy* would not be entirely out of line.

Texas comes into town for three games. Pettitte pitches a gem in the first game. Mussina looks like his old self in the second. But the finale on the 10th results in an embarrassing 14–2 loss in which Wang allows seven runs in 6⅓ innings. He is supposed to be our ace, but his inconsistency is emblematic of the team as a whole. We cannot get a streak going. We are stuck in mediocrity while the Red Sox are cruising. I grind my teeth so hard that I knock my jaw out of alignment.

⌇

The Yankees fly to Seattle for the start of a nine-game road trip. The change of scenery will be good for the players, the way a change of scenery is good for people who are sick and convalescing. But the Yanks lose two of three to the Mariners. What is alarming about all three games is that we don't score. First the pitching was impotent. Now the bats are limp. As for me, I am descending into a state of perpetual crabbiness, as if I have a chronic case of PMS. I am short with people. I don't return phone calls right away. I curse a lot—for no good fucking reason. This is what the Yankees are reducing me to. They are not holding up their end of the bargain. They were supposed to be my escape, and they are not doing their job.

What do I have to escape from? That is what you are probably asking yourself. I write all these funny novels and live in paradise and am married to the sensitive manly-man from *The Bridges of Madison County*. What's the problem?

Crohn's disease. That is what Michael has. It is an autoimmune disease that can cause the intestines to become inflamed and, ultimately, obstructed, and it is not pretty. I had never heard of it when Michael and I met in 1991. When he told me he had it, I shrugged and said, "Love conquers all." Love does not conquer Crohn's. He has had more than 30 surgeries, been hospitalized more than 50 times, and taken countless drugs, including steroids. He has spent more time doubled over in pain than anyone I know. He is at constant risk from complications. He is always one step away from the emergency room. He is the one who suffers and soldiers on, and I am merely the helpmate. But I would be lying if I said that living with a spouse who has a chronic, incurable illness is not difficult and often depressing. It is hard on a marriage, in other words. When the Yankees are winning, it gives me the illusion that there is no Crohn's and life is beautiful. But the Yankees are not winning. They are not delivering my required dose of denial.

AL EAST STANDINGS/MAY 13

TEAM	W	L	PCT	GB
BOSTON	25	11	.694	—
BALTIMORE	18	20	.474	8.0
NEW YORK	17	19	.472	8.0
TAMPA BAY	15	22	.405	10.5
TORONTO	15	22	.405	10.5

Week 7
May 14, 2007

When you scuffle and hit adversity, you bond together stronger than ever. It's easy to play the game when you're winning every day. It's tougher when things aren't going well. You've got to find your way to: "I'm not gonna take this anymore."

The Yankees fly to Chicago for three against the White Sox. The May 15 game is rained out. We split a doubleheader against them the next day, then lose the finale on the 17th. There is no excuse for dropping two of three to the 2007 White Sox, a team that bears no resemblance to the 2005 World Series champions. They are even more pathetic than we are, and yet we can't seem to beat the fucking shit out of those cocksuckers.

And it gets worse. Our first interleague series of the season pits us against the Mets at Shea.

We lose game one on Friday night despite Pettitte's solid outing.

We lose game two on Saturday night despite A-Rod's homer. Cano's three errors don't help. Neither does the fact that Darrell Rasner only pitches to two batters before breaking his index finger.

It is this particular game that unravels me. In the fourth inning, I explode in frustration—I want to rip the plasma screen off the wall. I start flinging objects everywhere—the TV remote, a copy of *Newsweek,* a hunk of Gorgonzola from my Cobb salad. The cheese lands in Michael's beard and nests there.

"What's the matter with you!" he shouts. "You're being a complete asshole!"

"It's the Yankees' fault."

I *am* being an asshole. But I feel betrayed by these 2007 Yankees. They are pretenders, not contenders. I am spending my days and nights watching these clowns, and for what? So they can keep me from writing my novel, which is how I earn my living? So they can ruin my social life, which I no longer have since I traded dinners out with friends for turkey burgers with the YES Network? So they can create tension in my marriage, which is now on shaky ground because I have been driven to throwing hunks of cheese at my husband?

I sit quietly, like a good girl, and watch the rest of the game. I am the model of decorum—until the Mets start high-fiving each other.

"That's it!" I stand and face Michael, who is skimming through the latest issue of *WoodenBoat*. If he were a real Yankee fan instead of the Connecticut-born Red Sox fan I suspect him of being, he would be throwing cheese, too.

"What's 'it'?"

"My relationship with the Yankees. It's over. I'm done with their injuries and their excuses and their dysfunctions. I'm divorcing them."

This gets his attention. "You don't mean it. You'll be back tomorrow."

"I will not be back. I am suing them for divorce. Mental cruelty."

He laughs. "Divorcing a baseball team—that's funny."

I can still hear him snickering as I storm down the hall into my office.

I plop down at the computer, open the Word program on my MacBook, and begin a new document. I am in a fury, my fingers flying across the keyboard. If smoke really came out of people's ears when they were fired up, it would be coming out of mine.

"I am no stranger to divorce," I write. "I thought I was over that particular brand of heartbreak, but now I am divorcing the New York Yankees—all 25 men on the active roster, in addition to the manager, the coaches, and the general manager. Oh, and the trainer, too. And, of course, the owner and all his baseball people. I made a commitment to these guys and they betrayed me."

I go on to explain why I am cutting the Yankees loose and how I just might throw my affection to the Tampa Bay Devil Rays. When I finish venting, my eyes light on the *New York Times* sports section on my desk—on a column by Harvey Araton. His e-mail address is right there at the end of the piece. I don't know him and he doesn't know me, but what the hell, I think. I like his stuff.

Maybe he will like mine. I configure my divorce essay into an e-mail to him and hit "send." I sit back in my chair and exhale.

I continue to watch the games but with a definite detachment, as if I am legally separated and just waiting for the paperwork. On Sunday the Yankees salvage the series against the Mets by beating them 6–2. Our latest rookie starter is named Tyler Clippard, and he looks too young to drive a car. He is the beneficiary of homers by A-Rod, Jeter, and Posada, the only three Yankees in the lineup who are hitting.

AL EAST STANDINGS/MAY 20

TEAM	W	L	PCT	GB
BOSTON	30	13	.698	—
BALTIMORE	20	24	.455	10.5
NEW YORK	19	23	.452	10.5
TORONTO	19	24	.442	11.0
TAMPA BAY	18	25	.419	12.0

Week 8
May 21, 2007

No, there isn't extra pressure playing the Red Sox. Pressure is what those kids overseas feel when they've got bombs whizzing over their heads. Baseball is a game. There's a lot riding on these games, but that's not pressure. If you can't handle 55,000 people screaming at you, come on. The fans and the media hype up this rivalry a heck of a lot more than the players do.

The Red Sux are so familiar to me at this point that it feels like incest. Thanks to the relentless close-ups you get on Fox, I can count Kevin Youkilis's nose hairs.

We actually beat them in Monday's opener on the 21st. Wang pitches really well, and A-Rod homers for the third straight game.

On the 22nd it is back to losing hell. Mussina is just—well, he is hopeless. He is supposed to give us a quality start, and instead he gives them seven runs. The good news is that I get an e-mail from Harvey Araton! He says he enjoyed my "tale of betrayal" and passed it on to Tom Jolly, the editor of the *Times'* sports section. I am about to rush into the living room to tell Michael when I notice another e-mail in my in-box. It is from Tom Jolly! He says he will definitely find a place for my essay in Sunday's paper, provided the Yankees don't go on a winning streak.

"We have to root against the Yankees until Sunday!" I tell Michael.

"So you'd sell them out for a chance to be in the *Times*?"

"Yes," I say, "I would."

We beat Boston in the finale on Wednesday, and I am nervous that my article will not run on Sunday after all. We hammer Schilling, and Pettitte pitches a beauty. Rotten luck.

But then the Angels arrive for a weekend series, and I know my essay is as good as published. The Yankees are allergic to the Angels. Joe rationalizes our dismal record against them with sound bites like "They always play us tough." But the truth is the Yankees always spaz out against them. "Figgy." "Vladie." "K-Rod." Give me a break.

The three games this weekend go exactly the way I expected.

We lose game one on Friday night. A-Rod hits his 19th homer, but the bullpen is horrendous, giving up seven runs in two innings.

We lose game two on Saturday afternoon. Wang throws eight solid innings, but our bats need Viagra. I get an e-mail from a copy editor at the *Times* saying that since the Yankees have cooperated and lost two in a row, my divorce story will run the next day. I also get an e-mail from Richard Sandomir, who covers the media and business scene for the *Times*' sports section.

"I sneaked an early peek at your essay, and I think it's terrific," he writes. "I'm hoping the Boss reads it and offers you some alimony."

Game three on Sunday completes the Angels' sweep. Mussina does his job, but Proctor can't record an out in the seventh. My divorce piece runs in today's *New York Times*, so I am much too excited to care. The *Times* places the essay on the section's back page and adorns it with a clever illustration showing a woman sawing herself free of a ball and chain—a ball with the Yankees' logo on it.

The huge response to the piece stuns me. I have a Web site that promotes my novels, but I didn't expect the *Times*' readers to seek it out.

There are supportive e-mails from other Yankee She-Fans. Like the one from Evalyn, who writes, "Only another female can understand the emotional attachment we have to the team."

There are funny e-mails from people I grew up with but have not seen in years. Like the one from Ken, who writes, "As I read your article, I recalled our trip to Yankee Stadium when the Mick had 499 home runs and we were hoping we'd see number 500. I certainly remember that you are as nuts as I am about the Boys in Blue."

There are interesting e-mails from people I have never met. Like the one from Sandy McCartney, who writes that she, too, lives in Santa Barbara and that her husband is not only a lifelong Yankee fan but also the best friend of Yankees radio broadcaster John Sterling. And the one from Matt Silverman, the president of the Tampa Bay Devil Rays, who wants to send me a Devil Rays care package and asks for my home address.

There are smirking e-mails from Red Sox fans. Like the one from John, who writes, "As a lifetime BoSox fan, here's hoping you see the light and join the Nation."

Most upsetting are the angry e-mails both to me and to the *Times* from Yankee fans that crucify me for being a traitor. Like the one from Stan, who writes, "Too bad Jane Heller has given up on the Yankees. True fans never give up. True fans die harder and root harder. We don't need her." And the one from Adam, who writes, "It is because of triflers like Jane Heller that Yankee supporters have the bum rap of not being genuine fans of the game of baseball." And the particularly articulate one from Rob, who writes, "Suck dick you whore."

I am stung by these vicious e-mails.

"They're questioning your loyalty," Michael says.

"This has nothing to do with loyalty," I say. "I wrote an essay about divorcing the Yankees because all the losing has taken an emotional toll on me. You get that better than anyone."

"Yeah, well, people hate you for being a bandwagon fan."

My nostrils flare with indignation. It stinks that I am hated by perfect strangers, especially strangers with whom I share a passion. And here is another thing that stinks: People are jumping to conclusions about me. How dare they question my legitimacy as a fan? I am not one of those people who abandoned the Yankees when they were bad. I hung around during the Horace Clarke years and the Mel Hall years and the year that Luis Polonia had sex with that 15-year-old girl in Milwaukee. I was there even when the cokehead Mets were the toast of New York. Sure, I drifted away. I went to college and protested the war in Vietnam and listened to Led Zeppelin. I got married and divorced twice. I launched my career in publishing. I went through periods when I did not follow baseball as obsessively as I do now. But I never stopped rooting for the Yankees, never stopped loving them.

"I am the opposite of a bandwagon fan," I say, standing up very straight. "And the injustice of it all is infuriating."

"They're just reacting to what they read in the paper," says Michael. "They don't know you."

"Yeah, well, I wish I could show them."

"Show them what?"

"That I'm the best fan the Yankees have ever had."

AL EAST STANDINGS/MAY 27

TEAM	W	L	PCT	GB
BOSTON	34	15	.694	—
BALTIMORE	23	27	.460	11.5
TORONTO	22	27	.449	12.0
NEW YORK	21	27	.438	12.5
TAMPA BAY	20	28	.417	13.5

Week 9
May 28, 2007

Ninety percent of the media people are right on. But the worst things that happened to sports are ESPN and talk radio. They don't report the sports. They report the dirt.

On Memorial Day the Yankees lose the first of a three-game series against the Blue Jays at Rogers Centre. On Tuesday night, they waste a fine performance by Pettitte and lose to the Jays again. It is killing me that they are flushing themselves down the toilet, but I can't help watching, the way you can't help rubbernecking. Wednesday is a newsy day in Yankeeville. No, Joe has not been fired. It is A-Rod who is in the headlines.

The *New York Post* has dubbed him Stray-Rod and Yankee Doodle Randy. As is clear from the story's accompanying photos, he has been a naughty, naughty boy in Toronto. He is shown cavorting with a woman who is not his wife. The woman is a platinum blonde with big jugs and even bigger biceps—more *Hustler* than *Playboy*. She is not particularly attractive. Surely he can afford better. According to the story, she is a stripper, and she and A-Rod went to a lap dance club together. And—here is the real bombshell—she has been spotted with him in other cities besides Toronto.

A-Rod also makes news during the game against the Blue Jays. He shouts something that distracts third baseman Howie Clark, who drops the ball. The Blue Jays claim he yelled, "I got it!" or "Mine!" but A-Rod claims he said "Hah!" Replays are inconclusive, and Michael and I discuss whether A-Rod has a tendency to do bush league things. He is carrying the Yankees on his back this season, bush league or not.

The Yanks go on to beat the Jays 10–5, avoid the sweep, and snap their five-game losing streak. Mo gets his first save since May 3.

Thursday is an off day before the Yankees open another series against the Red Sox at Fenway. I focus on the e-mails about the divorce essay that continue to flood my in-box. Mixed in with the ones telling me that I am a despicable person are suggestions that I expand the saga of my relationship with the team into a baseball book.

A career in baseball is all I ever wanted. When I got out of college in the '70s, I wrote a letter to Michael Burke, president of the Yankees, asking for a job. He passed it along to Bob Fischel, who was head of PR then. I got my interview with the Yankees, but the job Bob Fischel offered me was secretarial, and I had bigger ambitions. I also interviewed with a vice president at ABC Sports, thinking I could be an on-air baseball reporter. The job he offered me was "sponsor hostess"—I would serve cocktails to sponsors at sporting events and "look pretty." This was before such jobs were not only objectionable to women but also illegal. And then there was my interview at Major League Baseball. Bowie Kuhn was the commissioner, and baseball was losing young men to other sports, to college, to the military. His office needed a recruitment campaign along the lines of the army's "Uncle Sam Wants You!" I said I would be thrilled to work on the campaign. But a few weeks later they explained that Major League Baseball was just not ready to hire a woman to promote it. I was disappointed, but I could not afford to be a pioneer and go door-to-door trying to break through any glass ceilings. I needed to make money. I answered an ad in the *New York Times'* classified section for an assistant in the publicity department at a book publishing company. I spent 10 years climbing the ladder in publishing, promoting dozens of novelists before becoming one myself.

But here I am in the present, and the novel I am supposed to be writing is going nowhere. Writing a book about the Yankees, however, would prove to those people who trashed me that I am not a bandwagon fan; that I am the most devoted fan a person can possibly be.

If I were Derek Jeter, I would not want to begin the month at a miniature park stuffed with Red Sox fans chanting, "Yankees suck!" The infield at Fenway is what sucks. I bet Jeter sees more bad hops there than anywhere.

Actually, I wonder what Jeter is thinking these days. His offense, unlike that of most of the hitters, has been very reliable. I am dying to know whether he really thinks this team will pull out of the hole they have dug for themselves or if he is just bullshitting the media when he says, "We'll be fine." I would also like to know if he still hates A-Rod or if they are good teammates now. And what is up with all the high-profile women he dates? Mr. and Mrs. Jeter always look so down-to-earth when the camera finds them in their seats. I can't picture them embracing a Mariah, Jessica, or Scarlett as their daughter-in-law.

The Yankees win the June 1 game in Boston 9–5. Wang struggles through five-plus innings, but it is in the fourth when things get heated. Wakefield hits Phelps, and Kyle Snyder hits A-Rod. In the top of the ninth, Javier Lopez hits Cano. And in the bottom of the inning, Proctor, the enforcer, throws at Youkilis's head. Both benches empty, but no punches are thrown. They all just stand around looking pissy. Typical Yankees–Red Sox.

Boston takes the Saturday game 11–6. Neither starter, Mussina or Schilling, gets the decision, as it is a battle of the pens and a sloppy display by the Yankees, who blow the lead three times. Jeter commits two errors, and Proctor gives up five runs for the loss. But that is not the worst of it. In the bottom of the seventh, Lowell is running to first and collides with Mientkiewicz, who not only has been playing stellar defense but also has started to swing the bat well. Doug goes down and stays down. Eventually, he is carted off the field and bound for the hospital. And Clemens, who was supposed to make his much-anticipated debut in Chicago, has a "fatigued right groin." I'll give that motherfucker a fatigued right groin.

On Sunday the New York tabloids report that A-Rod has been dining with a blonde in Boston but that this blonde is Cynthia—a.k.a. C-Rod. Unlike his stripper, C-Rod is attractive and well-groomed and very fit—more *Prevention* than *Playboy*. I guess she has been deployed by the Yankees to keep her husband out of trouble. Or maybe she has decided to step in and fight for her man. I am forever fascinated by Yankee marriages, since I used to dream of being in one. As for the game, the Yankees win it 6–5. Again, it is a battle of the bullpens as Pettitte can't get out of the fifth inning and Beckett is foiled by his closer, Jonathan Pap Smear, who gives up a homer in the top of the ninth to A-Rod. Divorce or no divorce, that is sweet. What is not sweet is the medical report on Mientkiewicz. He has suffered a concussion, a cervical sprain, and a broken bone in his right wrist and could miss 6 to 8 weeks.

And in an article in the sports section of the *Santa Barbara News-Press*, Tommy Lasorda weighs in on my divorce essay.

"If she is dropping the Yankees, she should pick up the Dodgers," he tells reporter Mike Takeuchi. "There is a saying in this country: If you don't pull for the Dodgers, you may not get to heaven."

AL EAST STANDINGS/JUNE 3

TEAM	W	L	PCT	GB
BOSTON	37	18	.673	—
TORONTO	27	29	.482	10.5
BALTIMORE	27	30	.474	11.0
NEW YORK	24	30	.444	12.5
TAMPA BAY	23	31	.426	13.5

Week 10
June 4, 2007

My dad taught me that if you want something bad enough, you go get it. His favorite thing was: "If you didn't get dirty, you didn't play hard enough." When I was growing up, the game was only fun if you won. He instilled that in me right out of the chute.

The Yankees move on to Chicago for a four-game series. This time they actually play well against the skanky ChiSox and win three out of four. A-Rod is smacking homers again. Wang pitches his first complete game of the season. Mussina has a great outing, despite not getting the decision. And Mo gets a couple of saves. I perk up. I watch the games without grinding my teeth. Michael is preoccupied with a photographic project he is doing in LA, and he is missing the games. It is like I have lost my Yankee buddy. I bet he is relieved not to be around me. I feel guilty for having taken his company for granted once the season started and putting the Yankees first. If he sent me an e-mail like all those *New York Times* readers did, he would probably call me a bandwagon wife.

Interleague play resumes on Friday with a series at home against Pittsburgh. The Yankees should be able to bury a joke of a team like the Pirates, and they do, in a sweep. Clemens makes his debut on Saturday and goes a respectable six innings, striking out seven and benefiting from the suddenly smoldering bat of Abreu. By the end of the weekend, the Yankees have won six in a row. I get e-mails from friends who suggest that the Yanks are playing well because I threatened to divorce them. I think it is more likely that they are finally beating teams they should beat and that the 2007 season could get interesting if they keep it up.

AL EAST STANDINGS/JUNE 10

TEAM	W	L	PCT	GB
BOSTON	40	22	.645	—
NEW YORK	30	31	.492	9.5
TORONTO	30	32	.484	10.0
BALTIMORE	29	34	.460	11.5
TAMPA BAY	28	33	.459	11.5

Week 11
June 11, 2007

I met my wife on a blind date. We lived a block and a half from each other for 3 years at school and never crossed paths. One day I was talking to a guy I played minor league ball with. I said, "Hey, you got anybody I should meet?" He said, "Yeah, I do." Next thing you know, we're married for 8 years with a 2-year-old son.

It is the interleague series at the Stadium against the Diamondbacks that convinces me this season is definitely worth writing about. We sweep Arizona. Wang pitches a beauty on the 12th. Mussina goes his longest outing on the 13th. And Pettitte pitches eight brilliant innings on the 14th. Oh, and A-Rod belts his major-league-leading 25th homer.

With the Yankees reeling off nine straight wins, I call Ellen Levine, my literary agent in New York, and suggest that I write a nonfiction book about their 2007 season.

"I'll get on a plane after the All-Star break, follow the team to every game, and chronicle the season from a female perspective," I tell her.

"It sounds very promising," she says, even though she is not the least bit into baseball and could not tell you what the All-Star break is. "The response you got to the *Times* piece indicates a market for a book."

"I'll write about what it really means to be a fan," I add.

"Great," she says. "Give me a proposal as soon as you can. Will you be able to get access to the players?"

I hesitate. "Absolutely."

Over the weekend, while the Yankees are winning two of three against the Mets in the Bronx, I sit at the computer and make my case for why a publisher should pay me to fly all over the country with the Yankees. I state that I will learn life lessons by going to Baltimore, Detroit, and Kansas City, the way the author of the bestseller *Eat, Pray, Love* learned life lessons by going to Italy, India, and Indonesia. Okay, it will not be the same thing, because she was writing about spirituality and I will be writing about baseball, but we will both be searching for something.

Since what I really hope to do in this book is to prove to my detractors that I am a true fan—such a true fan that I will become pals with Jeter and A-Rod and all the guys—I boast in the proposal that I have contacts within the Yankees organization. (Well, I must know someone who has contacts.) I pledge that I will gain access to the players and interview them for the book. I will be a true fan *and* a fearless journalist.

The Yankees win the finale of the series against the Mets. Wang strikes out 10—his career high. A-Rod hits home run number 27 and drives in three runs for a major-league-leading 73 RBIs. And the Yankees notch their 11th victory in 12 games.

AL EAST STANDINGS/JUNE 17

TEAM	W	L	PCT	GB
BOSTON	44	24	.647	—
NEW YORK	35	32	.522	8.5
TORONTO	33	35	.485	11.0
TAMPA BAY	30	37	.448	13.5
BALTIMORE	29	40	.420	15.5

Week 12
June 18, 2007

I always thought the majors were an unattainable goal for me. It wasn't until I got to college when I realized I could make it. We had five or six guys—pitchers—who became number one, first-round draft picks. I started hitting against those guys and having a lot of success. I thought, "If I'm holding my own against these first-round picks, maybe I have a chance of becoming something."

Ellen loves the proposal and sends it to publishers, asking them to respond quickly since the All-Star break is approaching and she would like to have a deal in place by then. While I wait to hear, I watch the Yankees get swept by the Rockies in Colorado. The Rockies! What is with these guys? Just when there is a glimmer of hope that they are not dead after all, they pull crap like this.

On Friday they move on to San Francisco, where they lose two of three to the Giants and become participants in the Barry Bonds circus. In the first game, which the Yankees win 7–3, Bonds hits his 749th homer off Proctor and is only six away from tying Aaron's record. In the second game, Proctor again figures prominently, taking the loss in a 6–5 defeat in 13 innings. The 7–2 loss to the Giants on Sunday has about 1 minute of drama. Clemens comes in to relieve Mussina in the seventh and faces Bonds. It is a showdown between two gun-slingers, except that both are past their prime. The only question is whether

Clemens will throw a strike to Bonds or walk him. He walks him. Drama over. So are the Yankees. They lose five of six and are sinking fast.

AL EAST STANDINGS/JUNE 24

TEAM	W	L	PCT	GB
BOSTON	48	26	.649	—
TORONTO	37	37	.500	11.0
NEW YORK	36	37	.493	11.5
TAMPA BAY	33	40	.452	14.5
BALTIMORE	32	43	.427	16.5

Week 13
June 25, 2007

When you sign with a new team, you're always really anxious to get to spring training and meet the guys. You have such a short period of time to get to know everybody before you start to work. But the Yankees were so easy. I met Derek and he said, "If you ever need anything, let me know." He made me feel right at home. Everybody did. I kept telling my wife, "Pinch me. This is the dream of all dreams."

The Yanks land in Baltimore for three games against the Orioles. They lose game one on Tuesday by the score of 3–2. Pettitte pitches well, but Proctor starts the ninth and walks in the winning run. *Walks in the winning run.* There is never an excuse for that. Joe has overused Proctor, and his arm is hanging by a thread, but what is so fucking hard about throwing strikes?

The O's shut out the Yankees in Wednesday's game. Erik Bedard makes it look easy, as opposed to Roger Clemens, whose fatigued groin fails to get a strikeout for the first time in over 200 starts. Thursday's contest ends in a suspension of play due to rain, with the Yankees up 8–6 in the top of the eighth. The game will be resumed on July 27, the next time the Yankees are in Baltimore.

While I wait to hear about the book, I pass the time reading Peter Abraham's blog on LoHud.com, the Web site offshoot of the *Journal News* in Westchester. Almost all the Yankee beat writers have blogs, but Peter actually gives you dishy, behind-the-scenes stuff. I can't go 2 hours without checking to see what he has to say.

❦

On Friday the Yankees open a home stand against Oakland. They beat the A's 2–1—only their second win in nine games. Mussina pitches seven strong innings, but Farnsworth takes the mound in the eighth and gives up back-to-back singles. Joe replaces him with Mo. Farnsworth storms into the dugout and hurls his glove against the wall like a 5-year-old.

Saturday's game is a shutout by the A's. The Yankees manage only one hit. Igawa, back up from the farm, gives up three homers, and Proctor and Myers are responsible for the rest of the damage.

I don't get this 2007 team, I really don't.

Michael is finished with his assignment in LA, and it is good to have him back. But now he is busy on his computer Photoshopping every single shot he took. He is not present even though he is home, the way I am not present when I am watching the Yankees on TV. I put on makeup and something sexier than my sweats and sashay into his office.

"Hi," I say, wrapping my arms around his neck and kissing him on the cheek. "How about a little break?"

"Not now," he says in the same tone I use when A-Rod is up with men on base and I can't look away.

I sigh and leave him to his photographs.

On Sunday the Yankees finish up their series against Oakland with an 11–5 loss at the Stadium. Pettitte is just plain awful. Regarding the continuing side-show that is Alex Rodriguez, his wife, Cynthia, takes her seat in the players' family section and places her 2-year-old daughter, Natasha, on her lap. She is wearing a tight-fitting white tank top—one of those designer shirts with a mes-sage on the back. Usually they say Zen things on them like "Breathe" and "Simplify" and that old standby "Peace." Not C-Rod's. Her shirt says "Fuck you." The parents of small children sitting nearby on this summer Sunday afternoon are offended. Several alert the security guards who regularly patrol Yankee Stadium in search of people wearing, carrying, or yelling obscenities; such peo-ple are routinely ejected. Not C-Rod. Throwing out the wife of the team's home-run king is tricky. But the New York Post has no compunction about putting Cynthia and her tank top on the back page of the next day's paper with the headline: "Mrs. A-Rod Is a Bronx F-Bomber." They also ask the question I can't help but ask, which is: Why? Is Mrs. A-Rod saying "Fuck you" to the fans who booed her husband last year, particularly in the postseason? Is she saying "Fuck you" to the Yankees, who have stated that they will not negotiate with her husband if he opts out of his contract and becomes a free agent at the end of the season? Is she saying "Fuck you" to the media who exposed her husband's adulterous behavior? Is she saying "Fuck you" to the stripper who went lap dancing with her husband? Or is she saying "Fuck you" to her husband? Maybe she is the one who wants a divorce.

AL EAST STANDINGS/JULY 1

TEAM	W	L	PCT	GB
BOSTON	49	31	.613	—
TORONTO	39	42	.481	10.5
NEW YORK	38	41	.481	10.5
BALTIMORE	35	46	.432	14.5
TAMPA BAY	33	47	.413	16.0

Week 14
July 2, 2007

Sports fans act like the money we make comes out of their pockets—like the Yankees were stealing little Johnny's college money to pay for Clemens to come here. As a player, you never think about that stuff. No one says, "Wow. He's making whatever." Do we all want to make $30 million? Yeah. It sounds crappy, but money is respect in this game.

The Yankees begin a four-game series at home against the Twins on Monday and win three out of four. Clemens gets win number 350 in game one. Game two marks the debut of the latest call-up, Edwar Ramirez, who is wiry, wears Malcolm X glasses, and throws a mean changeup. Johan Santana overmatches Mussina on Wednesday. And Matsui hits a two-run homer that wins the game on Thursday.

Everyone in publishing is away for the July 4 holiday, so I don't hear any news about the book. But I write another essay for the *New York Times,* in which I say I am holding off on the divorce from the Yankees and instead going to couples counseling to talk about them. Tom Jolly says he will run it in Sunday's sports section, and I am thrilled. I am a sportswriter at last, albeit one whose style is more Bridget Jones than Harvey Araton. The piece is meant to let people know that I still love the team with all my heart. It is not as convincing as a book would be, but it is a start.

❦

The Yankees host the Angels again on July 6, 7, and 8—the last weekend before the All-Star break.

In the first game, Pettitte gives up eight runs for the second straight time. But A-Rod hits his 29th homer of the season and his 493rd overall, tying Lou Gehrig and Fred McGriff, and the Yankees win 14–9. Posada has three RBIs of his own, and I have to say he is having a career year, both offensively and behind the plate. He doesn't seem as hotheaded as he was a few years ago when he had that fight with El Duque in the dugout. He is more of a leader now. He even has his own cool nickname: JoPo.

The Yankees lose the Saturday contest 2–1 in 13 innings, spoiling Clemens's one-run performance. They continue to be up and down, sending me on a roller-coaster ride. Roller coasters make me nauseous.

My *New York Times* article runs on Sunday, and I get lots of e-mails about it. I don't win people over about being a true fan. They take the essay literally and tell me it is about time I went into therapy.

As for the finale against the Angels on the 8th, the Yankees win it 12–0. Wang throws almost seven scoreless innings and the bats come alive. Matsui, Cano, and A-Rod all hit three-run homers.

It's nice that the Yanks end the first half of the season on a high note. It will be even nicer if I get the book deal and can congratulate them in person. I will walk right over to, say, JoPo. I will shake his hand and introduce myself and tell him what a fabulous catcher he is. He will thank me for coming all the way from California and promise that the team will play good baseball now that I have joined the party. We will have a long, heart-to-heart conversation, and I will put every word in my book.

AL EAST STANDINGS/JULY 8

TEAM	W	L	PCT	GB
BOSTON	53	34	.609	—
NEW YORK	43	43	.500	9.5
TORONTO	43	44	.494	10.0
BALTIMORE	38	50	.432	15.5
TAMPA BAY	34	53	.391	19.0

Week 15
July 9, 2007

Everybody in sports today is so stats oriented, and it's asinine. You look at my numbers against 10 guys and you say, "Wow. He hits them really well." Well, that 4-for-11 stat could mean that I hit four broken-bat bloopers. You could see a 0-for-11 stat and it could mean that I lined out seven times. They put stats on your defense, too—your "range factor." Come on. If you have a pitcher who throws strikes, I'm always in the right place. If they miss a spot, I'm a half a step out of position. Does that mean I have no range?

The players are back from the All-Star game in San Francisco, and publishers are back from vacation. Ellen says she has interest in the book! I should know very soon whether I will be packing a suitcase.

On Thursday the Yankees open a series against the Devil Rays at Tropicana Field. I really do like the Rays, as I wrote in my first *Times* essay. With guys like Crawford and Upton and Pena and Kazmir, they are no pushovers. And yet I feel sorry for them. Hardly anyone comes to their games, and the ones that do cheer for the Yankees, who win tonight 7–3.

Game two is Kazmir's night. He gives up only one run in Tampa Bay's 6–4 win over the Yankees and Clemens.

Wang pitches six solid innings for a 6–4 win on Saturday. There is a lot of first-pitch swinging by the Yankees, which makes me nuts. But what annoys me the most is Farnsworth, who relieves in the eighth and gives up a homer. I stand right in front of the TV and curse him out.

"I could hear you ranting from the garage," says Michael, who walks in armed with bags of groceries. "Bad news about the book?"

"Just Farnsworth again." I help him put away the coffee filters and the paper towels and all the rest. "Sorry I've been so checked out lately. How about a movie tonight?"

"I still have work to do."

"Oh."

He gives me a hug before he goes to his office. I love his hugs. He never scrimps on them. He pulls me in tight and folds me in his arms and squeezes me. He doesn't do phony hugs, in other words. They are as sincere as he is.

In the Sunday game, the Yankees are ahead of the Devil Rays 7–5 when Joe summons Farnsworth in the bottom of the eighth. Kyle gives up a run. It is now 7–6, which becomes a final, thanks to Mo's 13th save.

AL EAST STANDINGS/JULY 15

TEAM	W	L	PCT	GB
BOSTON	55	36	.604	—
NEW YORK	46	44	.511	8.5
TORONTO	45	46	.495	10.0
BALTIMORE	41	51	.446	14.5
TAMPA BAY	35	56	.385	20.0

Week 16
July 16, 2007

How do I handle all the crazy things people scream at me from the stands? Mostly I try to play with the fans. A guy yells, "You suck!" and I go, "No shit! Tell me something I don't know. But you paid your hard-earned money to come watch my sorry ass play, so who's the idiot? You or me?" They die laughing, and I turn them from hating my guts to loving me.

On Monday the Yankees are home for the first of four games against the Blue Jays. We win the opener 6–4, and A-Rod hits his 496th homer. It will be beyond exciting if I get the book deal and am right there when he hits the big 500.

Game two is a fantastic matchup of Pettitte versus Halladay. The score is deadlocked until Joe brings in Farnsworth in the eighth. Kyle gives up a leadoff single to the Big Hurt, then tries this lame pickoff move to first, allowing the go-ahead run to cross the plate. What a loser. I switch over to HBO, where Gary Sheffield is essentially calling Torre a racist on *Real Sports*. He is wearing matching diamond earrings and looks like a transvestite. The Yankees win 3–2 in the bottom of the 10th.

The Yanks and Jays split the final two games. Clemens has a good outing on Wednesday night and gets run support. Wang has a good outing on Thursday night and does not.

On Friday Ellen calls with the news that the book is a done deal! I am definitely going on the road to write about the Yankees! That is the good news. The bad news is that I need to figure out how to pull the trip together in about a week. I am talking about flights and hotels and all the details that go with being away from home from the end of July to—I am not sure when the trip will end. If the Yankees make the postseason, I could be gone until the end of October. That is a long time not to sleep in my own bed. But I am not complaining! I am getting paid to watch baseball games! Well, the publisher's advance will not be on my doorstep right away, so I will have to lay out my own traveling expenses. Lay out our traveling expenses. Michael and I decide to embark on this journey together.

We acknowledge that we have coexisted in parallel universes lately, and our marriage is stale. A trip is exactly the way to rejuvenate us, to put the spark back. Thanks to all those movie options on my novels, we have enough in the bank for him to take the time off from his freelance work—if we budget correctly. The only hitch is that it poses a health risk for him to come along; he has no immune system and is prone to infection if he so much as catches a cold. Stadium crowds and airplane passengers could be perilous, and I am nervous that he will get sick while we are in some strange city. But he is unfazed.

"Going to all the games with you is an adventure I'm not passing up."

"You have serious medical problems." I am always the one who worries, and he is always the one who waves me off.

"Remember the broken ankle when I was 13? I didn't let that stop me from watching Maris hit number 60."

"You have Crohn's, not a broken ankle."

"I'll pack a lot of Imodium."

I give up. He is coming with me, and that is that. The truth is, I am thrilled that he wants to come. This trip is the solution to everything. I can prove what a true fan I am *and* have a second honeymoon with my husband. What could be better?

I print out the Yankees' schedule and mull it over. Michael and I will join the team in Baltimore on July 27. But that is all we agree on because I am suddenly paralyzed by the logistics of this trip. Which do I arrange first: the flights or the hotels? And how the hell do I get access to the Yankees, to the clubhouse, to the games? I told my publisher that access was a no-brainer, that I would meet the players and persuade them to spill their guts, but I have no clue how to make any of that happen.

I call my friend Marty Bell, a successful Broadway theater producer who used to be an editor of *Sport* magazine back in the '70s. He is my go-to person when I have crises large and small. He tells me I must contact the Yankees' media relations director and ask for a press pass to all the games. I hop on the Yankees Web site and find the name of the media guy. It is Jason Zillo. I e-mail him right away, introducing myself as the author of 13 published novels so he gets that I am not some kid writing for my high school paper. I tell him I have a contract for a nonfiction book about being a Yankee fan and would like press passes. I also mention the divorce article that ran in the *Times* and make sure to explain it was meant to be tongue in cheek. I get a quick reply.

"Thanks for your inquiry," Jason writes. "Unfortunately we receive scores of similar requests throughout the season, and because of the overwhelming demand of media coverage, this is simply not something we can pursue."

Oh, God. He is blowing me off. Now what? If I don't get access, my publisher will dump the book—and me. I call Marty again.

"You can find a way around this Zillo guy," he says. "Just go to Baltimore and the other cities, buy tickets for the first week of games, start hanging out at the hotels where the team is staying, in the bar and the lobby, wherever they are. You'll find a player who will talk to you. There's always one. You are beautiful and charming and funny. You will pull this off."

Now you know why Marty is my go-to person. He not only says flattering, reassuring things, but he reminds me not to take no for an answer. He adds that I should reach out to any other contacts I can think of—people with a relationship to the Yankees or Major League Baseball who may be able to help with access to the players and the games. He also gives me the contact information for his friend Lisa, who gets discounted hotel room rates for the actors traveling with his touring productions.

I e-mail Lisa. Within 24 hours she has Michael and me booked at all the hotels at very reasonable rates. One crisis resolved.

I compile a list of everybody I know who might conceivably have a connection to the Yankees. The list comes to a staggering three people.

The first person is Jane Heller. No, that is not a misprint. Michael and I refer to her as the Other Jane Heller. In the spring of 2000, I wrote a novel called *Name Dropping* about two women with the same name whose identities get mixed up. The Other Jane Heller e-mailed my Web site to tell me that she had my same name. She said she was the largest private banker in the country and that her clients included Martha Stewart as well as *George Steinbrenner and the New York Yankees*. She invited me to a Yankees game if I was ever in New York and added that she had the best seats in the house. Fast-forward to the fall of 2000 as the Yankees and Mets were about to begin the Subway Series. I took her up on her offer. Michael and I flew to New York and joined the Other Jane Heller and her husband for game two. She did, indeed, have the best seats in the house—in the first row next to the Yankee dugout—and watching the Yankees win was the greatest night ever. I e-mail her now, hoping she will help me bypass Jason Zillo and gain access to the Yankees' inner sanctum.

Next is Sandy McCartney, the Santa Barbara woman who wrote to me after the divorce essay was published in the *Times*—the one whose husband is the best friend of John Sterling. I tell her my problem and ask if she thinks John might be willing to open doors for me.

I e-mail Larry Brooks, the much-respected sports columnist for the *New York Post*. Over 30 years ago, Larry and I were counselors at a day camp in Mamaroneck. We have stayed in touch sporadically ever since. I ask if he knows Jason Zillo and could offer any advice about how to infiltrate the Yankees.

I e-mail my mother. She lives in Westchester. I ask if Michael and I can stay with her during the Yankees' first home stand. She is 90, but you would never guess it. She walks 5 miles a day on her treadmill and drives around in her little Subaru with the spoiler and leads a monthly book group whose selections are by authors like Proust and Balzac. She has a boyfriend named Cy. He is in his eighties. They watch Yankees games together.

I make progress on the travel front. Dorothy Darr, my friend and neighbor, is an artist and filmmaker who is also the wife of Charles Lloyd, the jazz legend. She is experienced at setting up complicated itineraries because Charles performs with his group all over the world. She suggests I call Charles de L'Arbre of Santa Barbara Travel Bureau and let him solve the puzzle.

So. Flights are booked. Hotel rooms are reserved. All that remains is for me to get press passes from the Yankees.

I hear back from Sandy McCartney, who gives me John Sterling's phone numbers and tells me he is happy to speak to me. I thank her profusely and call John. When he answers in his deep baritone that is as familiar to me as a family member's, given all my years listening to him on the radio, I half expect him to launch into his trademark "Theeeeee Yankees win!"

"How can I be of help?" he asks.

"Jason Zillo won't give me access to the press box," I say.

"Of course you should be in the press box," he booms. "I'll put in a good word for you."

"That would be great." What a nice guy!

"While you're waiting for Jason," he adds, "I would contact the media relations directors at all the teams the Yankees will be playing. It may be easier to go through them."

"Good idea."

He also says I should stay at the hotels where he and the Yankees stay in each city and gives me the names. I gulp when I see that there are Ritz-Carltons and similarly upscale spots on the list. The Yankees and I don't have the same budget.

I hear back from Larry Brooks, who says he is excited for me about the book but warns that the Yankees are harder to deal with than any other organization in any other sport. He says he wishes he could help me with Zillo but doesn't know how.

I hear back from my mother, who is delighted that Michael and I are coming to stay with her and assures me we will not cramp her style.

I hear nothing from the Other Jane Heller.

I research the names of Jason Zillo's counterparts at some of the other teams. I fire off e-mails to Jay Stenhouse of the Blue Jays, Brian Britten of the Tigers, Bill Stetka of the Orioles, Jeff Sibel of the Indians, Nancy Mazmanian of the Angels, and John Blake of the Red Sox.

Here are their responses.

Jay Stenhouse of the Blue Jays writes, "As your interest is specifically regarding the Yankees I would ask that you run your request through them first."

Brian Britten of the Tigers writes, "After consulting with the Yankees Media Relations department, we will not be in a position to credential you for the games at Comerica Park against the Yankees this season."

Bill Stetka of the Orioles writes, "The Yankees have informed us that they are not cooperating on the book, and therefore I will not be able to provide a credential for you."

Jeff Sibel of the Indians writes, "After speaking with Jason Zillo of the Yankees, we will not be able to credential you."

Jennifer Hoyer in the Angels' media relations department writes, "We received your request for credentials for the Angels/Yankees series in August. However, this series is one of the busiest series of the year and unfortunately we only have space to accommodate our regular media who attend throughout the season. So we are not able to provide a press pass for you for any of the Angels/Yankees games. Sorry about that and best of luck in your endeavors."

As for John Blake of the Red Sox, he does not have the decency to reply at all.

I am about to call Marty and report that the Yankees are blackballing me when my phone rings.

"Hello?"

"Jane Heller, please," says a male voice.

"This is she," I say.

"Hi, Jane. It's Jason Zillo."

He has changed his mind! John Sterling must have spoken to him! I am getting access to the Yankees after all!

"I've been hearing from the other media relations directors," he says. "I need to let you know that nobody will be granting you a press pass."

My shoulders sag. "Why not?"

"It's nothing personal. I recognize that you've written all those novels, but we don't credential authors of books about the Yankees unless they're authorized biographies of one of the players. John Feinstein is writing a book about Tom Glavine and Mike Mussina, so he has access to Mike. But that's it. So good luck."

I don't sit around feeling sorry for myself. I e-mail Matt Silverman, the president of the Devil Rays. I tell him about the book and ask if he would be willing to comp me for tickets to both the series against the Rays at Yankee Stadium and the games at the Trop. He writes back that he would be glad to and will put me in touch with his director of VIP relations. The Rays *are* worthy of affection, because look at how well they treat people. To them I am not an undesirable to be kept out at all costs. I am a VIP.

Speaking of the Devil Rays, the Yankees open a three-game series against them this weekend at the Stadium. It is weird to think that I will soon be in the Bronx, watching the Yankees from a hard wooden seat, instead of sitting in Santa Barbara, watching them from my comfy green chair. As excited as I am about the trip—

Oh my God. I will have to fly to New York and Tampa Bay and everywhere else, and I don't do flying. Well, not without a lot of alcohol and not on scary little commuter planes. Somehow, the reality of my actually getting to all these cities never occurred to me, not even when Charles at Santa Barbara Travel was charging the flights on my American Express card. What was I thinking? I am the Yankees' number one fan, but I am not prepared to die for them.

Mussina is pitching atrociously in tonight's first game. Joe comes out to get him with the score at 5–0 in the fifth. Edwar Ramirez takes over and walks the bases loaded, then finally throws a strike to Navarro—for a grand slam. He looks despondent as he trudges to the dugout, where the camera finds Jeter consoling him as he is doubled over sobbing. There is subsequent discussion by Michael Kay on YES about whether there should be crying in baseball. As far as I am concerned, all the Yankees should be crying. We lose to the Devil Rays 14–4. The only bright spot is the first major league hit by our latest call-up, Shelley Duncan.

The Yankees defeat the Devil Rays in game one of Saturday's doubleheader 7–3. Shelley Duncan hits a homer—the first of his big league career—and he takes an exuberant curtain call. He is a big, tall, blond kid with so much enthusiasm that he practically tears the arms off the other players when he high-fives them.

The nightcap is a 17–5 laugher for the Yanks. Matt DeSalvo, still no relation to the Boston Strangler, is back from the minors for the start. Michael Kay and Al Leiter, today's YES duo, discuss the fact that in his spare time DeSalvo reads books. They say this as if reading books is akin to eating raccoon intestines. The score is 10–5 in the sixth when A-Rod comes up. The crowd is chanting "MVP!" and it is only July. He responds by hitting his 33rd home run. He is now just three away from 500. In the bottom of the seventh, Wil Nieves doubles, and it is his last hit as a Yankee. Michael Kay announces that he has been designated for assignment and that the Yankees are replacing him with Jose Molina, the Angels' veteran catcher. Nieves is out. Molina is in. Baseball is a cruel business.

In the finale, the Yankees beat the Devil Rays 21–4. Shelley Duncan caps a 10-run fourth inning with a home run and then adds another homer in the sixth—his third in two games. Is he the new Shane Spencer, who was the new Kevin Maas—the rookie who comes to the big club late in the season and reels off a streak of homers, never to be heard from again? Or will this kid have staying power? A-Rod also homers and is now two shy of 500.

After the game, I e-mail the friends of friends who have recently come forward to say they have connections to baseball. The Yankees may be barring the door, but the "regular people" who find out I am writing the book are only too happy to put me in touch with someone they know who might help with access. One friend knows someone with the White Sox. Another knows a guy with the Indians. And so on. I contact all the names I am given because you never know—and because I am completely desperate.

AL EAST STANDINGS/JULY 22

TEAM	W	L	PCT	GB
BOSTON	59	39	.602	—
NEW YORK	52	46	.531	7.0
TORONTO	48	50	.490	11.0
BALTIMORE	44	54	.449	15.0
TAMPA BAY	38	60	.388	21.0

Week 17
July 23, 2007

I was a free agent, but I pretty much shut off all talks with everybody else when the Yankees came calling. Now, when players from other teams ask, "Hey, how is it over there?" I tell them that what makes it tough to play here also makes it great. One, the people who come to see you expect you to play well. Two, the owner, the manager, and your teammates expect you to play well. And three, the team in the other dugout is gonna give you their "A" game every single time.

On Monday I hear back from all my friends' friends, and none is in a position to help me with tickets or anything else. I am beginning to feel like Typhoid Mary. Does Jason Zillo's reach extend to everyone everywhere?

Out of ideas, I call StubHub to buy tickets. I explain to Jeremiah, my "tele-sales specialist," that I am writing a book about the Yankees and need the cheapest seats available for the first 10 games starting on the 27th, plus all forthcoming Yankees–Red Sox games. I tell him I am just biding my time until the Yankees grant me press credentials.

I am on the phone with Jeremiah for well over 2 hours. While he is finalizing our transaction, he informs me that my American Express Platinum Card has blocked it. This has never happened to me before, and I am humiliated. Well, I have never charged hundreds of dollars' worth of tickets to baseball games before, on top of 2 months' worth of hotel deposits and airline tickets— all in the span of a week. I tell Jeremiah not to cancel everything we have just labored over and hang up to call American Express. I speak to a customer service representative in the Platinum Card department. She has the reserved, snooty voice of one of those women hosts on NPR. I expect her to reprimand me for being such a profligate spender, but when I tell her about the Yankees book she turns giddy and squeals, "Oh, what a jolly time you shall have! I love Derek Jeter!" I call Jeremiah back and authorize him to go ahead with all the purchases.

After I finish liquidating my entire savings, the phone rings. It is my friend Bruce Gelfand, a writer and writing coach. He sent my *New York Times* articles about the Yankees to his producer pals, Howard Burkons and Brenda Friend, who specialize in TV movies based on real-life subjects.

"Brenda is a huge baseball fan," Bruce says. "She's the flip side of you. She's crazy about the Red Sox."

"I won't hold that against her."

"She's dying to make a fictionalized TV movie based on you divorcing the Yankees," he says. "She's already approached Lifetime, and they're very interested."

I rein in my excitement.

"Apparently, Brenda knows the person who works directly under Brian Cashman and could get you tickets to all the games."

"Excuse me?!"

"She knows Jean Afterman, the Yankees' assistant general manager," says Bruce. "She's offered to call Jean for you."

The game tonight in Kansas City, the first of four against the Royals, results in a 9–2 Yankees' win. Clemens goes seven. Shelley gets another hit. And A-Rod drives in his 100th RBI while remaining two short of the 500-homer mark.

On Tuesday I try to get organized and figure out what to take on the trip, since Michael and I are leaving on Thursday at the crack of dawn. My friend Dorothy advises me to pack light. "You end up wearing the same thing every day," she says. I believe her, but I empty the contents of my closet and throw everything into suitcases.

Brenda Friend calls. "Jean Afterman is the assistant GM—one of the few high-ranking women in baseball," she says. "She'll love your approach to writing about the Yankees and help you with tickets."

Brenda tells me how she stalked Jim Lonborg, the Cy Young Award–winning Sox pitcher, when she was in high school. She really is the flip side of me. As for the Lifetime movie, I ask her to speak to Amy Schiffman, my agent at Gersh in LA, who teams with Ellen on my movie options.

I call Amy and fill her in. She suggests I also seek help with tickets from Joe Longo, a sports agent at Gersh.

"There's only one person I deal with at the Yankees," says Joe, who represents several professional baseball players.

"Who?" I ask.

"Jean Afterman," he says. "I'll e-mail her right away. Since she's a woman, your book will probably be right up her alley."

I am one of those believers in signs and portents and omens. If two people in 2 days tell me that Jean Afterman is the key to my access to the Yankees, there must be something to it.

The Yankees win tonight's game against the Royals 9–4. Wang is shaky through six, but Jeter goes four-for-six, Abreu and Posada drive in two runs each, and the Yankees notch their fifth straight victory.

On Wednesday Brenda Friend sends me a copy of the e-mail she sent to Jean Afterman about me. I write back to thank her and say how much fun it would be if she, Jean, and I could attend a game as a threesome. Everything is coming together!

Everything except Michael. He is coming apart. This morning he announces that he has an infected toe and is limping.

"This is exactly what I was afraid of! Roger Maris all over again!" I say, going ballistic. He knows a simple infection in his toe could turn into something much worse, and yet he leaves the vigilance to me.

"I'll be fine," he says, sounding like Jeter, who could have an ax sticking out of his head and tell the media it doesn't hurt.

"Why did you wait until the last minute to deal with this?"

"We're not leaving until tomorrow morning. I'm dealing with it today."

"What if we're in Detroit or Kansas City and you get worse?"

"They have emergency rooms," he says and heads to the emergency room at our local hospital. He comes back a few hours later with a bandaged foot and a prescription for an antibiotic.

We spend the evening circling each other, not exactly fighting but not exactly jumping into each other's arms. I repack for the 100th time, taking enough clothes for 6 months instead of 2. Michael packs quickly, then buries himself in the latest issue of *Small Craft Advisor*.

The Yankees beat Kansas City 7–1. Mussina shuts down the Royals until the sixth, and A-Rod homers in the eighth for number 499. The Royals' announcers speculate about whether he will hit 500 in tomorrow night's game. I hope not because I will be in Baltimore. They also say it will be "Gals' Night" at Kauffman Stadium, and women will receive free pink caps. I hate pink. I hate that women are supposed to wear pink. But mostly what I hate is the "Yankees suck" chant coming from the previously docile crowd in KC. Do people really do that in places other than Boston? I guess I will find out.

After the game, I watch the local news. They are reporting that the Zaca Fire, a wildfire that started on July 4 in northern Santa Barbara County, is spreading because of the severe drought and high winds in the area. Officials don't expect containment until September, and they caution residents to be on the alert.

I am on the alert, all right. My house could go up in flames, and my husband can hardly walk, and I am leaving to watch baseball games.

Book Two

but
I still
love
you

Week 17
Continued

It is middle-of-the-night dark as Michael and I scramble to get dressed, close our bulging suitcases, and lock up the house. We are off to LAX for our 8:55 a.m. United flight to Baltimore.

At the United terminal, I march up to the customer service counter. Because I am neurotic about flying, I like to confirm things—the type of aircraft, the location of my seat, the fact that the flight is nonstop—but there is a long line of people waiting to speak to the lone representative. A storm in Chicago has delayed all flights in and out of O'Hare, and everybody is missing their connections. Realizing that my concerns are trivial in comparison, I relinquish my place in line and join Michael at the gate.

Our Airbus A320 takes off on schedule, and we are offered snacks. There is turbulence and I need alcohol, not trail mix. When the flight attendant comes around with her cart, I order white wine even though it is 9:30 in the morning.

"That'll be $5," she says.

"What kind is it?"

"Your basic screw-top chardonnay."

"Is it dry?"

"People drink it."

I am an expert in plane wine, so I know not to expect anything transformative, but this wine tastes like mouthwash. I consume the entire bottle.

We land in Baltimore. After collecting our suitcases, we look for the Marriott shuttle, which does not come. We are rescued by a large man driving a rundown van that has plastic bags full of garbage in the front seat. He offers to take us to the Marriott for the same price as the shuttle, so we hop in. He talks non-stop about Cal Ripken, whom he likens to God.

We check into the Marriott Inner Harbor. I ask the woman at the desk for a quiet room. She laughs.

"There's a convention of over 17,000 firemen this weekend," she says. "They get pretty rowdy."

"How rowdy?"

"They love to pull fire alarms at 2 in the morning." She nods at the throng of people in Yankees caps and T-shirts who have congregated in the lobby. "They're pretty noisy, too. They come whenever there's a series at Camden Yards."

The bellman takes us to our room, the sort of space that should be photographed in a shelter magazine as a "before" shot. The wallpaper is yellowed and peeling. The closet doors are mirrored sliders straight from the '60s. And the pillows on the bed are the appropriate size only if you are a very small child. But we are happy to have begun our adventure. And we have a night to ourselves before the Yankees come into town and open their series against the Orioles tomorrow night.

We venture out for dinner. It is 90 degrees and very humid. My hair frizzes instantly, and I curse it for not being the hair of, say, Reese Witherspoon. We stroll along the harbor area, which is packed with firefighters in T-shirts displaying their local communities. When we pass the Renaissance Harborplace Hotel on Pratt Street, I stop in my tracks.

"Let's go in," I tell Michael. "John Sterling said the Yankees will be staying here."

"I'm hungry," he says. "I thought we were eating."

"I just want to see what it's like." I waltz through the front door. The lobby is way nicer than ours.

I approach the concierge, a man in a conservative dark suit. "Do you have any rooms available this weekend?" I ask. "We're staying down the street, but would rather be here."

"The Yankees are coming. We're full."

"Maybe if you just take a minute to check the computer, you'll—"

"I don't have to check. No rooms."

I have been thrown out of better places.

Michael and I continue our stroll outside and peruse the restaurant options. We choose California Pizza Kitchen because it is the only place with empty tables. I order a veggie pizza, and Michael orders a pizza with pepperoni, onions, and spicy sausage.

"You must have a death wish," I say, knowing this stuff is poison for someone with Crohn's.

"Let's get something straight," he says. "I came on this trip to support you, but I also came to have a good time. So I'm eating whatever I want and going wherever I want and staying up as late as I want."

Fine. I am not his mother.

Back in our room, I check how the Yankees did in their finale against the Royals. They lost 7–0. Igawa sucked, and A-Rod remained at 499.

"Sounds like we didn't miss anything," I say to Michael.

When he doesn't answer, I turn to look at him. He is stretched out on the bed, his head on the infant-size pillow, groaning from heartburn.

Friday is our first full day on the road, and I am stoked. At breakfast we sit next to two beefy guys from New Jersey.

"Are you firefighters or Yankee fans?" I ask them.

"Both," the beefier one says. He is digging into a steak. "I remember the first game my father ever took me to. I was 7, and I thought I died and went to heaven."

"Me, too," says the other one, whose hair is cut like a Marine's. "It was a game against the Red Sox, and we beat the assholes."

"My wife is writing a book about the Yankees!" Michael blurts out.

Both men suddenly regard me with shimmering respect.

"I wish I had your job," says the beefier one.

"Yeah, give us some inside information about the Yankees," challenges the Marine.

I pretend I have some by dropping John Sterling's name, as if he and I are old friends. They are impressed but want more.

"The Yankees are staying at the Renaissance," I say, like that's a bombshell.

"No kidding," the Marine says. "I thought they were at the Sheraton."

"Not according to John Sterling."

By midafternoon the temperature has reached 100 degrees. Michael's toe is throbbing, so he hunkers down at the Marriott while I go stake out the Yankees.

There is a big crowd in the driveway of the Renaissance, with everybody jockeying for position behind a velvet rope, hoping to spot the players as they leave the hotel for Camden Yards. There are young boys brandishing baseballs. There are firefighters taking a break from the convention. There is an old guy who introduces me to his Yorkshire terrier. He tells me he and the dog drove down from Staten Island yesterday because the dog is a Yankee fan whose favorite players are Melky and Cano. And there are middle-aged women bearing digital cameras. They are not groupies; they are wholesome, soccer-mom types wearing Yankees T-shirts.

"A security guy said they were coming out at 2 o'clock," one of them whispers to me. She loves the Yankees and will die happy if she gets a picture of Jeter.

There is a sudden commotion near the hotel's front door.

Okay. Here they come: Yankees in the flesh.

Torre appears first. He looks awful. Pale. Haggard. Balder than I realized. It has been a tough season, and he is wearing it on his face. He ignores the chants of his name and the outstretched balls of the kids and does his peg-leg walk to the parking garage where the team bus must be waiting.

Farnsworth *does* stop to sign and chat. Sure, he needs good PR, but I am surprised he is so friendly to the kids. I will not boo him tonight—unless he fucks up.

Wang walks past the crowd without a smile or a wave, but I give him a pass for it. He is painfully shy, according to Peter Abraham, who tells us this sort of thing on his blog.

Molina comes out of the hotel, and everyone yells, "Melky!" Well, Jose is still pretty new to the Yankees, so mistakes are inevitable.

Michael Kay not only walks right over to the kids standing behind the rope but also stays for several minutes to sign autographs for them.

I sense that A-Rod will not be coming through the front door like the others. It is probably in his contract that he has his own special exit.

The crowd is beginning to disperse when a stocky dark-haired man in his early forties makes his way out of the hotel and waits for a cab. It is Peter Abraham. I recognize him from his picture on the blog.

Forgetting that I am not wearing makeup or a bra, never mind that my hair is a fright wig and my clothes are soaked with sweat stains, I rush over.

"Hi, Peter," I say, extending my hand. "I'm a big admirer."

He regards me with caution. For all he knows, I am the local bag lady. But he shakes my hand.

"I read your blog religiously."

"That's great. Thanks."

"I'm writing a book about the Yankees!" I blurt out, just like Michael did this morning. "I'll be following them the rest of the way."

"I wrote a book about Wang," he says. "It was a bestseller in Taiwan."

"Congratulations." I am about to ask him if Jason Zillo is really the devil, but his cab pulls up.

"Nice meeting you," he says and drives off.

I should have suggested a drink after the game tonight or lunch tomorrow. I need to be more social.

I go back to the Marriott and call John Sterling on his cell phone. I leave him a message asking if he wants to get together with Michael and me over the weekend. I also leave a message for Peter Abraham at the Renaissance asking if he would let me interview him for the book.

John returns my call. He is busy this weekend but proposes that we have dinner in New York next week with Sandy and Doug McCartney, the Santa Barbara couple who put us together. He says that Thursday is a day game, so we could all meet in the city that night. He also apologizes for not being able to help me with Zillo. I thank him for trying and tell him not to worry about it because I might have a way in through Jean Afterman. He is impressed and says he hopes it works out.

We arrive at Camden Yards for the 7:05 game. It is everything everyone says about it—the perfect place to play baseball. With its historic brick warehouse in the background and its high-tech scoreboard in center field, it is old-fashioned and state of the art at the same time. *Field of Dreams* meets urban downtown.

We pass Boog's Barbecue, the food concession owned by former O's first baseman Boog Powell. The line is too long. We settle for Attman's Deli. We take our trays of food and ride the escalator to the top level of the park, where kindly ushers point us in the direction of our seats.

We find row LL, section 308, on the right-field side. We are about to bite into our turkey sandwiches when a group of firefighters appears and insists we are in their seats. "This is row L, not double L," one of them says after we show him our tickets. "Your seats are up there." He points skyward.

I can't believe there is an "up there" because we are already up there as far as I am concerned, but we apologize and go in search of our correct seats, which are near the very top of the stadium. If the first seats were in the nose-bleed section, these seats are in the brain aneurysm section. It is hot and sticky and close up here, and it smells like the inside of a beer can. Jean Afterman better come through. I can't spend days and nights like this, so far away from the field that the players are microscopic. Camden Yards is beautiful, no question, but I miss my green Barcalounger in the living room.

As we wait for the game to start, we are forced to watch a Cal Ripken video on the scoreboard. He *is* God here.

First up is the resumption of the June 28 game that was suspended by rain with the Yankees up 8–6 in the eighth. Myers is on the mound. He does his part and makes way for Mo, who gets the save, and the Yankees win.

Pettitte is the starter for the "real" game, and he pitches in and out of trouble. By the end of the third, it is 3–1 Orioles.

I get tapped on the shoulder.

"Is anyone sitting there?" a woman asks, pointing at the empty seat to my right.

"Not that I know of."

"Do you mind if I take it? Somebody vomited on the seat behind me."

Guthrie, Baltimore's pitcher, has the lowest ERA in the league right now, and all the Yankees can do with his 98 mph fastball is ground out. The only excitement comes whenever A-Rod steps to the plate. Thousands of flashbulbs go off simultaneously, and it is like a fireworks show on the Fourth of July. Everyone wants a shot of him grooving his 500th, but he does not oblige. He goes 0-for-2. He is pressing. At least that is what it looks like from up-up-up here.

In fact, all the Yankees look flat, feeble. They go down 4–2. The only good thing they do tonight is to demote Igawa again.

On Saturday Michael comes with me to watch the players exit the Renaissance, but he doesn't hide how bored he is.

"It's like watching grass grow," he says.

We leave and walk over to the Babe Ruth Museum, where we admire all the memorabilia. I choke up when I watch the video of the Mick talking about the Babe. The Yankees are deities for sure.

After a quick nap, Michael and I are back at Camden Yards. We go early tonight so we can watch the Yankees take batting practice. There are 48,000 other sweaty people with the same idea waiting for the gates to open. The vast majority of them are dressed in Yankees gear. The man behind me is from Bellport, Long Island, and drives down for every Yankees–Orioles game. The man to my left is from the Bronx and makes the pilgrimage, too.

The gates open, and there is a crush to get to the food concessions. I am dying to try Boog's Barbecue, so we wait in line for 20 minutes. Boog's is clearly the most popular spot, and after one bite of my pit turkey platter, I know why. The food is outrageously good. The platter comes with a roll stuffed with smoked sliced turkey that is smothered in spicy barbecue sauce, baked beans, and coleslaw. Michael, who should not even be looking at spicy food, loads up his plate and wolfs everything down. I keep my mouth shut about what he is putting into his inflamed intestines.

We are in section 354, row AA—above the Yankee dugout instead of way out in right field. We have missed batting practice but are in our seats in time for warm-up exercises and yet another Cal Ripken infomercial on the Jumbo-Tron. Melky is doing leg kicks as if he were auditioning for the Rockettes. Matsui is performing sort of a *Riverdance* routine. Jeter plays long toss with Cairo. A-Rod sprints. It is both disconcerting and reassuring to see the players without the benefit of TV cameras. They are no longer characters in some long-running prime-time series.

After their warm-ups, they take refuge in the dugout while the rest of us swelter. The announcer welcomes us to tonight's game and reports that it is 94 degrees. The people sitting next to me are a sweet middle-aged couple who took a 3-hour bus ride from Easton, Pennsylvania. The young punks on Michael's side are drunk even before the national anthem begins.

In the top of the first, the flashbulbs go off when A-Rod is batting, but he doesn't hit the big one. In the bottom of the inning, Clemens serves up a double to Brian Roberts, and the Yankees are down 2–0 before I know it.

Two male Orioles fans behind me are debating Kevin Millar's role with the 2004 Red Sox.

"Wasn't he the one who wouldn't give the championship ball back?" one of them says.

I turn around and say, "No, that was Doug Mientkiewicz. He plays first base for the Yankees now, but he's on the DL. He had a cervical sprain, a slight concussion, and a broken bone in his wrist as the result of a collision with Mike Lowell."

They look at me as if I have six heads.

A twentysomething woman in the section below us is wearing a white veil and carrying a sign that says "Bride to be would love to kiss Joe Torre." Next to Michael, one of the punks—they are now stinking drunk—throws a cell phone at the girl with the sign. He escapes ejection by telling the security guard that the phone "just slipped." When the coast is clear, he laughs and says to his friends, *That's* how you're supposed to get a wife: Throw a cell phone at her and knock some sense into her." I think longingly about my green chair in the living room. When I watch games at home, the only obnoxious person I have to deal with is me.

The Yankees look indifferent at the plate until the top of the ninth. With the O's ahead by 7–1, Abreu comes up as the potential tying run, with A-Rod on deck. He strikes out. Game over.

On Sunday we discover why Jorge does not catch day games after night games. Who wants to get up early after going to bed late?

There is a light drizzle as we ride up the escalator at Camden Yards at 12:15. The announcer comes over the speakers to tell us the game will be delayed until 2:05 and that in the meantime we are welcome to watch live coverage of Cal Ripken's induction into the Hall of Fame on the JumboTron. I am sure Cal is a terrific guy, but I am getting sick of him.

Eventually, the sky brightens, the tarp comes off, and we find our seats in section 332, row LL—still in the upper deck, but the best ones yet. We are in the midst of a "Wang section." There are over a dozen Taiwanese fans waving Taiwanese flags.

"People in Taiwan idolize Wang the way Americans idolize Elvis," one of them tells me.

In the first inning, A-Rod comes up with bases loaded and strikes out. He comes up again with bases loaded in the second and grounds out. He must be seriously constipated.

It is a seesaw battle the rest of the way. Farnsworth serves up a two-run homer in the bottom of the eighth, but the Yankees win 10–6 and avoid the sweep. After the game, Kyle complains to the media that he has not been used enough and did not come to the Yankees to sit on the bench. He may have signed balls for those kids at the Renaissance on Friday, but he is a big stupid crybaby.

The good thing about a day game is you get to go to an actual restaurant and have dinner that night. Michael and I take a cab to Obrycki's, Baltimore's famous crab house. The waitress delivers the crabs on a tray and dumps them onto our table, which she has covered with brown paper. She covers us too—with bibs—and brings us wooden mallets and a garbage pail. We pound our crabs. Pieces of meat fly into our eyes, our hair, everywhere but our mouths.

We have survived the first stop on our long journey and are in the mood to celebrate.

AL EAST STANDINGS/JULY 29

TEAM	W	L	PCT	GB
BOSTON	64	41	.610	—
NEW YORK	56	49	.533	8.0
TORONTO	52	52	.500	11.5
BALTIMORE	49	55	.471	14.5
TAMPA BAY	39	65	.375	24.5

Week 18
July 30, 2007

Pop-ups are Alex's kryptonite. He dropped one in the first inning on open-ing day. Derek and Robbie hid their faces in their gloves and died laugh-ing. Derek looked over and yelled, "Jesus Christ! Catch the ball!" Last year Alex would have beaten himself up and the game would have gone to hell. But this year he laughed it off. This game is so hard and so hum-bling that if you can't laugh at yourself it'll bury you. I've been there.

Thunderstorms are forecast for Monday, the Yankees' off day and our getaway day. We are supposed to take some claustrophobic little US Airways Express flight up to New York this morning, but I can't summon the courage. We rent a fire-engine-red Toyota Matrix from Hertz, drive north on I-95, and pull into my mother's driveway in Westchester by midafternoon. She has lived in the same house for more than 30 years. Most of her friends have either downsized or moved into assisted-living facilities, but she will not hear of leaving. That house is home to her. I am envious. I have lived in so many places—New York, Connecticut, Florida, California—that I have no real sense of "home" anymore.

"Hello!" I say as Mom waves to me from the front door. She looks adorable in her jeans and sweater and pink lipstick. She has shrunk another half inch since my last visit, but she is otherwise a miracle of nature.

She hugs me, then Michael. "I bought cold cuts and potato salad and an Entenmann's coffee cake."

Later, she drives me into the village, where she drops me at her hair salon. I have a blow-dry with Katya. I could have washed and dried my own hair, but a few years ago I came to the sobering conclusion that I have absolutely no command of a blow-dryer. So I seek out professionals.

I spend the rest of the afternoon doing laundry and talking to my mother while Michael naps. I tell her about all the cities we will be going to and all the teams we will be playing, and she gives me a look like she thinks I am crazy.

"What?" I say.

"I know you love the Yankees, dearie. I love them, too. But it sounds so exhausting."

"I'll be fine."

"Do they feed you at those baseball stadiums?"

"Yes, Mom."

"How will you get enough sleep going from hotel to hotel?"

"I just will."

"There are a lot of maniacs out there," she says, wagging an arthritic finger at me. "You have to be so careful these days."

"Mom! I'm excited about this trip! It's a good thing, okay?"

When Michael and I are alone in the guest room later, he tells me his cell phone is missing. "I must have dropped it at Camden Yards."

"So it's sitting in the middle of a ballpark where any maniac can use it! You have to be so careful these days!"

❧

Tuesday begins promisingly. I get an e-mail from Susan Tofias, who became my best friend in the sixth grade when we danced to "The Loco-Motion" in the gym. She moved to a Boston suburb after college and raised a family while I moved around the country and wrote books. But she is my Scarsdale friend and I am her Scarsdale friend, and we keep in touch via e-mail. She is one of the people I wrote to after Jason Zillo barred me from the press box. She has a large social circle in Boston, and I asked her if she knew anybody with Red Sox tickets. She writes back that her friends, Steven and Joan Belkin, are willing to part with their four field-box seats for the Sunday game at Fenway in September. This means there is an extra seat for Michael's brother Geoff, who lives in New Hampshire and is, of course, a diehard Red Sox fan.

"There is only one caveat," writes Susan in her e-mail. "The game will probably be nationally televised and the Belkins' seats are VERY VISIBLE ON TV. SO NO YANKEES CLOTHES! YOU MUST NOT EMBARRASS THEM!"

"They're being so generous. I wouldn't dream of embarrassing them," I write back. "I will happily bury all evidence of my Yankee-ness."

Michael and I leave at 3:30 for tonight's 7:05 game against the White Sox. He takes 684 to the Hutchinson River Parkway to the Cross County Parkway to the entrance to the Major Deegan—except it is not the entrance to the Deegan.

"I know you hate asking for directions," I say to Michael, "but could you please ask for directions?"

"Okay," he says grudgingly. "But I have to find the right person."

He pulls into the parking lot of an Irish pub where three gray-haired men in black suits are standing around smoking unfiltered cigarettes. They look like undertakers or *Sopranos* cast members or both. Michael gets out of the car and speaks to them. He returns after a few minutes and off we go. I know we are nearing the Stadium because the black Jeep in front of us has a decal on its rear window with a man in a Yankees cap pissing on a Red Sox cap.

I turn on WFAN to find out if there is any trade news now that the 4:00 p.m. deadline has passed. There is. The Yankees have traded not Farnsworth but Proctor—to the Dodgers for infielder Wilson Betemit. I have never heard of Betemit, so I don't know what to make of this deal. The FAN also reports that the Red Sox traded a minor leaguer to the Rangers for Eric Gagne, who is more famous than Wilson Betemit.

We arrive at Yankee Stadium at 4:30 and can't find a parking lot that is open. They all have gates that are locked. As we wind our way through the narrow, serpentine streets—161st, 162nd, 163rd—it's clear we're not in Baltimore anymore. The streets are teeming with people who are serious about getting the most bass out of their boom boxes.

We park in Lot 16. It is about a mile from the Stadium, but it is open and it only costs $14 as opposed to the $28 they charge at the valet lots.

Michael takes a photo of me in front of the Stadium. We plan to document that I have actually gone to every ballpark.

Afterward I scan the crowd and recognize Freddy, the man who encourages people to bang a spoon on his pan to bring the Yankees luck. He has been around forever—a legendary character in the Bronx—and I have to meet him.

He is sitting on a bench in his pinstriped shirt and Yankees cap, pan in hand, along with a sign that reads: "Freddy Sez Yankees Can Improve!" He is stooped over, and his face is covered with gray grizzle, and he looks 100 years old. But he smiles and lets Michael take his picture with me.

"How did you become the Pan Man?" I ask.

"I grew up in the Bronx," he says with the accent to prove it. "I was always a Yankee fan. About 20 years ago I started bringing a pan to the games for luck. In the beginning I bought my own tickets, but now they let me in for free."

"You've become a celebrity."

He grins proudly. "Did you see me in *For Love of the Game*?"

"Of course I did." I am lying, but I don't have the heart not to. Before I can find out more, another fawning woman sidles up to him, and I am history.

Michael and I enter the Stadium through Gate 6, where the snarling security guards check our bags and clothes and pat us down as if we were going through security at the Baghdad airport. Even the ticket takers bark at us. The people who work here are not touchy-feely like the employees at Camden Yards. They are like bouncers at a nightclub.

We forage for food before finding our seats. We find an outpost of Bronx's famous Mike's Deli on Arthur Avenue. I order a turkey sandwich known as the Sweet Bird, and Michael, who is determined to sample the hot dogs at every ballpark, gets his first Yankee Stadium dog, which he rates an F.

We take the escalator to Tier 17. Well, several escalators. It is one thing to be at the very top of Camden Yards. It is another to be at the very top of a stadium that holds over 55,000 people. I flash back to the night we went to the World Series with the Other Jane Heller and sat behind the on-deck circle. You can't even see the on-deck circle from up-up-up here. It is not for people with vertigo.

Tier 17 is between first base and the right-field foul pole. Our seats are in row C, on the aisle. I now understand why this ballpark is being torn down. It is butt ugly, except for the immaculately kept field and the distinctive facade. The seats up-up-up here are truly uncomfortable—hard and bare with no legroom—and their blue paint is faded and sad looking. And the aisles themselves are so narrow that you have no choice but to step on people to get anywhere. Still, this is Yankee Stadium—the cathedral in which I have worshipped since I was a child.

"Disorderly conduct will not be tolerated and will lead to immediate ejection," intones Bob Sheppard, the longtime voice of the Yankees. This place has history, but it is not warm and fuzzy.

Sheppard announces the Yankees lineup accompanied by the theme from *Star Wars.* I get a kick out of how he lingers over each name, particularly "Der-ek Jeet-ah." And he is funny with the names of the Latino players. He rolls his r's, but his dentures get in the way. A-Rod elicits a huge hand from the crowd. They have come to see him hit 500.

Tonight is the first of a three-game series against the White Sox. Mussina is on the mound. He has a nice, clean first inning and gets a loud "Moooose" call. In the bottom half, A-Rod steps in to chants of "MVP!" and the flashbulbs go off. It is an absolutely blinding spectacle, and I can only imagine how daunting it must be for him to try to hit a baseball with all those lights popping. He flies out. But Matsui homers, and the Yankees jump ahead 4–0. The Stadium may be dilapidated, but there is no place more electric. When the crowd rocks, the cathedral rocks, too.

Before the top of the seventh, we applaud the grounds crew and their "YMCA" dance routine. But we turn solemn during the seventh inning stretch and Kate Smith's "God Bless America." When I watch the games at home, the song is my cue to disappear into my office to check phone messages and e-mails, but now that I am here, I am touched by it. I feel very patriotic singing along with 54,999 others.

In the bottom of the seventh, the Yankees are up 16–3 and here comes A-Rod. He flies out yet again, and there is a collective sigh of frustration. He is now in an 0-for-16 slump.

After the game, Michael and I are pushed and shoved and elbowed as we attempt to leave the ballpark. Even after we make it to the parking lot, it is pure madness—gridlock, horns honking, people telling each other to go fuck themselves.

We are back at my mother's by 11:30. She is still awake.

"I looked for you in the stands," she says. "I don't understand why I couldn't see you."

"We have to sit very high up."

"You can't get seats right down in front?"

"Not yet," I say. "I'm working on it."

In the Wednesday *New York Times* there is speculation that since the Red Sox got Gagne, the Yankees will call up a rookie from Scranton named Joba Chamberlain to be our setup man. Supposedly, this Joba person has a live arm and can strike batters out. I will believe it when I see it.

Joe Longo at Gersh e-mails that he has not heard back from Jean Afterman and suggests that I should just call Jean at her office. He gives me her number. "Tell her you're the one who's doing the book."

I swallow hard and dial her number. A young woman answers.

"Is Jean there, please?"

"Who's calling her?"

"Jane Heller. Joe Longo suggested I call."

"Oh. Joe. Sure. Please hold."

I am on hold for several minutes when the assistant returns.

"Can I get a number where Jean can call you back?"

I give her my cell number and go on and on about how important it is for me to talk to Jean as soon as possible, but she has already hung up.

At 3:00 p.m. Michael and I leave my mother's for tonight's game against the White Sox. We don't get lost this time. We drive straight to parking lot number nine. It is easily 100 degrees.

Inside the Stadium we check out the food court, but I will not pollute my body with hot dogs or chicken fingers. We keep walking—until we see something called the Pinstripe Pub.

"Let's go in," I say to Michael.

"It's a private club."

"So?" I turn to the guard stationed outside the door. "Can you take two?"

"Sorry," he says. "You need a special pass to get in."

Michael gives me a look, but I am not budging. I am hot and I am hungry and I am determined.

"A special pass?" I say. "But we came all the way from California for tonight's game."

"Don't tell anyone," he says, then opens the door and whisks us inside.

I give Michael a look and find us a table. The restaurant is air-conditioned and has waiters and menus and, best of all, serves wine.

After dinner, we search for our seats. They are in Tier 18, row C—above third base and much better than last night's. At 6:58, right on schedule, Bob

Sheppard's voice booms with the lineups. He really gets a workout trying to maneuver around the White Sox's "A. J. Pierzynski."

Pettitte is on the hill tonight. He strikes out two of three in the top of the first. In the bottom of the inning, A-Rod comes up and the 500 Show starts all over again: the flashbulbs, the chanting, the holding up of signs and banners. He flies out.

It is 7–1 in the bottom of the seventh when A-Rod gets another turn. He has done nothing in this game. Nothing in days. He looks completely unnerved by the attention and pressure, and I feel sorry for him. Sure, he is a gazillionaire and the best player in baseball, but he is a psychological wreck right now. You can see it in his body language even from Tier 18. For this at-bat, everybody in the Stadium stands. He works the count to 3–1, then grounds out. I hear a few boos.

The 8–1 final is the Yankees' third straight win. We are on a roll.

Thursday brings another day game after a night game—and another trip to a hair salon. It is time to touch up my roots. Bruce, my colorist in Santa Barbara, applies my shade of blond every month, but he has given me my "formula," and I hand it over to Trish at the Peninsula Hotel's Mélange Salon in the city. I want to look my best for dinner with John Sterling later.

Michael and I have brought our dress-up clothes in garment bags and plan to leave them at my sister Susan's high-rise apartment on the Upper East Side while we go to the game. She meets us in the lobby and introduces us to her doorman. His name is Hilton, and he is a Yankee fan.

"I heard about your book," he says with a big smile. He is a handsome young man in his uniform. "Pretty cool."

"Thanks, Hilton."

"I heard about the hassles with the tickets, too." He nods at my sister, who has apparently told him my life story. "I'll keep my ears open. I think one of the tenants here works for WFAN."

"You really shouldn't go to the game," my sister says once we are upstairs in her air-conditioned apartment. "It's too hot. You can watch it here, and we'll order lunch, and you'll be more comfortable."

My sister is 7 years older than I am. She is also a mother, a grandmother, and a preschool teacher—very nurturing and much nicer than I am. I don't see her that often, since we live on opposite coasts. And we don't share the same interests—she is a show-tunes person and I am a rock-and-roll person, for example—but we share an interest in the Yankees, and that is no small thing.

She and Michael persuade me that it would be silly to go to the game. So we watch it in her living room.

Clemens falters badly, departing in only the second inning after giving up eight runs. I am amazed at my sister's lack of anger at the Rocket. She doesn't throw cheese at Michael or me. The Yankees tie the score at 8–8 in the bottom of the frame, but the White Sox win the 4-hour contest 13–9 after Farnsworth watches two homers sail over his head and Cano lets a ball dribble through his legs for his second error of the day. A-Rod is still stalled at 499, but at least he got a couple of hits.

Bob, my brother-in-law, emerges from his office in the apartment.

"How's the book going?" he asks. He is trying to quit smoking, but I detect a whiff of cigarettes on his clothes.

"I'm having trouble getting access to the Yankees," I say.

He thinks about this. He always tries to help. He drove me around to look at colleges when I was a teenager and found me my first car and, of course, introduced me to the groupies who lived next door. "A friend of mine knows Bob Watson," he says, referring to the Yankees' former GM, who is now the disciplinarian at Major League Baseball. "I'll ask him to put in a good word for you."

I love that I have this grassroots support for my cause.

The Post House on East 63rd Street is a dark, clubby steak house filled with Upper East Side power brokers and their trophy wives. Michael and I arrive in our dress-up clothes and Sandy and Doug McCartney come along soon after. Sandy is attractive, with intelligent eyes and a warm smile. She jumps right in and starts talking, so there are none of the awkward silences that often accompany first meetings. Doug is tall and tanned and handsome, and he laughs easily. I am so glad they let us horn in on their dinner.

John shows up looking not the least bit weary from the marathon game he has just broadcast. He is nattily dressed in a dark suit with a white handkerchief in his jacket pocket. He is taller and trimmer than he appears on TV, but what gets me is the Voice. Unmistakable.

Since he is an Important Personage in New York, we are led to the Post House's best table. Once we are seated, I remind myself that this occasion is a social get-together, and I rein in my impulse to grill him about the Yankees. Well, I do ask a few questions. He is very affable and charming and doesn't seem to mind.

"What if you have to go to the bathroom while you're on the air?" I ask, after having established that he has not missed a single game since he started with the Yankees in 1989.

"I hold it in until the game is over."

"What do you do to relax after a game?"

"I watch tapes of *The Young and the Restless* and *The Bold and the Beautiful*."

I notice his World Series ring. It is gold with diamonds studding the interlocking N-Y. He lets me try it on, and it is so heavy I can hardly lift it. He says the new versions are even bigger and gaudier. This one is big and gaudy enough.

The dinner is very cordial. As we are leaving the restaurant, John pledges his help with the Yankees once again.

"I don't know exactly what I can do, since Jason Zillo won't let you into the press box. Maybe you could interview the beat writers and ask them about the players."

"Thanks. I'll do that."

During the drive back to Westchester, Michael and I crack each other up doing impressions of John.

"It's an A-Bomb! From A-Rod!" I say in a mock baritone.

"Theeeee Yankees win!" Michael says in his deepest voice.

"Except they didn't win today," I say in my own voice.

On Friday morning, I try Jean Afterman again at her office. Her assistant is brusque. She takes my number. I have a bad feeling about this.

I send Jean an e-mail, explaining who I am in case she is confused by all the info from Joe Longo and Brenda Friend.

My heart stops a few minutes later when I see her name in my in-box. She will be my advocate, I tell myself. She will understand the emotional component of being a She-Fan. She will "get" this.

I open the e-mail.

"Ms. Heller," she writes. "This is a Media Relations matter and you should address any inquiries to that department. I have nothing to do with these issues."

Talk about curt. She regards me as an "issue." And she copied Jason Zillo. I am sure he is thrilled that I went over his head.

What is wrong with the Yankees? Don't they understand that I am their number one fan?

At first I panic that my publisher will void the book contract if I don't get access. But I call Marty, and he reminds me that this kiss-off is just a minor setback.

"Remember what I told you. There's always one player who will talk, and you'll find him—with or without their cooperation."

He gives me the name of a ticket broker he has used in Toronto: Mike Chivlelli at Kangaroo Promotions. I call Mike and buy tickets for the games against the Blue Jays at the Rogers Centre next week. They are not cheap, but they take 5 minutes as opposed to the 2 hours I spent on StubHub.

Tonight the Yankees open a three-game series against Kansas City. My niece, Lizzie, and her husband, Aaron, will be at the game, and I look forward to seeing them. It is very hot and humid with a forecast of thunderstorms, so I stick my collapsible umbrella in my bag.

At the Stadium we take the escalators up to Tier 5, row V, the highest we have been so far—only three rows from the very top. We are directly above home plate, but we might as well be up in the blimp.

Wang is pitching, and once again there are rows full of Taiwanese people waving Taiwanese flags. I also notice that there are several groups of women sitting together. They are laughing and drinking and having a carefree night out with the girls. Has the ballpark replaced the singles bar? Is beer the new Cosmo?

Wang looks sharp tonight, his sinker making suckers out of the Royals batters. In the bottom of the sixth, the Yankees are up 5–1 and the bases are loaded for A-Rod. It is sheer bedlam. Flashbulbs. Cheers. Stomping. Is this his moment? Will he finally hit number 500? He doubled in the third. Does he have his stroke back? No. He flies out.

Lizzie calls in the top of the seventh from the Loge section, where she and Aaron are sitting. She says there are plenty of empty seats and we should come and join them. We are only too happy to move down.

"Nice seats," I tell her. "You can actually make out the players' faces from here. How much did you pay for them?"

"Sixty apiece on StubHub." Like her mother, she has a calm, nurturing demeanor. She is a Yankee fan but takes their winning and losing as part of the natural order of things. I am the freakish She-Fan of this family. I wonder if I was adopted.

It is 7–1 in the bottom of the eighth when A-Rod steps in. A loud clap of thunder erupts and everyone jumps. If he hits number 500 now, with all the sound effects, it will be really dramatic. He flies out.

In the top of the ninth, the speakers blare Mo's theme song, "Enter Sandman." As he finishes off the Royals, there are bolts of lightning in the sky. The crowd hurries out of the Stadium to avoid the sudden storm.

Lizzie, Aaron, Michael, and I head down the ramps along with 55,000 others. I have never experienced such a crush of hot, sweaty bodies. The ramps are totally backed up, and once we inch down to the main level I see why. It is now pouring outside, with ferocious thunder and lightning. Nobody wants to go out in such a violent storm, including us. We are not worried about getting wet; we are afraid of getting electrocuted.

"Everybody out!" yell the security people in their yellow shirts and menacing voices as they literally try to herd us out the doors. "You have to leave *now!*"

We are not budging. The four of us huddle together with hundreds of others who refuse to be thrown out. We have rights. We are not living in a police state. We are united in our refusal to be bullied.

"*You people have to leave!*" one of the security guys screams, as another Yankee Stadium employee actually shoves a woman outside and does nothing when she slips and falls on the wet pavement.

Small children cry hysterically, which is enough to rouse the normally mild-mannered Michael. He gets in the security guy's face: "It'll be your ass if somebody is hurt!"

He is not alone in his anger. But as if to show who's boss, the security guy grabs the handles on a man's wheelchair and pushes him out the door.

Our collective rage explodes. We are on the verge of an actual riot, and the security people don't have a clue what to do. There is no crowd control, no one in charge—until a big, burly guy with a shaved head yells at us through a megaphone.

"Everybody quiet down!" He glares at his own employees. "No one's going anywhere until I say it's okay to leave!"

"I hate this place," I say to Lizzie.

"Welcome to Yankee Stadium," she replies.

After about 30 minutes, the guy with the megaphone announces that the storm is supposed to continue for the rest of the night, so we do have to leave. He instructs the security people to hand out large garbage bags to everyone in the crowd. The idea is for us to poke a hole in the bags for our heads and wear them as raincoats. I am amazed they don't make us pay for the bags.

Saturday is another day game after a night game. And since the night game was such a bummer, I am not in a rush to drive back to the Stadium. But we do. We take the escalators to Tier 27, row M. The section is not quite as high up as last night's, but it is farther away from the action—in right-field foul territory. I can't see the scoreboard, which really irritates me.

Phil Hughes is making his return to the team since coming off the DL. He is throwing strikes in the top of the first and sets the Royals down in order. When A-Rod comes up in the bottom half, 55,000 people stand and scream, "Let's go, A-Rod!"

"God, I hope he does it already," I say to Michael, who is giving the hot dogs at Yankee Stadium another try.

Here is the first pitch from someone named Kyle Davies. A-Rod golfs the ball toward left field. It is not one of his towering bombs, but it could be long enough. The question is will it stay fair? Will it? Will it? YES!!!

The Stadium literally shakes as A-Rod rounds the bases. We are on our feet clapping, chanting, waving our arms in a kind of delirium. Now the entire Yankees team spills out onto the field waiting to congratulate A-Rod. On his way toward home plate, he looks up into the stands and blows a kiss to someone. His wife? The stripper? Scott Boras? After he is mobbed by his teammates, he joins them back in the dugout, then comes out for a curtain call. But it is not the usual doffing of the cap. His arms are outstretched in appreciation of the crowd—and probably with relief that the whole ordeal is over. He is the third player, after the Babe and the Mick, to hit 500 homers in pinstripes. What is more, the Yankees trounce Kansas City 16–8.

We listen to A-Rod's press conference in the car on the way back to my mother's. He sounds awed both by his feat and by the fans' support. "To wear this uniform and do it here, that is so special," he says. "I've had some good times and had some rough times, and a day like today brings it full circle, and maybe there's a happy ending for me somewhere."

"What do you think?" I ask Michael as we pull into Mom's driveway. "Will he opt out of his contract and leave New York?"

"I could care less," he says. "I wouldn't mind taking a night off from baseball."

I pat his arm. "We'll have dinner and focus on other things."

When we get inside the house, we see that my mother has set up tray tables in front of the TV in her bedroom. "I heard about A-Rod's homer on the news!" she says, her face flushed with excitement. "I missed the game this afternoon, so I was hoping we could eat dinner and watch the rerun of it tonight. You don't mind, do you?"

Sunday is getaway day. There is a 1:05 game in the Bronx, the finale against Kansas City, but we will not make our flight to Toronto if we go. So we watch it on TV with Mom. Mussina is sharp over six-plus innings, and Matsui and Melky homer. The Yankees win 8–5 and sweep the Royals.

We finish packing, load up the car, and say good-bye to my mother.

"Thanks for having us." I hug her. She is so small, and I feel a lump in my throat the way I always do when I leave her. At 90, every visit with her is a gift. But I will be back in New York for the next home stands.

I hug her again. We endured the usual mother-daughter power struggles over the years, but now we are much more than mother and daughter; we are friends, too. In fact, she is probably my best friend other than Michael. I know with absolute certainty that she would do anything for me; that I could tell her anything; that she is always in my corner. There is only one lingering issue between us: She insists that Bernie Williams should still be on the Yankees. I try to explain that his numbers suggest otherwise, but she will not yield on this point.

When Michael and I arrive at the Air Canada terminal for our 6:30 flight to Toronto, I ask the agent about the flight's equipment, our seats, my usual routine. She says the equipment is an Embraer 175. I gasp, having only heard of Boeings and Airbuses.

"You don't like small planes?" she asks.

I tell Michael I will meet him at the gate and go in search of the bar.

I sit between two overweight guys downing scotches and order a glass of

Pinot Grigio. Facing me is a bank of TV screens, one of which is tuned to the YES Network. YES is showing one of their "classics," and it happens to be the game the Yankees played right after Thurman Munson was *killed in a small plane crash*. All I need now is a retrospective on the career of Cory Lidle, who was also *killed in a small plane crash*. I polish off my glass of wine, then race back through security to the gate. Michael is standing there, pissed. People have already begun to board. I am not getting on this piece of *equipment*. But then I see Michael Kay boarding the plane.

"Maybe I can interview him during the flight," I whisper to Michael.

"I thought you were worried about dying."

"It would be great to get his take on the Yankees before we all go down."

Unfortunately, this dinky plane has an even dinkier first-class cabin, and Michael Kay sits in it; we are banished to coach.

After we land in Toronto we go through customs, then on to our baggage-claim carousel. There is Michael Kay waiting for his suitcase.

I put on some lipstick, fluff my hair, and hope to God I don't stink of Pinot Grigio.

"Michael?"

He turns to face me.

"Hi. I'm Jane Heller." I stick out my hand to shake his. He is tall and has an extremely large head. "I'm writing a book about the Yankees and following them for the rest of the season."

"Really?"

I notice another man approaching him. Oh, wow. It is Al Leiter.

"Hi, Al."

He is quite handsome but seems less than thrilled to be accosted by me at the Toronto airport. I refocus on Michael Kay.

"Are you staying at the Park Hyatt?"

"Yes."

"Me too! John Sterling says it's *the* place to stay in Toronto." I must stop dragging poor John into every conversation.

"Yes, it's a great hotel." He starts looking for his suitcase.

I follow him. "I was really touched by the way you took the time to sign autographs for the kids outside the Renaissance in Baltimore."

"The ballplayers are so busy," he says with an air of modesty. "Signing autographs is the least I can do." He laughs. "Maybe you'll write in your book that I'm a nice guy."

"Absolutely!"

I am about to suggest we get together, when Al points to their bags. They hurry over to retrieve them, and before I know it they are out of the terminal.

We take our own cab to the Park Hyatt, which is a swanky establishment in Toronto's swanky Yorkville neighborhood. A battalion of foot soldiers rushes to greet us. I spot Cano, Melky, and Betemit in the lobby. They are all dressed up for a night on the town. I overhear Cano asking the concierge for dance club suggestions.

While I am at the front desk requesting a quiet room, Michael Kay is speaking to another front desk clerk. I catch his eye and wave. He does not wave back.

"We have a package for you, Ms. Heller," the front desk person says and hands me a delivery from Mike, the broker. I open the package. Inside are all the tickets to the games at the Rogers Centre, along with a couple of Fila shirts and a box of chocolate candy. Who needs StubHub?

Our quiet room at the Park Hyatt is, in fact, a lavish suite that Marty's friend Lisa somehow managed to finagle at a reasonable rate. On the coffee table is a plate of scones with blueberries and cream along with a "Welcome" card from the hotel management. This is more like it.

AL EAST STANDINGS/AUGUST 5

TEAM	W	L	PCT	GB
BOSTON	68	43	.613	—
NEW YORK	61	50	.550	7.0
TORONTO	56	54	.509	11.5
BALTIMORE	52	58	.473	15.5
TAMPA BAY	42	68	.382	25.5

Week 19
August 6, 2007

Clemens was pitching a two-hitter when he hit Rios. But that's what being a teammate is all about. You don't care about your numbers. You care about taking care of your guy. The average fan will never understand the magnitude of what he brought us.

I wake up on Monday morning from an odd dream. I was trying to solve a mystery, and the person who was helping me was Eric Berson, my college boyfriend from the University of Rochester. Since I believe in signs and portents and omens, I took Eric's presence in the dream as my cue to track him down. Never mind that I have not seen or spoken to him in years. He once told me he had a part ownership in some pro sports team. Maybe he can get me access to the Yankees.

I Google him and find his Web site. I e-mail him and he calls me!

"Holy shit!" he says. "This is a surprise."

"How are you?"

He reels off all his successful business ventures, including Greeniacs, an international organization that educates the public about environmental issues. In college he was the kid who never studied, never even bought the textbooks, and still ended up with a 4.0 average. It is not a shock that he has done well in his life.

I explain about the book and ask if he has any influence with the Yankees.

"I'm still semi-involved with the 49ers, but it gets me restaurant reservations and not much else."

"Too bad. The Yankees won't give me press passes to the games."

"Oh, kid," he says as if he is my much smarter, older brother. "Don't torture yourself. Just buy the tickets."

At noon, Michael and I take a cab to the Rogers Centre, where the first pitch is scheduled for 1:07 p.m. We gaze up at the mammoth domed stadium, which is directly behind one of the world's tallest structures, the CN Tower. We follow the crowd up the stairs and around and around in search of our gate. We pass a panhandler wearing a wool plaid kilt and playing the bagpipes. The temperature is in the 90s.

Inside the stadium, whose roof is open for the sunny day game, we find a food court and buy lunch. Our cashier charges us $120 for a couple of subs. We point out his mistake.

"I had a brain cramp, eh?" he says, changing our tab to $20.

We find our seats, which are excellent. We are right on the field, on the third base side, about 20 rows back. After being in the up-up-up there section for so many days, I am in heaven.

The Rogers Centre is hardly charming like Camden Yards. It is a functional dome with a retractable roof, not an old-timey-looking ballpark, and there is artificial turf where real grass is supposed to be. But it is comfortable and easy to navigate, and the scoreboard is a technological wonder, as sleek as a plasma TV monitor with perfect resolution. And there are glass-enclosed restaurants overlooking center field that I put on my list of places to try.

David Beckham and some of his Galaxy teammates throw out the first pitch, since they are in town to play the Toronto team. Becks gets booed. He is the A-Rod of soccer.

Next up: two national anthems are sung—ours and "O Canada."

This is the first game in Toronto since A-Rod yelled something in May that made Howie Clark drop the ball, and the Jays waste no time in retaliating. Jesse Litsch throws his first pitch behind A-Rod.

Toronto scores three runs off Pettitte, who gets lifted in the sixth for someone named Jim Brower. Apparently, Myers has been designated for assignment—his punishment for not getting lefties out—and Brower is his replacement. Mo comes on in the ninth and strikes out the side: Rios, Wells, and the Big Hurt. Impressive, even for Mo. The Yankees win 5–4 and are only a half game behind Detroit for the wild card.

Back at the Park Hyatt, I leave a message for John Sterling inviting him to join us for dinner at Spuntini, the Italian place the concierge recommended.

He calls right back. "The bad news is I'm busy for dinner tonight. The good news I'm going to Spuntini. It's one of Joe Torre's favorite restaurants, and he's having a team dinner in a private room. So I'll come out and say hello."

I pump my fist.

"What's going on?" Michael asks.

"The Yankees are having dinner in a private room at Spuntini! This is my big chance to meet them!"

"Are you planning to pop out of a cake?"

I take a great deal of time with my clothes, hair, and makeup. Tonight is the night I will strike up a conversation with a Yankee.

We walk to the restaurant. As we step inside, I catch a glimpse of Jeter and Jorge. They are in the private room John mentioned. I crane my neck to see which other players I can spot until the maître d' comes over to show us to our table.

"I can't believe they're all here," I whisper to Michael, who is sitting across from me. "If we stay long enough, they'll wander out and I can—"

Jorge emerges from the private room and stops to talk to the father and son who are sitting a few tables away from us. They all chat for a few minutes—the boy is adorable, managing to look both excited to be hanging out with an actual Yankee and sophisticated enough not to make Jorge sign his napkin—before Posada goes back to his party.

"I wonder who they are." I nod at the father and son.

Michael is more interested in the menu. "Must be associated with the team somehow."

"Let's order a lot of food so we don't have to give up the table anytime soon."

We order as many courses as I pray my American Express card will allow, and the food keeps coming. But I don't want my Yankee to see me with spinach between my teeth, so I keep opening my compact to inspect myself in the mirror.

We are on our main course when John Sterling stops by. He slides in next to me.

"What do you guys talk about in there?" I say.

"This and that. Everybody in there is someone Joe trusts."

After a few minutes, he excuses himself and goes back to Joe and the guys. I am sipping the last of my wine when I glance up at Michael. There is a large—

no, massive—figure moving behind him. It takes me a second before I realize that it is A-Rod who is walking directly in back of his chair en route to the men's room and that he is making eye contact with me. I actually choke on my saliva. It is one thing to see him in his uniform, on the field. It is another to see him in jeans and a polo shirt, inches away. He is an amazing specimen—not an ounce of flab, just a hard, sculpted, athlete's body—and his sheer physicality makes him a commanding presence.

"What's wrong?" Michael asks. "You look like you're having a stroke."

"That was A-Rod," I whisper. "He was right behind you. He went to take a leak."

"So?"

"You have to follow him in there."

The rest you know.

At the hotel after dinner, we take a ride up in the elevator to the 18th-floor lounge. One tidbit John dropped is that the players like to go up there for a drink. We walk into the dimly lit room, and there are Jeter and Jorge sitting at a little cocktail table.

"I'm going over," I tell Michael.

"And say what?"

"That I'm writing a book and would like to interview them."

"They'll tell you to call Jason Zillo."

"Maybe," I say. "And maybe not."

I open my compact one last time to check for food between my teeth. I can't smile at Jeter and have green things showing. Jorge would be a great catch, too, don't get me wrong. But Jeter is the Captain.

I close the compact and glance up—only to find that both catches have vanished.

On Tuesday I meet Peter Abraham at 12:30 in the lobby of the Renaissance Hotel at the Rogers Centre. He is stocky with dark, close-cropped hair; a goatee; and a serious expression. He is not unfriendly, just businesslike. I am businesslike, too. I did not come to swap recipes or discuss my favorite chick flicks. I came to find out about the Yankees from someone who has the access I don't.

Peter and I ride up in the elevator to the concierge lounge where he says it will be quiet. We sit at a table and I turn on my tape recorder—only to have a maintenance person start vacuuming the carpet.

Peter has already told me he needs to be at the ballpark by 2:30. I begin by asking him about his background.

"I'm from New Bedford, Massachusetts," he says. "I got my start in journalism at the hometown paper. After covering UConn men's basketball for the *Norwich Bulletin,* I went to work at the LoHud chain, which used to be called the Gannett Suburban Newspapers, and covered the Mets for a couple of years. I inherited the Yankees beat at the end of the '05 season."

"So you're relatively new on the beat," I say.

"Relatively. There's a lot of turnover with baseball writers because it's such a hard job. Guys get married and their wives don't want them to be away for a hundred and fifty days a year."

He is obviously single.

"Was it difficult to get to know people in the Yankees organization?"

"One advantage I had was that the previous beat writer from my paper wasn't the most popular guy. The Yankees were happy I was replacing him."

"Tell me about some Yankees."

"Andy Phillips is one I root for. I hope he hits 1,000 home runs. His poor wife almost died and his mom almost died, and he never once wouldn't talk to us."

"Is that why you like some players? Because they talk to you?"

"How helpful they are to me is a factor. When I was covering the Mets, they were a bad team, and bad teams want to get out of the clubhouse after the game and go home. But Cliff Floyd never once said, 'Sorry, fellas. Gotta go.' Glavine was the same way. David Wright, too. Totally professional. The Red Sox aren't like that at all."

"Really?"

"Manny won't talk to anybody. And Beckett swears at the writers all the time. He's just a really mean guy."

"Did you ever have a run-in with a player?"

"Al Leiter—when I was on one of my first road trips with the Mets. He hadn't pitched well. I asked, 'Do you think it was something with your stuff today?' He said, 'What do you mean by *stuff?*' I said, 'Your pitches, Al.' He said, 'What pitches?' I said, 'Al, you pitched the game. You tell me.' He started giving it back to me, trying to intimidate me because I was a new writer. But I wasn't afraid of Al Leiter. So I said, 'You know what? I'll go ask somebody else,' and walked away. We had this contentious relationship for a while but ended up friendly. We both like Springsteen."

"I'm guessing Mussina isn't fun to interview."

"No, I love Mussina. He's really quite funny and smart."

Smart, okay. But funny? "What about Jeter? He always gives the same pat answers. He must be tough to interview."

"In a group session it's impossible. He won't say much more than 'Bottom line: We want to win' and all that clichéd stuff. You have to be around awhile to build up credibility."

"What about A-Rod?"

"Alex tries too hard," he says. "Someone must have told him that swearing would make him seem cool. So he went through this period where he couldn't talk to us without swearing. It was weird. But then someone else must have told him to stop swearing because we wouldn't print what he was saying."

"That *is* weird."

"Here's the difference between Derek and Alex," Peter goes on. "When I show up at the clubhouse, A-Rod is always there. He works out before every game. He works out after games, too. He's the hardest-working guy on the team. Jeter is the next-to-last guy to show up in the clubhouse. He and Jorge come in together with their Starbucks coffees. They put on their basketball shorts and are ready to go."

"Do you think A-Rod will opt out of his contract?"

"In spring training I was convinced he would leave. But now I think the finances are such that he'll stay. The Yankees can offer him more than anybody else."

"What about that remark he made after hitting his 500th homer? He said he was hoping for a 'happy ending somewhere.'"

Peter rolls his eyes. "Alex likes to play the put-upon guy, like 'Everything's so hard for me.' He tries to make himself a sympathetic figure. He wants everybody to like him."

"Tell me about some of the other players."

"Andy Pettitte is the sweetest, nicest guy. Wang is great but really shy. Roger is professional."

"What about Mo?"

"He doesn't realize how good he is. He'll strike out the side and say, 'No big deal. That's what I do.' He has the perfect closer mentality, never letting what happens carry over to the next day. He just turns the page."

"Doesn't sound like there are any really bad apples in this group."

"Randy Johnson was a bad guy—just mean and nasty all the time. Now that he and Sheffield are gone, everybody gets along with everybody pretty much."

"On your blog you wrote about how Edwar Ramirez cried after a bad outing. Do you really believe there's no crying in baseball?"

"No crying on the Yankees. Look, Ramirez pitches 1 day in the majors and he has health insurance for the rest of his life. The players union is strong, with great pensions. Nothing to cry about. With the Yankees, it's either you help us win or you get out. No sentimentality."

"You actually like covering this team?"

He gets this beatific look on his face. "When they play at Yankee Stadium, I have a great seat—in the front row of the press box, two seats over from the middle of home plate. Every time I sit down I say, 'How great is this? A baseball game at Yankee Stadium. A big crowd with a lot of people who really care.' I love that."

Back at the Park Hyatt I call Mike, the ticket broker, and ask if he can get us seats for the series in Cleveland this weekend.

"Sure," he says, "but they won't be good seats like the ones you have here in Toronto, eh?"

"Why is that, eh?"

"Because I have better connections here in Toronto. I'll have to put you in the bleachers in Cleveland."

I was hoping to be done with the up-up-up there seats. Still, I need to be at every game, so I take his bleacher seats and buy Tier tickets for next week's series at Yankee Stadium against Baltimore and Detroit.

When we are finished, I check e-mail. There is one from my friend Kandy in Santa Barbara. She alerts me that the Zaca Fire has spread closer to where we live. I had forgotten all about it! She says residents in the area have been advised to be prepared in case of a mandatory evacuation.

Suddenly, the issue of tickets, never mind the Yankees, is the last thing I am worrying about. I e-mail Dorothy, my friend and neighbor, and ask her what is happening. Is the house in danger? Is there a state of emergency? Should we come home right away? She writes back that the situation is serious and that everything depends on the direction of the winds. She says for us to wait another day before deciding what to do. She reminds me that she has a key to the house in case there is an evacuation and we are not back. She asks which possessions of ours she should grab and where she should look for them. She is not an alarmist, which alarms me all the more.

I fill Michael in. Naturally, he is as worried as I am.

"We could lose all your photographs and all my books," I say.

"Everything we own."

"But we've only just started our trip."

"And you've got a contract to honor."

"What do you think we should do?"

"Maybe give it another day, like Dorothy suggested."

We sit together in silence, holding each other. We are connecting in a way we haven't connected in months.

By 7:00 we are in our seats at the Rogers Centre. They are only five rows from the field, and the proximity to the players is thrilling. I can practically pluck Jorge's eyebrows. The roof is closed because of the steady rain, and it's like watching a game in a gymnasium. There are many Yankee fans in our section, although next to me is a Blue Jays fan and his 7-year-old son. I ask the father if he minds that there are so many fans rooting for the Yankees. He shrugs and says, "That's just how it is, eh?"

Clemens is on the hill tonight. He is coming off his two-inning "performance," so he should have plenty of gas in the tank. In the top of the third, A-Rod comes to the plate and the Jays' pitcher, Josh Towers, hits him in the calf with a fastball. Having been thrown at last night, A-Rod has had enough. He takes a few steps toward Towers and says something along the lines of "You want a piece of me?" or maybe just "What the fuck?" Both benches empty, but no punches are thrown. Eventually, the inning resumes—for a second. Before Towers throws another pitch, he and Tony Pena get into it, and both benches empty again. It is fun to see which players are itching for a fight and which hang back. I have never seen Jeter clock anyone, for example, or even look menacing. Shelley Duncan, on the other hand, has a rookie's lack of fear and puts himself right in the thick of things.

Clemens has a shutout going into the seventh—a two-hitter. But when Rios steps in to lead off the inning, the Rocket plunks him in the back. He has clearly and without remorse retaliated for A-Rod getting drilled and is tossed for it. As his teammates gather around him on the mound, he argues with the umpire before departing. I read his lips. He is telling the ump, "I know you have a job to do and I respect that, but I have a job to do, too."

As I watch Clemens walk off the field, I feel this keen sense of admiration for him, and it floors me. I have never liked the man. I pegged him as an egotistical asshole. I thought he was a jerk for hitting Mike Piazza in the head. I thought his whole tough Texan act was bullshit. But he is suddenly and unexpectedly my hero. Even though he was pitching a shutout, he risked ejection and defended his teammate. He stood up to the Blue Jays and their fans. He used the pitch to Rios to say "Leave my guy alone." If I were A-Rod, I would kiss him full on the mouth.

The rest of the game is anticlimactic, except for the major league debut of Joba Chamberlain. He was brought up today from Scranton, and Bruney was sent down. A big tall 21-year-old, he relieves in the eighth and fires fastballs at 96, 97, and 98 mph along with a few devastating sliders, stunning the Blue Jays. He is back for the ninth, reaches 100 mph on the radar gun, and records his second scoreless inning.

The Yankees win 9–2 for their fifth straight victory. I bet Boston fans are starting to look in their rearview mirrors.

I wake up on Wednesday and e-mail Dorothy to see if there is news about the fire. She responds right away, and the news is good. The winds cooperated last night and did not cause the fire to spread. She says that it's still a threat, but the area that borders our houses will be secured soon. She thinks the crisis has been averted.

Michael and I are relieved, to put it mildly. We take an afternoon walk. Just down the street from the Park Hyatt is an imposing stone-and-brick residential complex. A shiny black Bentley pulls out of its motor court. In the driver's seat is Frank Thomas.

"It's the Big Hurt," I whisper to Michael as the car stops for oncoming traffic.

He peers into the Bentley. "It is *not*."

"You know I'm always right about this stuff." And I am. I have this uncanny, rather bizarre ability to recognize famous and even marginally famous people, baseball players especially. Michael, on the other hand, recognizes no one. "Check out his license plate. It's HRTTT."

He looks at the plate and concedes it is Thomas.

"I should go talk to him," I say. "I'll interview him about playing the Yankees."

"I bet he won't stop for you."

This time he is right. The Big Hurt practically runs me over, speeding away as I approach his car.

We go back to the Park Hyatt, where we split a club sandwich in the 18th-floor lounge. We are the only two guests there. As we pay the check, I ask the waiter what it's like having the Yankees stay at the hotel. He laughs and says, "No other team or sports star—not even Gretzky—has so much security. It's like they're really serious about keeping people away."

"I'm one of those people," I admit.

"So you camp outside and wait for them to come out?" he asks.

"I have a legitimate reason. I'm writing a book about them."

"Sure you are, eh?"

It is a beautiful, clear night for the finale of this three-game series, so the roof at the Rogers Centre is open. Again, Mike has gotten us seats that are only five rows from the field. They are just past first base, not far from the visitors' dugout.

A-Rod is sitting out this game with a sore calf, thanks to the pitch from Josh Towers, and Betemit is playing third. Wang is facing Halladay—no easy matchup.

In the first inning, it is obvious how this game will go. Halladay has great stuff and Wang is leaving his sinker up, allowing the Blue Jays to spray hits all over the turf. By the end of the sixth, it is 14–2 Toronto. The Yankees make an attempt at a comeback in the top of the seventh on homers by Matsui and Cano. But the final score is 15–4—a drubbing. Torre always says it is tougher to lose a close game than a blowout, but I don't agree. Blowouts are humiliating.

Back at the hotel, I get an e-mail from George King of the *New York Post*. I had asked my friend Larry Brooks to put in a good word for me. George has been covering the Yankees the longest of all the beat writers, so I am thrilled he has agreed to an interview—until I read the rest of his e-mail. He suggests I meet him in the press box at 2:00 on Friday afternoon in Cleveland. I feel like a dork as I write back that I am not allowed in the press box.

I go to bed thinking that while Jason Zillo may only be doing his job by refusing me access, he is also thwarting me from doing mine.

⋎

Thursday is getaway day. At the Toronto airport, I grill the ticket agent at the Continental counter. We are on a commuter partner called ExpressJet Airlines, and I ask about the equipment.

"It's an Embraer 135," she tells me.

"How big is the plane?"

"It holds about 30 people. You'll definitely feel the bumps."

After a stop at the Currency Exchange to give back our Canadian money, it is on to Customs. The inspector is stern, as if he expects to nab our cache of stolen diamonds.

"What business have you been conducting in Canada?" he asks.

"I'm writing a book about the Yankees, and I came to watch them play the Blue Jays. I'm following them to every game."

"No kidding." His face lights up. "How long will it take to write the book?"

"I'm not sure. I'm still in the research stage."

"Will it be out soon? I'm a big reader. My wife is, too."

"It's up to my publisher when it'll be out." There is a line of people waiting behind us.

"Is Jeter still dating Miss Universe?"

"I'll ask him the next time I see him."

He winks at Michael. "You get to travel everywhere with her. Not bad for you, eh?"

Michael gives the guy his best game face.

As we board the flight I gasp. "This isn't a plane. It's a sedan."

"Pretend it's Steinbrenner's private jet," Michael suggests.

During takeoff the pilot tells us there is rain in Cleveland. Luckily Rhonda, our lone flight attendant, is selling screw-top chardonnay.

After we land, we wheel our bags outside to the airport taxi stand.

"Where to?" asks the attendant.

"The InterContinental Suites on Euclid Avenue, please," I tell him.

"Oh, you're going to the Cleveland Clinic?"

"That's a hospital," I say. "We're going to a hotel."

"Same place." He whistles for the next cab to pull up.

"Something's wrong," I whisper to Michael as the driver is loading our suitcases into his trunk.

"Maybe Lisa got us a good rate at the Cleveland Clinic," he jokes.

Neither of us is laughing when we get to the InterContinental. It is in the middle of nowhere, not even close to Jacobs Field, and it is, indeed, part of the Cleveland Clinic's complex of buildings. Judging by the condition of the guests in the lobby, the hotel is sort of a halfway house for people who have had surgery or are about to.

I tell the front desk clerk I would like to cancel our reservation. She suggests we try the Marriott Key, and off we go. The Marriott is more expensive, but we grab a room. We are relieved to be free of people walking around with their IV poles.

After we unpack, I check e-mail. George King says he will come to the Marriott for lunch tomorrow, and I can interview him then. And Dorothy e-mails with even better news. The Zaca Fire has been contained on its southern border where it was threatening our houses, so we are in the clear. She says the air is full of soot and ash, but that is the worst of it. Oh, and she says our tomato plants are dead.

Speaking of tomatoes, I am starving. All I have had today is plane wine. As soon as the rain lets up, we have dinner at the Blue Point Grille in the Warehouse District, a section that has been renovated and now boasts the best nightspots in downtown Cleveland. The restaurant is having a special on lobster tonight, and Michael orders it. I can't believe it. Lobster gives him a bellyache like almost no other food, and yet here he is, dipping a claw into melted butter. I dread how bad he will feel later, but the smile on his face right now is a beautiful thing.

On Friday morning George King calls to cancel lunch.

"There's a lot of stuff going on with the Yankees," he says.

"Like what?"

"The whole A-Rod steroids issue."

What issue? Chipper Jones made a harmless remark after a game against the Mets the other day. He said that anybody who approaches Bonds's numbers will be asked the steroids question, including A-Rod. He never accused anybody of anything.

"I have a conference call with my editor around noon," says George. "Let's try again for tomorrow, same place."

I try to think of another way into the Yankees and come up with Suzyn

Waldman, who has been covering the team for over 20 years—from WFAN to WCBS, where she is now John Sterling's color commentator. She has been a pioneer for women in the field of sports broadcasting. She will get how badly I need information about the Yanks.

I leave a message on John's cell, asking if he will put in a good word with Suzyn. And then I call Mike, the broker in Toronto, to buy tickets for the Boston series at Yankee Stadium. He tells me he can get me some up-up-up-there Tier seats—for a steep price. "It's a big series, eh?"

Michael and I ask the concierge how to get to the Rock and Roll Hall of Fame, and he gives us a map. We also ask where we can find the nearest drugstore so Michael can buy Pepcid for his post-lobster-binge heartburn, and he points us in the direction of a CVS/pharmacy. While Michael is shopping, I notice the magnificent Roman Catholic cathedral across the street and hurry over. Inside the church, which was built in the 1940s and smells like incense and flowers, I dip my fingers in holy water and take a seat. I bow my head.

"Dear God. Thank you for sparing my house from the wildfire, for keeping all my flights from crashing, and for putting me back in touch with family and old friends. Please let Michael make it through the trip without an emergency-room visit. Please let the Yankees get into the play-offs in spite of their miserable start. Please let all those judgmental *New York Times* readers come to realize what a true fan I really am."

I pause, trying to be sure I am not leaving anything out.

"And please grant me an interview with a Yankee, so my publisher won't stop payment on my advance. Amen."

Michael and I spend the afternoon at the Rock and Roll Hall of Fame. Even in the "Hall" there are Yankee fans. A twentysomething woman in a Jeter jersey tells me she is going to the game tonight. I am about to ask her what makes Jeter her favorite player when a fat guy in an Indians T-shirt puts his arm around her. She introduces him as her husband. As they walk away, I wonder if I could be married to a man who roots for a team other than the Yankees and decide that I could not. My ex-husband was a Mets fan, and, although I sat through a game at Shea and tried to look riveted, I was not meant for Shea or, I later realized, him.

Back at the Marriott, John Sterling returns my call about Suzyn Waldman. He tells me I should call her in her room at the Ritz-Carlton and gives me the number.

"Or you could just stop by the booth tonight and meet her," he says. "We're right in the press box."

"I'm not allowed in the press box."

"I forgot. It's not fair, but I don't know what I can do about it."

I call the Ritz and leave Suzyn a long message.

I lengthen my list of beat writers to contact. Tyler Kepner covers the Yankees for the *Times,* so I e-mail him.

At 6:30 Michael and I are off to the Jake. It is a breezy, brisk night—the heat and humidity having cleared out—and the 10-minute walk from the Marriott is a pleasant one.

Jacobs Field, which was built in the '90s, according to our program guide, is a pretty park. It has good sight lines and is well maintained—a contemporary stadium with an old-fashioned feel. And the vendors and ushers and security people are so polite that I think it must be true what they say about Midwest-erners: They *are* friendly.

Our seats in the bleachers are on benches and, remarkably, nobody invades your personal space by squeezing onto your lap. And although we are at least 350 feet away from home plate, we have a decent view of the field. What is odd is that the Indians have not been able to draw big numbers this season; even with the Yankees in town, the Jake is not filled to capacity.

Hughes is pitching against Fausto Carmona. Both teams are in the wild-card hunt, so there is excitement in the air—and noise. An Indians fan sits in the top row of the bleachers and bangs on a drum to rally his team. He is about my age—old enough to know better—and I keep turning around to glare at him. Also in the house is LeBron James, the star of the Cleveland Cavaliers. The Indians fans cheer wildly when he is shown on the scoreboard until they realize he is wearing a Yankees cap.

A-Rod goes deep in the top of the second to put us in front. Hughes pitches six very solid innings, and it is 4–1 when Joba Chamberlain takes over in the bottom of the seventh. The Tribe fans sitting behind me gasp when Joba's fast-ball hits 99 mph on the radar gun.

"Where did this guy come from?" says a college jock type.

I spin around. "Nebraska. He's Native American—from the Winnebago tribe. His father had polio but raised him to play baseball. He hardly spent any time in the minors; that's how good he is. And in case you're wondering about his name, his niece called him Joba because she couldn't pronounce his real name, which is Justin."

He stares at me for a second, then thanks me. He is impressed that I am such a fount of information.

Just when I am thinking how friendly Midwesterners are, the Yankees score another couple of runs and a "Yankees suck" chant breaks out.

Joba is back for the eighth and strikes out all three Indians he faces. Mo pitches the ninth and gets three up, three down. The Yankees win six of their last seven games and are tied with Seattle for the wild-card lead.

As we file out of the bleachers, I ask the drummer, "What's up with the drum?"

"I've been bringing it to the games for 34 years," he says. "Win or lose, I never miss a chance to root for my team."

"You have to admire his loyalty," Michael says on our walk back to the hotel.

"If not his musical ability," I say, rubbing my throbbing temples.

On Saturday I wake up with a Yankee hangover from the dream I had last night—my first Yankee one of the trip. It is about A-Rod. He is living in the apartment next door. We are friends. He comes over to ask which set of dishes he should use when he entertains his girlfriend for dinner that night. (This Dream A-Rod is single.) I have a look at his dishes, and together we decide on a white pattern with a cobalt blue border. I ask if he will introduce me to this special lady, and he says, "Stop by at 7:05."

"His girlfriend in the dream looked like Jennifer Lopez," I tell Michael. "Isn't that weird?"

"The fact that you're dreaming about A-Rod is weird," he says.

George King calls this morning to cancel lunch again today. He says he has to talk to Harlan Chamberlain, Joba's father, plus he has to chase down the rumor that Igawa is being traded to the Padres.

"Ordinarily I could do it tomorrow after the day game," he says, "but I'm flying out on the 6:45 into Newark."

"Me, too," I say.

We agree to meet at the Cleveland airport at the Continental gate and do the interview there.

I e-mail Mark Feinsand, who covers the Yankees for the *Daily News*, and

Sweeny Murti, WFAN's beat reporter, and ask if they would let me interview them for the book. And then I try Suzyn Waldman again at the Ritz-Carlton. This time she answers.

"Is this something we can just do over the phone now?" she says in a voice that is almost as familiar to me as John's. There is no mistaking the Boston in it, since she was born and raised there.

"I'd rather do it in person," I say. "I would only need an hour or so."

"John mentioned that you want to discuss the Yankees from a female perspective. Frankly, I'm sick of that subject. The words alone make me cringe. I've been covering the team for a long time and have gotten way past the gender thing."

Yikes. "The book will be from the female perspective, but I'd ask you the same questions I'll ask Tyler Kepner and Peter Abraham."

"Oh." There is a thawing. "Why don't we get together in Detroit next week-end? We can have a drink after the Sunday-afternoon game. There's a nice bar at the Townsend."

"Perfect." The Townsend is where the Yankees are staying.

"Who else have you talked to for the book?"

I mention that I was supposed to talk to George King yesterday, but he was working the A-Rod steroids story.

"Alex has never done steroids," she says firmly.

"Jose Canseco claims to have something on him," I say.

"It's just about women, and so what? Wade Boggs had the whole Margo thing, and yet he had his best year on the field."

"I can't imagine A-Rod talking to the *Post* after they printed those pictures of him and the stripper."

"He doesn't talk to them anymore. He talks to me, though. Being a woman is a double-edged sword. It's hard sometimes, but it also works to my advantage. The players know I'm not confrontational."

She laments that coverage of baseball has changed since she started in the business—how writers, especially bloggers, are not accountable the way report-ers used to be.

"Anyone can write whatever they want, and it doesn't have to be true," she says. "And once they write it, it takes on a life of its own."

The conversation moves back to my book and the trip, and I explain that

I have been buying tickets to every game. I mention that my friend got us great seats for the Sunday night game at Fenway next month but told me not to wear Yankee clothes.

"Your friend's right," Suzyn says. "When you're in another ballpark, never wear the Yankees hat or T-shirt and call attention to yourself. Root with your heart. In Boston you could get hurt if you say the wrong thing."

As soon as I am off the phone, I go back on the computer. There are responses from Tyler Kepner, Mark Feinsand, and Sweeny Murti. They all suggest getting together in Detroit next week. I am suddenly very popular.

Michael and I take a stroll and have lunch. It is another sunny, breezy day, and the fresh air feels good. As we wait for the elevator to go back up to our room at the Marriott, a burly man with a weathered face gets off.

"Excuse me," I say. "Aren't you Jim Fregosi?"

Michael is nonplussed, not only because Jim Fregosi has not played on a big league team or managed one in years, but also because he is not exactly a household name.

Fregosi himself can't believe someone recognized him. "Yeah, it's me," he says in a gravelly voice.

"That was your most obscure call yet," Michael commends me on our way up to the room.

For tonight's game we are at the very top of the bleachers, right near the drummer. He starts banging away to get loose.

Mussina is on the hill against Paul Byrd. He gives up a run in the bottom of the first but quickly becomes the beneficiary of the Yankees offense. They send 10 batters to the plate in the top of the second, seven of them coming in to score. When A-Rod hits his 38th homer, Indians fans respond by chanting "Gay-Rod!" in one section and "A-Rod hires prostitutes!" in another. A drunken Yankee fan gives them all the finger and is escorted out of the stadium by two cops.

Matsui scores another run in the top of the seventh, and the friendly Midwestern bigots in the crowd chant "Go home, Chop Suey!" A-Rod hits his second homer of the night in the top of the eighth—a two-run shot.

The Yankees beat the Indians 11–2 and Mussina, who is doing his best imitation of the pitcher he used to be, gets his 100th win in pinstripes.

On Sunday, our last day in Cleveland, I regard myself in the mirror before applying makeup. I want to look decent for my interview with George King at the airport later. Either it is the lighting in the room or I have aged 20 years in 17 days. My face is hollow, haunted. I have been passing up the food at the ballparks. My mother was right: I need to eat and sleep more. And I need to find someone to blow-dry my hair. I did it myself and used too much spray, and it is as stiff as the cotton candy at the ballparks.

For today's finale at the Jake, we are back in the bleachers but in row G, only six up. The pitching matchup is Pettitte versus Westbrook.

In the bottom of the seventh, with the Yankees ahead 4–0 and the Indians threatening, the two Andys—Pettitte and Phillips—make a spectacular pickoff play on Peralta at first that kills the rally. The Indians pull to 4–2 with Viz on the mound in the eighth, so Joe calls for Mo to get four quick outs—again.

With the 5–3 final, the Yankees sweep the Tribe for their eighth win in the last nine games to stay tied with Seattle for the wild card. The big news is they gain a game on the Red Sox and are now only four back. The image of Red Sox fans panicking thrills me.

Michael and I take a cab to the airport and hurry to the gate for our flight to Newark and my interview with George King. I e-mailed Larry Brooks earlier in the day to ask what George looks like.

"He's a good-looking guy in his early fifties with blondish-grayish hair and a blondish-grayish beard and mustache," Larry wrote.

There is no such person at the gate.

The attendant announces we are starting to board. I hang back for a few minutes in case George shows up. He does not.

We walk down the gangplank. When we reach the open cabin door I do my crazy preflight ritual, which is to rap my knuckles on the side of the plane to make sure it is not falling apart. Once aboard the Boeing 737, we move toward the rear. Our row is three across. Michael takes the window. I take the middle seat. As I am strapping my seat belt on, a good-looking guy in his early fifties with blondish-grayish hair and a blondish-grayish beard and mustache throws his carry-on bag onto the empty aisle seat.

"Are you Jane, by any chance?"

"George!" I whip out my tape recorder.

Where Peter Abraham was serious and businesslike, George King has an entertaining, seen-it-all attitude. When there is turbulence after takeoff and I squeeze the arms of my seat, he laughs and says, "You'd better get over that if you're traveling with the team."

I ask George how he got started in the business, and he tells me he covered the Phillies in Trenton before getting hired by the *Post* in '97.

"This is my 11th season there," he says. "It's long hours and a long year—February to November—but it's a blast."

"February to November *is* a long year," I say. "How does your wife feel about all your traveling?"

"She's gone a lot, too. She's a vice president of Bloomingdale's in charge of women's shoes."

"Do the players ever invite you out with them?"

"When I was younger, with the Phillies, yeah. But I'm 51 now, and the players are 30. It's different. And let's face it. I work for the *New York Post*. Do the players really want me around at the Limelight club?"

We both laugh. "Is it true A-Rod won't talk to you since the *Post* printed the stuff about the stripper in Toronto?"

"He doesn't talk to me," he says with regret. "We were very close, too. I had the best relationship with him of anybody. But after that story ran, he made it very clear that we were done. He doesn't freeze me out during group interviews, but if he's by himself, he'll ignore me."

"Does that surprise you?"

"Not really. He warned us. He said, 'Hey, if you want to write stuff that's off limits, it's gonna hurt.'"

"How did the story even come about?"

"Those pictures fell into our lap. But if it hadn't been that story it would have been another story. With the Yankees there's always another story."

"Do you think A-Rod will opt out?"

"I think he's gone, yeah. He did it in Seattle, and he did it in Texas. Now he's done it in New York for 4 years and hit his 500th home run. Time to go find something new."

"He didn't get a World Series ring in New York."

"He's not gonna get one with this team. The pitching isn't good enough, and it hasn't been all year. The kids will make the staff better but not enough."

"My impression of the Yankees has really changed. They're a cold, unfeeling organization."

"A professional sport is a very cold business—probably the coldest business outside of the Mafia."

"You're comparing the Yankees to the Mafia?"

"In the sense that it's cold."

"What's the most bizarre thing that ever happened to you while you were covering the Yankees?"

"It was the last day of spring training in '98. Hideki Irabu was pitching. I came into the clubhouse, and Steinbrenner showed up. I said, 'George, what did you think of Irabu?' George said, 'That fat pussy toad.'"

"Do you miss George being around?"

"The *New York Post* misses him. He made the telephone ring at 7:00 in the morning. He'd be screaming at you. 'Wait a minute, George,' I'd say. 'I don't work for you. Why are you calling?' He'd say, 'I'm calling to tell you I'm never calling you again.'"

I laugh. "What's the best part about being a Yankee beat writer?"

"It was February—3 days before spring training and probably the deadest time for the beat writers. The phone rang. A friend of mine said, 'The Yankees are trading for Alex Rodriguez.' I said, 'You know this how?' He said, 'I know a company that's advertising with the Rangers, and they just pulled out of the deal because Alex won't be there.' It was Friday night at 5 minutes to 6:00. At 6:00 I was on the phone to Cashman. I didn't get him. I called the agent, Scott Boras. I didn't get him, either. I called the Rangers. Didn't get them. So I needed a story for 7 o'clock, and we decided to go with it. The point is that one day the Yankees tell me a journeyman like Enrique Wilson is their third baseman. Within 24 hours it's 'We got the best player in baseball.' I wouldn't be surprised if Mickey Mantle walked in tomorrow. That's the best part of covering the Yankees. You never know."

"What's the worst part?"

"What's the worst $1,000 bottle of wine you ever had?"

As our flight lands, George and I talk briefly about my situation with Jason Zillo.

"I just need to interview a player," I say. "One player." I tell him about my plan to get together with Suzyn Waldman in Detroit.

"There you go," he says. "She'll probably introduce you to someone."

As Michael and I collect our baggage, I realize I didn't drink any wine on the plane. I completely forgot to be nervous.

We take a cab into Manhattan. We are staying in the city for this home stand as well as the next three. Lisa has booked us a very inexpensive room at a boutique hotel in the theatre district. It is 10:00 by the time we pull up in front of the hotel, and we are exhausted.

"This is it," says the cab driver.

As Michael and I drag our suitcases inside—where is the bellman?—my heart sinks. The lobby, which is as big as a phone booth, consists of a beat-up desk at which a man sits behind a computer. No gift shop. No concierge. No guests.

"I see your reservation," he says in the sort of deadpan that makes me think he is drugged. "We don't have any deluxe rooms with king beds available."

"But we booked the deluxe room."

"I only have the little one with the double bed."

The little one with the double bed.

The room is tinier than my bedroom closet at home. I know people say things like that and they exaggerate, for the most part. I am not exaggerating. There is a tiny bed, a tiny desk, and a tiny bathroom with a tiny sink and an even tinier toilet. There is not enough room for two adults, let alone their luggage. But what puts me over the edge is the not-so-tiny roach that skitters across the floor.

I call my sister. "We need to get out of here."

She rouses herself—it is late, after all—and suggests places for me to call. I call them. Either they are booked or their reservations office is closed for the night. I call my sister back and tell her we will have to look for another hotel in the morning.

Michael and I barricade ourselves in by stacking our suitcases next to the door. Then we place ourselves very gently across the bed, so as not to stir up the roaches or crab lice or other vermin that reside here. Fully clothed, we lie with our arms around each other.

"Tell me a story," I whisper. "One of your sailing stories." I love Michael's sailing stories. He tells me the same ones over and over, and they are never boring to me. Not the one about the time he fell overboard on the way to Bermuda. Not the one about the time he sailed to Block Island just before a hurricane hit. Not the one about the time he sailed to the Caribbean on a big old schooner and was marooned on the island of Canouan. I am not sure whether it is his voice that soothes me or if it is the fairy-tale quality of his tales.

"After our Atlantic crossing, we restocked the schooner in St. Thomas and headed south toward the lower Caribbean," he begins.

Within minutes, I am asleep.

AL EAST STANDINGS/AUGUST 12

TEAM	W	L	PCT	GB
BOSTON	70	47	.598	—
NEW YORK	66	51	.564	4.0
TORONTO	59	57	.509	10.5
BALTIMORE	54	62	.466	15.5
TAMPA BAY	45	72	.385	25.0

Week 20
August 13, 2007

Farnsworth is having one of those years where even when he makes a good pitch, the balls find holes. And when he makes a mistake, he gets hammered. But how do you expect the guy to play well when he's announced and you boo him? I don't get that. He's still trying to help us win.

By 8:00 a.m. on Monday I am on the phone, attempting to find us a hotel that does not cost a fortune and does not have roaches.

My sister calls with a suggestion: the Marmara on 94th Street and Second Avenue, not far from the 86th Street subway station that will take us directly to the Bronx. We flee the hotel-that-shall-remain-nameless.

The Marmara is a converted apartment building that rents furnished studios and one-bedroom apartments by the night and by the month. Our one bedroom is clean and bright and cheerful. I would have chosen a different decor—we are talking about a '60s look with Swedish blond wood furniture and a platform bed, the corners of which keep barking my shins—but I am in no position to quibble.

Tonight is the first of a three-game series against Baltimore. At 6:00 the 86th Street subway station is jammed with both rush-hour commuters and Yankee fans, but we squeeze onto the #4 train. I am sandwiched between two men with deadly breath.

When the train finally stops at the Stadium and we spill out onto the platform, I turn to Michael and say, "I don't think I'm a subway person."

"It'll get easier," he says, rearranging his Yankees cap, which is askew from all the bumping and shoving.

We enter the Stadium at Gate 4 and go through the usual security check-point. Only this time the guard takes issue with the black bag I have given to Michael to carry. It is filled with rain gear—an umbrella and two slickers. We are not about to get caught in another thunderstorm.

"You can't bring that bag in here," yaps the guard, who has an angry scar across his cheek.

"Why?" I say.

"Because you can't."

"You already looked inside," Michael points out. "We're not hiding any bombs."

"You're not getting in with that bag. Walk back to the parking lot and leave it in your car."

"We didn't drive," Michael tells him. "We took the subway."

"Then you'll have to throw the bag out," says the guard with a little grin. He is enjoying this.

I tell him to look at the woman at the next turnstile. She is lugging a large leather tote. "Why are they letting her in with that?"

"It's a purse."

"Men can't have purses?"

"Oh, now you wanna report me for sexual discrimination?" He flashes me his ID badge. "Make sure you spell my name right."

I know New York is a tough town and the Yankees are a tough organization. But this guy bites.

"You win," I tell him, then grab Michael's hand. When we are far enough away I whisper that we will enter through another gate and try again. I am not letting the Yankees keep me out.

The security guard at Gate 2 is nicer and waves us through.

We are in Tier 17, row H—familiar territory for me now. The seats don't seem so up-up-up anymore and the aisles not so narrow. When the speakers blare "The Boys Are Back in Town," I sing along.

Wang doesn't have the good sinker in the first inning, allowing three runs. But he settles down. The Yankees are up 6–4 by the time he makes way for Villone in the seventh. Ron promptly hurls two wild pitches, and the score is 6–5 for Joba in the eighth. He shuts the Orioles down and pumps his fist. Mo blows the save in the ninth, but Melky scores on Jeter's slow roller in the bottom half, and the Yankees win 7–6.

Tuesday brings new challenges on the hotel front. At 7:00 a.m. we are awakened by construction noise outside our window. And I don't mean a little construction noise. I mean drilling and digging and jackhammering. I call the front desk. Nobody speaks much English here. But I do glean from the woman that the noise outside is the construction of a new subway line on Second Avenue—a project that will take, oh, 12 years.

I call my mother to tell her we are at a different hotel than originally planned. "Susan found it for us," I say. "It's called the Marmara."

"The Marinara?" she says. Her hearing is remarkable for a 90-year-old. But every now and then she mixes up names, like when she refers to A-Rod as A-Rot.

I tell her we will be staying here for the next few home stands, so I hope she will come into the city and visit.

"Are you taking care of yourself?" she asks. "There must be all kinds of crazy people at that stadium."

"I'm fine," I assure her.

It is a beautiful day, and Michael and I take a walk. I had forgotten how much I enjoy that you can walk everywhere in Manhattan.

Back at the hotel we learn that Phil Rizzuto has died. According to the YES Network, there will be a moment of silence before tonight's game, and all the players will wear number 10 on their sleeves. I am sobered by the Scooter's death. It reminds me how fragile the Yankees are. I would be grief stricken if something happened to Jeter or A-Rod or even Farnsworth.

Now that I am stacking up Yankee media people to interview, I zero in on Kim Jones, who does the TV postgame interviews with the players for YES. I e-mail Peter Abraham to ask if he will pass along her contact info.

At the Stadium for tonight's game against Baltimore, we go right to our gate as if we have been doing this for years. The mean security guard is not around, and we waltz in. Our seats are in Tier 13, row D, which turns out to be a nonalcohol section. It will be a nice change of pace to sit with people who are not drunk.

After the moment of silence for Rizzuto, the Yankees take the field. I can see Jorge kneeling at home plate, praying silently and crossing himself. I have seen Mo pray, too, turning his back to home plate and bowing his head before throwing his first pitch. These small observations are what make watching a game in person so much more interesting than watching it on TV. I also love the interactive "roll call" at the top of the first inning of every game at the Stadium, when the Bleacher Creatures yell out a rhythmic cheer for each starting player. I don't miss my green chair anymore.

Karstens is starting in place of Clemens, who is serving his suspension for hitting Rios. Jeff goes sour in a hurry, giving up five runs over three innings. The crowd boos him. A pigeon shits on Michael's head. I have a bad feeling about this game.

Baltimore's pitcher, the hard-throwing Daniel Cabrera, is throwing strikes for a change, and the Yankees don't get a hit off him until the fourth. Brower allows three more Orioles runs, and Villone serves up four more. Only Farnsworth is effective, retiring the side in order in the eighth. If he could do the same thing when the score is not 12–0, he would be on to something. It is a blowout for the Orioles, and I am pissed.

On the subway back to the city, a tall, disheveled, bearded man asks for our attention. He tells us he has kicked booze and heroin and crack, survived a stroke, lost his twin babies at birth, and watched his sister get hacked to death by her knife-wielding boyfriend. He would like our money. My mother is right: There *are* crazy people out here. But he also tells us he is a Yankee fan, so I reach into my bag for a dollar and hand it to him.

Wednesday is a day game after a night game. Our seats are in Tier 13 again, the nonalcohol section. The man in front of us is an emaciated old dude with a bleached blond ponytail and white-gray sideburns. He is wearing a T-shirt that says "God, Country and Notre Dame" and a green cap with a sham-rock on it.

The Yankees are facing Erik Bedard, a tricky left-hander. Hughes is on the mound for us. I know Phil is a rookie coming off an injury, but he never seems to go deep into a game. With the Yankees down 3–0 in the top of the sixth, he is pulled for Sean Henn, who has been recalled from Scranton along with Edwar Ramirez.

"Ice cold water!" shrieks the female vendor Michael and I have come to rec-ognize. She has a great pair of lungs and works her ass off. She is the most exciting thing about this game, which is over 3 hours old.

But then Shelley hits a three-run homer to tie the game in the bottom of the ninth, and we all leap to our feet, cheering and clapping and chanting, "Let's go, Yankees!" Here is Mo for the top of the 10th. He is coming off a rocky outing, so the crowd is wary—with good reason. He gives up three runs. As he trudges off the mound, people boo him. They are assholes. The Yankees lose 6–3.

On Thursday the construction on Second Avenue knocks out our Internet service. I march down to the lobby and ask the woman at the front desk why we were not told about the construction when we checked in, particularly when I asked for a quiet room. She offers to move us to a deluxe apartment for the same price.

I hurry back upstairs to tell Michael, and we grab handfuls of clothes and bring them down the hall to Room 505, which faces 94th Street instead of Second Avenue.

I have been thinking about the three girls who lived next door to my brother-in-law in the '60s and had ballplayers from every team at their feet. They didn't get pushed away. They knew how to make the players pay attention. It occurs to me I should track them down.

When my Internet service is fixed, I Google Barb, the ringleader, and find out where she lives. I dial Information, get her number, and call. Her husband answers.

"Hello," I say. "Is Barb there, please?"

"She's not home," he says. "Who's this?"

"My name is Jane Heller, and my sister Susan is an old friend of Barb's. It's been a long time, but I'd love to catch up with her." I don't bring up that Barb was a baseball groupie. I have no idea whether she has told her hubby about this aspect of her past.

"She'll be home in an hour."

"Great," I say. "I'll call back then."

An hour later, Barb picks up the phone on the first ring. I tell her who I am and she laughs.

"Of course I remember Bobby and Sue," she says of my brother-in-law and sister. "I remember you, too. You wanted to meet a baseball player so badly. A Yankee, especially."

"Not much has changed." I explain about the book. "Is there any chance I could get you and Diane and Patty together and interview all three of you? I'm really interested in how you came to know so many players."

"What a coincidence. I was out of touch with Diane and Patty for a long time, but we recently agreed we should plan a reunion."

"Great." I give her the dates of the next home stands. She promises to talk to the others and arrange something.

"Didn't I introduce you to Ruben Amaro?" she asks, as we are about to hang up.

"No," I say, "you introduced me to Jack Hamilton. I met Ruben Amaro all by myself."

⚜

Tonight is the opener of a four-game series against the Tigers. It is hot and muggy, and the subway station is a sauna. We slip into the train just before the doors close on us.

I am kind of getting into the subway experience. On the #4 train to Yankee Stadium, the majority of passengers are Yankee fans. I love riding along with them, listening to how cocky they are one minute and panicky the next. They can boast about the Yankees, then bash them, in one head-spinning sentence. I get that. I get them. I am them.

Our seats are in Tier 7, row W, which is the second row from the top. The players are little tiny ants from up-up-up here, but we are behind home plate, along the first-base side, so we have a view of the balls and strikes.

When the lineups are announced, we all boo Sheffield for calling Torre a racist. But the one who could be trouble for the Yankees is Detroit's starter, Justin Verlander, who pitched a no-hitter earlier this year.

Mussina looks honest-to-God-terrified of the Tigers, giving up six runs over five innings. The Yankees mount a minor charge in the bottom of the ninth, scoring two runs, but they get beaten 8–5. They have now lost three straight.

On Friday the New York papers are full of doom and gloom about the Yankees' chances of making the postseason. Mussina's performance last night is critiqued, and there is talk that he might skip a start to work on his mechanics. Fine with me, but who will take his spot in the rotation? SpongeBob SquarePants?

It is raining as Michael and I are ready to leave for tonight's game. We decide to wait out the storm and then leave. We flip on YES, and Mike Francesca says the tarp is on the field and the game will not start at 7:05.

It is 8:30 when it suddenly dawns on me that YES is not televising the game against the Tigers tonight. I turn to channel 9, and there is baseball! They are in the bottom of the first at Yankee Stadium while we are sitting in our hotel!

Michael grabs his rain jacket and says we should get moving.

"But do we really want to go out in that?" I point to the window. There is still lightning out there.

He sits back down.

"Although it looks like it's cleared up in the Bronx," I say.

He stands back up.

"But even if we leave immediately, it'll be another 45 minutes before we're in our seats, which will put the game in about the fifth inning. Is it worth it?"

He sits back down.

"But I paid for the tickets. It would be a shame—"

He stands back up and yells at me. "*What the fuck do you want to do!*"

"Sorry, but this is not a simple decision!"

"Of course it is!"

"I'm not interested in us getting soaked and you getting sick! Plus, I'm supposed to be on this mission. I should be like the post office! I don't want to be a dilettante who runs for cover when the going gets tough. We spent all this time and money, and for what? To sit here watching on TV like we could be doing at home? True fans are willing to do anything for their team."

He smiles. "You know you're insane, don't you?"

"I know."

He walks over, sits down next to me and puts his arm around me. "The measure of a true fan isn't whether you scream the loudest or notch the most number of games. You need to let go of all that."

He takes off his jacket, turns up the volume on the TV, and settles in.

I regard him with wonderment. He sheds Rice Krispies and forgets to take out the garbage and talks over Anderson Cooper when I am trying to listen to the news. And then there are all his health problems. But he is the sanest, fairest, most loving person I know.

I kiss him, and he kisses me back.

"Here's a question for you," I say. "Can I be a good fan and still be a good wife?"

"I think there's hope for you."

We snuggle up together and watch the game. The Tigers only score one run off Pettitte, and Giambi homers twice. Joba relieves in the ninth and sends the Tigers home with a 6–1 loss. A happy ending all around.

The rain is gone on Saturday, and it is gorgeous and sunny.

Peter Abraham passes along Kim Jones's e-mail address. I send her a note asking for an interview. He says she is really nice, so I am optimistic.

Today's contest against the Tigers is being televised nationally on Fox, so it has a 3:55 start. We get to the Stadium early, in plenty of time for the Military Appreciation Day pregame ceremonies. I am so glad to be back after missing last night's game that I smile at everyone, even the mean security guard who gives me a pat down before letting me in.

We are in Tier 15, row S—not quite as high up as Thursday night's seats, but further up the right-field line. No matter. We are in the perfect spot to view the show by the US Army's Golden Knights Parachute Team.

Clemens is making his first start since his suspension. The Rocket gives up a homer to Maybin, Detroit's prized rookie, and expresses his displeasure by hitting him on the wrist his next time up. Abreu's two-run shot puts the Yankees up 5–2. Farnsworth relieves in the seventh. As usual, his reception from the crowd is chilly. But he strikes out Sheffield and Ordonez and leaves to chants of "Let's go, Farnsworth!" When Mo comes in for the ninth, you can feel everyone tense, as if fearing another uncharacteristic meltdown. But he gets his 20th save, and the Yankees win.

Michael and I linger for a while as the crowd files out. We hold hands and sing along to "New York, New York."

Sunday is our last day of this home stand. I sleep a little later, do some packing, turn on the YES Network, and watch the Yankees sweep the Padres in the '98 World Series. I love watching the "classics" where the Yankees never lose. It is like watching *Pretty Woman*, where Julia Roberts always ends up with Richard Gere.

For this afternoon's finale against the Tigers, the crowd is the biggest yet. We are in Tier 3, directly over home plate, but in row X, the very top row. I surprise myself by not bitching about getting stuck up-up-up there. What happened to the person whose idea of heaven was sitting in the front row next to the Other Jane Heller? What happened to the writer who thought it was imperative that she watch the games from the press box? What happened to the princess who would not be caught dead in the nosebleed section with the peons? She is sort of glad to be sitting exactly where she is.

Wang faces Bonderman today. With the Yankees ahead by 2–1 in the top of the fifth, he comes undone—a couple of singles, a balk, a walk, a wild pitch— and the Tigers go up 3–2. Joe lifts him in the seventh after Damon's solo shot has put the Yankees ahead 4–3. It is Joba Time. Chamberlain has yet to be scored on and has become a folk hero, eliciting huge cheers before he even gets to the mound. He has been mowing hitters down, and today is no different.

With our 9–3 victory, we take three out of four from the Tigers and are now *four* behind Boston.

AL EAST STANDINGS/AUGUST 19

TEAM	W	L	PCT	GB
BOSTON	74	50	.597	—
NEW YORK	70	54	.565	4.0
TORONTO	63	60	.512	10.5
BALTIMORE	57	65	.467	16.0
TAMPA BAY	47	76	.382	26.5

Week 21
August 20, 2007

During a play-off game, my wife got beer thrown on her—in Anaheim.
My God. People there don't even show up until September 15. I remem-
ber when I was on deck and we were getting eliminated in the ALCS
and some guy goes, "Hey, what's your tee time tomorrow? Or are you
going fishing?" I said, "I'll be the same place you are from April through
September. Not here." But you can't lump people together. Ninety-seven
percent of baseball fans are great.

On Monday morning we are off to JFK for our 8:40 United flight to
LAX. We are not flying into John Wayne Airport in Orange County, even
though the Yankees are playing the Angels tonight in Anaheim. We are not, in
fact, going to Anaheim—not yet. We are flying into Los Angeles, renting a car,
and driving to Santa Barbara.

We are going home so Michael can have a nurse administer the medication
he receives in an IV infusion every 8 weeks for his Crohn's. The drug, which is
called Remicade, helps him manage his disease, but it is also the reason he can't
fight infections. Medications have their downsides, but we are lucky that
Michael has been on the road for a month without incident. We are also lucky
that his scheduled infusion coincides with the three-game series in Anaheim.
We will watch the first two games at home, catch the last one at the ballpark,
and fly to Detroit with the rest of the Yankees' traveling carnival.

Aboard our Boeing 757, we are offered beverages, and I pass.

Michael is shocked. "No garbage chardonnay at 9:30 in the morning?"

I shake my head.

Once we land at LAX, we rent a silver Chevy HHR and drive 2 hours to our
house. We are relieved when we finally pull into the driveway—until we get out

of the car and inhale. The air is filled with smoke and ash. Apparently, the Zaca Fire is still burning. I call Dorothy to say we are home and ask her about the fire. She says that we're safe, but the air quality is awful, and we should keep our windows closed.

Although it is comforting to be home, it feels odd, too, almost as if I am a stranger in my own house. One of the things I love about where we live is its peacefulness, which is why I keep asking hotel clerks for quiet rooms. But now that I am back in paradise, I miss the noise, the hubbub, the tumult of the road. What is wrong with me?

By 7:05 Michael and I are in the green Barcaloungers, ready to watch the first game between the Yankees and the Angels. It is just like old times, except that I have outgrown the TV experience. I want to see what goes on during the commercials. I even miss the smell of beer and hot dogs.

Boston has already beaten Tampa Bay, and Seattle has trounced Minnesota. The pressure is on the Yankees not to lose ground.

Hughes goes six-plus and gives up three runs, but it is the relief pitching that does us in. After A-Rod's 40th homer puts the Yankees up 4–3, Viz allows three runs to score in the seventh. Posada hits a two-run shot in the eighth to tie the game. Hip hip, Jor-hay! Farnsworth is on the mound for the bottom of the eighth, and we go into extra innings.

The Yankees can't score in the top of the ninth off K-Rod, that little twerp, and the Angels can't score in the bottom of the ninth off Mo. This contest is not settled until the bottom of the 10th.

We lose 7–6. I hate the Angels almost as much as I hate the Red Sox.

When I wake up on Tuesday, I am disoriented. There is no slamming of guest room doors. No humming of elevators. No clattering of room service trays. Instead I hear birds chirping.

Michael has his Remicade infusion, and I have my first-ever telephone reading with Reverend Sandi, a spiritualist/psychic/medium with a church in Santa Barbara. My friend Deborah gave me her number back in May, when I was frantic about whether the Yankees would turn their season around. But then they started winning, and I figured I would stick with my lucky clothes and lucky food and daily prayers. But now, with the wildfire still burning and the Yankees still stonewalling me, I need metaphysical help.

I begin by asking Reverend Sandi about the Zaca Fire and whether it is safe for me to leave home again. She assures me that the fire will stay away from my neighborhood. My next question is about the book. Reverend Sandi does not like sports but says that her spirits tell her the book will be very successful.

"It will?" I say.

"Wrong answer!" she scolds. "You need to say: 'It *will!*'" She instructs me to picture the book at the top of the bestseller list and imagine myself at a signing where hundreds of people are lined up. She tells me to visualize the scene as specifically as I can, right down to what I will be wearing. I dress myself in a very fetching Armani suit.

"I'm having trouble with the Yankees," I say. "I need help getting access to the players. My book depends on it."

"Write a letter to the Universe," she advises. "Just jot down: *I need access to the Yankees!* Then put the letter in an envelope and keep it with you while you travel. The Universe will help you."

After she and I finish up, I realize that I did not press her enough. I could have asked her if A-Rod will stay in New York and if Mo will retire in pinstripes and if the Yankees will make it to the postseason and win the World Series. But I am not sure I want to know the answers.

While Michael rests after his infusion, I settle into the green chair and watch Yankees–Angels. The matchup tonight is Mussina versus Escobar.

Moose is off to a shitty start, and the Angels go ahead 2–0. A-Rod homers in the top of the second, and the bats do come to life. But Mussina gets shelled and the relievers are pathetic, and the Yankees lose 18–9. The pitching is just not good enough for the postseason. I don't need Reverend Sandi to tell me that.

We lock up the house on Wednesday and hit the road again. We drive south on the 405.

"Jason Zillo should be swinging open the door for me instead of slamming it in my face," I say to Michael. "The Yankees have been doing much better since I came along."

"They have," he agrees.

"I'm not only their number one fan. I'm their lucky charm. And yet he still won't deign to talk to me!" I am getting riled up—and with good reason. The other day I e-mailed Jason to ask if he would let me interview him. I thought it might be interesting to find out what the Yankees' media relations director actually does. No reply.

We arrive at the Hyatt Regency Orange County. A large bellman carries our bags up to our room.

"How far is it to Angels Stadium?" I ask him.

"You going to the game tonight?"

"Yeah."

"Should be fun." He laughs. "We always kill the Yankees."

We leave for the 7:00 game at 4:30—nice and early so Michael can take my picture in front of the stadium and we can have an early dinner at the Catch, the restaurant everyone has told us to try. I would have sampled the fare at the concessions, but the local TV news reported that there are rats running rampant at Angels Stadium.

Our seats are in section V 431, row C, in the upper-upper deck and next to the right-field foul pole—really crappy. Before the game starts, we are forced to watch girls in skimpy clothes loading air guns with balled-up T-shirts and shooting them into the crowd. This is what passes for entertainment in Anaheim.

Good old Andy is pitching tonight. He seems to pick the team up after every losing streak. His opposition is John Lackey.

A buxom blonde sings the national anthem, during which fireworks go off from the fake-looking rock pile in center field. As for the stadium itself, it is smack in the middle of an industrial park or corporate development. It has about as much charm as a hunk of concrete.

There is no score until the top of the fourth. A-Rod comes home on Lackey's errant throw to first. A little boy in the seats in front of us asks his father, "How come people are talking to each other instead of watching the game?" I want to step in and break the news to the boy that there is no Santa Claus and that Angels fans are easily distracted. But I keep quiet.

The Rally Monkey makes its first appearance on the scoreboard in the bottom of the sixth. For those who have never had the pleasure, it is a real monkey dressed in an Angels uniform, and it jumps up and down to cheer its team on. Does it get any worse than this? Where is the organ grinder? I think about calling the animal rights people because the poor primate is being humiliated.

The Yankees go up 4–1 in the top of the eighth. Lackey departs for Scot Shields, who gives up two more runs. A fight breaks out in the bleachers, and it is a drunken Boston fan that gets tossed. Angels fans chant, "Red Sox Suck!" and are enthusiastically joined by Yankee fans.

Joba comes in for the bottom of the eighth. He electrifies everybody by striking out Vlad on a 100 mph fastball to retire the side.

With the Yankees ahead 8–1 in the bottom of the ninth, I am surprised to see Mo on the mound. But he gets Mathis to fly out to end the game.

I hug Michael as the crowd files out.

"Was that because you love me or because the Yankees won?"

"Both." I hug him tighter. "And because it's good to be back on the road."

Thursday is getaway day and an off day. Our flight lands in Detroit at 8:30 p.m. We drive off in our rented Kia Sorento. It is raining and hard to see, and we take several wrong turns before finding the Hyatt Regency in the suburb of Dearborn.

Before joining Michael in bed, I check e-mail. There is still nothing from either Kim Jones or Jason Zillo.

"What do I have to do?" I rant. "I'm a writer, not a serial killer, and yet all I do is beg for crumbs from these people. I'm the Yankees' number one fan and I can't get near them."

Michael pats the side of the bed. "How about calling it a night, good wife?"

I get his drift.

The buzz in the New York sports media on Friday is how critical the series is between the Yankees and Tigers, because both teams are fighting for a wild-card berth. There is also speculation about what the Yankees will do about Mussina. He is said to have spoken with Joe after the disaster in Anaheim about whether he will lose his spot in the rotation or be given one more shot against the Tigers.

Today is my lunch with Tyler Kepner from the *New York Times*. I have only a vague idea of what he looks like, having checked out his photo on the *Times*' "Bats" blog this morning. I don't read the blog regularly, but I never miss his articles in the *Times*. He tells you everything you need to know about a story or game in a particularly intelligent, elegant style.

I meet Tyler at the Marriott's RiverCafe in the Renaissance Center downtown. In my last e-mail I had described myself to him as having long blond hair and dark circles under my eyes. He walks right over to my table, so I must be the only one here fitting that description.

He is a fresh-faced, 32-year-old man with glossy dark hair, large blue eyes, and a very neat, preppy appearance.

After we order lunch, he tells me about his childhood in Philly, how he covered the Angels and the Mariners before starting at the *Times* on the Mets beat, how he always tries to be fair to the players he writes about instead of resorting to cheap shots.

"What do you think about Mussina's situation?" I ask. "Do you think he'll stay in the rotation?"

"I think he's one of the most underappreciated pitchers of his era. The last two games got away from him real early. But for a long stretch he gave the team a chance to win every game."

"Do you like him as a person?"

"Yeah. He's so thoughtful in explaining himself and the reasons why things happen. People think he makes excuses, but I think he gets a bad rap. He's candid, and it's hard to get candor."

"I bet it's hard to get candor from Jeter."

"I think Jeter's got it all figured out. I wouldn't like it if everyone gave the same kind of answers, but I really appreciate having one guy like that."

"Weren't you surprised that he didn't speak up for Joe, after Sheffield's comments?"

"Derek thinks the less you say about something the quicker it goes away. But he could have said, 'I've always had a great relationship with Joe, and I've never experienced any of that stuff.'"

"Think A-Rod will opt out?"

"The Yankees will make him an offer that's so lucrative he'll look at it and say, 'What more do I really want?' If he turns it down after all the stuff about how he wants to stay in New York and how much his wife and his daughter love it, he's a huge phony."

"Do you find him easy to deal with?"

"I like it when I talk to Alex versus when I talk to A-Rod. I've known Alex since he was 23. I covered him with the Mariners. Alex is a very engaging, intellectually curious, very bright guy who loves baseball passionately and dissects everything that happens on the field. He'd be the best analyst if he ever wanted to go into the TV booth. But A-Rod is a corporate entity. You don't feel like you're dealing with a person so much as a corporation that's looking out for its own interests."

We eat and continue to talk about the team. Tyler asks what my book will be about. I say it will explore my emotional attachment to the Yankees.

"Think Yankee fans are different from other fans?" I ask him.

"They're always about to commit suicide." He laughs. "My son is 5, and he doesn't know he's supposed to hate the Red Sox."

By the time Michael and I arrive at Comerica Park for tonight's game, it is raining—hard. Actually, the rain is coming down sideways because there is also a lot of wind, not to mention ferocious thunder and lightning. This storm easily trumps the one in the Bronx. The crowd—and I am guessing we are 45,000 strong—is crushed together on the stadium's lower concourse level. We are all ducking under the same small overhang, and there is not enough room for even a fraction of us. Michael pulls me inside his big rain jacket and wraps me in it with him. We share its hood, too, like twins conjoined at the head. Still, my jeans are drenched and my sneakers are in a puddle of water and I am shivering. We keep expecting a voice to come over the loudspeakers to tell us if the game has been called, but there is none. We consider leaving but decide to stick it out to the bitter end. We wait for over 2 hours in the stinking rain. Who's a bandwagon fan, eh?

Eventually, the storm lets up, and there is an announcement that there will be baseball tonight. Everybody cheers.

We look for food. It is close to 9:30, and we are starving. The walkways are flooded, and I am not about to start foraging for healthy menu options. While Michael goes to buy a hot dog, I buy the chicken tenders and French fries I have so scrupulously been avoiding. And here is the big news: They are fabulous in the most guilt-inducing way. I dip those tenders in ketchup, and it is like savoring some rare delicacy.

"I can't believe you ate the whole thing," says Michael once we are in our seats, which are in section 338, row 10—our usual upper-upper deck location but on the left-field side. The tarp has been removed, so we must be minutes away from game time.

"I hope I don't die."

We swiped extra napkins from the concession and dried the seats as best we could. Comerica Park is, like Camden Yards, one of those new/old-timey parks. Along with the tiger sculptures, the requisite fountain in center field, and a Walk of Fame celebrating great Tigers players from the past, it also boasts theme park–type rides for the kids. But what attracts me from my perch in left field is its lovely view of the downtown skyline.

"I wish they'd get going," says Michael. "This could be a long night."

They have put the tarp back on the field. I look up, and there is more rain.

"Let's get the hell out of here," we say at exactly the same second, just as the scoreboard posts the words "rain delay." They will end up postponing the game and will play a doubleheader over the weekend.

Back in our room, we turn on the TV to discover that the game will be played after all, and the first pitch will be at 11:06. Maybe a true fan would have stayed at the park in her wet clothes. Maybe a true fan would have stayed up and watched the game in the comfort of her hotel room. But sleep hits when it hits, and it hits me before the national anthem.

It is still raining on Saturday morning. I bound over to the computer to see what happened in the game. Including the 2-plus hours we were at the ballpark, the rain delay lasted a total of 4 hours and 1 minute. The game itself lasted 4 hours and 24 minutes. Oh, and the Yankees lost 9–6 in the bottom of the 11th inning on the three-run homer Carlos Guillen blasted off Sean Henn at 3:30 a.m.

I get an e-mail from Mark Feinsand asking if we can postpone today's lunch until Monday. The time on his e-mail is 5:00 a.m. He says he still has not left the ballpark and plans to sleep as late as possible once he gets back to his hotel. He hopes I understand.

I also get lots of e-mails from friends who want to know if Michael and I stayed through the rain delay and the extra innings and were still there when the game ended at 3:30 a.m.

"Of course we stayed!" I write to everyone. "It was the most incredible experience—a baseball game that went on all night! Only the Yankees' true fans were still there at the end!"

Michael peers over my shoulder. "Why are you lying about this?"

"Because my mother wouldn't let me go to Woodstock."

I suddenly remember that I have an appointment at the mall across the street to have my hair washed and blown dry by someone named Betty. It is pouring and there is no point whatsoever in having my hair done, but the salon has a 24-hour cancellation policy, and I do not want to do two bad things in the same morning.

Michael comes with me to the mall. He takes a walk while I try to make conversation at the shampoo bowl with Betty, a very tall African American woman with hair that has a million tendrils. She is not very friendly.

"Did you get heavy rain last night where you live?" I ask.

"Yeah."

"The news said there were tornadoes in some places."

"Yeah."

"There was really heavy rain at the Tigers game."

She stops shampooing me. "You were *there*?"

"Until 3:30 in the morning. And you know what? I'm going back tonight."

Betty is now my best friend. When she finishes me up, she whirls me around in the chair so I can face the mirror and admire her handiwork.

I look like Dolly Parton, minus the breasts. I have big hair. High hair. Towering hair. I ask her if she could soften it a bit, hoping she will understand that by "soften" I mean "flatten."

"I have just the thing," she says and reaches for something called Molding Mud. It is in a jar and it is a yellow, waxy substance. She dabs some between her palms, rubs them together, and runs her fingers through my big, high, towering hair. "This will keep it looking good for 2 years."

Two years? I pick up the jar and read the label. It describes the product as "a sculpting fiber cream best used for dreadlocks." Maybe Manny Ramirez uses it.

I thank Betty and meet Michael at the entrance to the mall. He does not scare easily, but he jumps when he sees me.

"It'll only last 2 years," I say.

We go back to the Hyatt and take naps. Later, I e-mail Kat O'Brien, the beat writer for *Newsday*. I ask if I can interview her for the book. I think about sending another e-mail to Kim Jones, but then I see she has finally responded to mine.

"I will try to talk with you," she writes, "but I'm just not sure when. Things are crazy right now, but I will be in touch."

We arrive at Comerica Park at 6:00. The sun is out, and the air is dry and fresh—a perfect late-summer night for baseball. We check out the carousel with the tiger seats. We look at the sculptures of Al Kaline and Ty Cobb and Hank Greenberg. We wander around the Big Cat Food Court, which features a dizzying array of choices. Michael buys a hot dog and pronounces it his favorite among all the others he has sampled.

Our seats are in section 145, row H, which is essentially Comerica's bleachers. It is Wang against Bonderman for this second game of the four-game series—the same matchup as last week's in New York.

The Yankees jump out to a 2–0 lead in the top of the first, and the Tigers fans surrounding us are not happy. They are drunk already. When they start a "Yankees suck!" chant, they look like they want to kill somebody. We are glad we are not wearing anything with the interlocking N-Y on it.

When the Yankees score four more runs in the top of the sixth, a group of Yankee She-Fans cheers wildly.

"Jeter will never marry any of you because you're ugly tramps and sluts!" one of the boozy Tigers fans yells.

In the top of the seventh, there is an actual scrum between these jerks and a guy wearing a Mariners jersey.

"Hey, Seattle guy!" one of them taunts. "Are you a Jap lover?"

Another chimes in. "Do you eat sushi all the time, Ichiro?"

I turn to Michael. "Have they not heard about ethnic and racial tolerance in Detroit?"

"Apparently not."

"Hey, Seattle guy!" the first one yells. "You got a big nose. You must be a Jew!"

"Are you Youkilis's brother?" the second one yells. "Or are you just gay?"

Michael and I are stunned as the slurs keep coming at the Mariners fan, who makes a few attempts to defend himself but is outnumbered.

What amazes me is not the bigotry and prejudice I am hearing, particularly from a bunch of fans who have had way too much beer. I am surprised—and furious—that the usher in our section is sitting on his fat butt watching the game instead of taking care of business. What is the point of announcing that offensive behavior will result in ejection if the employees look the other way?

"This wouldn't happen at Yankee Stadium," I say to Michael. "Those assholes would be thrown out in a heartbeat."

The Yankees win the game 7–2. They move to within two of Seattle for the wild card.

Michael wakes up sneezing on Sunday. The person sitting behind him had a cold, but he also stood around in rain-soaked clothes on Friday night. I try not to worry, but it is in my DNA.

Today's game has a 1:05 start. Our seats are in section 339, row 18, which is back up-up-up there, down the left-field line. The good news is we are shielded from the hot sun, so I will not be sweaty and smelly for my drinks date with Suzyn Waldman later.

Hughes is on the mound today and gets bombed. Granderson hits an inside-the-park home run. And Guillen and Thames both smack two-run shots. Giambi and Cano go deep for us, pulling us to 5–4. But here comes the Tigers' flamethrowing reliever, Joel Zumaya, in the top of the seventh. The scoreboard announcer proclaims, "It's Zoooooom Maya!" and the speakers blare Jimi Hendrix singing "Voodoo Child." Zumaya shuts us down.

Farnsworth and Viz pitch scoreless innings, but the Yankees' bats go dormant. We lose the game but remain two behind the Mariners, who continue to cooperate by sucking whenever we do.

Back at the Hyatt, I change out of my game clothes and slip into a black cotton pantsuit—casual but not too. We drive to the suburb of Birmingham, where I am meeting Suzyn Waldman at the Townsend.

Michael drops me off at the hotel's entrance and goes exploring. He has spotted a Borders and wants to browse, then go have a greasy, disgusting burger somewhere. He thinks I should be alone with Suzyn so we will bond, but I think he is just dying for a night off from baseball and me.

I find Suzyn in the hotel bar, where she is having a glass of white wine and munching on nuts. She waves me over and I pull up a stool next to hers. Like a lot of people I have met, she is more attractive in person than on TV. She has beautiful blue eyes and a lot of energy for someone who has just been on the radio for over 3 hours. I order a glass of red wine. We chat like old friends.

"I wasn't a tomboy growing up," I say. "Were you?"

"No," she says. "But I remember going to my first game at Fenway at the age of 3 or 4 and loving it. I was sitting close enough to reach out and touch Ted Williams."

She tells me about her move to New York after college and her auditions for musical theater roles and the rejections she got when she was told she was not pretty and blond enough for the lead parts. Her blue eyes sparkle as she talks about landing the plum role in *Man of La Mancha* and touring with Richard Kiley.

"Is it okay if I turn on my tape recorder?" I ask.

"No tape recorder because I've had something to drink," she says. "Another time."

"We could do a more formal interview in Kansas City next week."

She shakes her head. "It'll be my birthday."

"How about Toronto, our stop after that?"

"It'll be Rosh Hashanah."

Suzyn and I move to a table and have dinner. We share a salad and sample each other's entrées and have another glass of wine. It is all very chummy.

Michael joins us as we are finishing up. Suzyn and I have talked a little bit about our personal lives, and she seems pleased to catch a glimpse of the husband she has been hearing about. When it is time to say good-bye, she and I give each other a hug. We have made a connection.

Ron Guidry walks by and takes a seat at the bar. He is inches away from us. I remember how George King predicted that Suzyn would be the key to my meeting a Yankee. Okay, so Guidry is a coach, not a current player. He is still a Yankee. This is my moment.

As Suzyn nods at him, I do some deep breathing, ready myself for the big introduction, and toss around a few possible opening lines in my head. I will be poised and professional. I will not gush. And I surely will not confront Gator about the Yankees' pitching problems. I will not even call him Gator.

"I'm going over to talk to him," Suzyn says. "Bye."

That is it. I have been dismissed.

I stand there, stunned. Michael takes my arm and leads me outside.

"Guidry was right there! I was right there!" I am ranting in a rental car in a suburb of Detroit. "Even if it didn't occur to her that a person writing a book about being a Yankee fan would kill to meet a Yankee, whatever happened to common courtesy? Whatever happened to sisterhood?"

"Maybe he doesn't like talking to fans and she knows that."

"But this was my chance! Time is running out."

"You've got the whole month of September to meet a Yankee. October, too, if they make the postseason."

He is right. There is time. My friend Marty told me there is always one player, and that player is out there waiting for me. Somewhere.

AL EAST STANDINGS/AUGUST 26

TEAM	W	L	PCT	GB
BOSTON	80	51	.611	—
NEW YORK	72	58	.554	7.5
TORONTO	65	65	.500	14.5
BALTIMORE	58	71	.450	21.0
TAMPA BAY	51	79	.392	28.5

Week 22
August 27, 2007

Why do ballplayers spit? Nobody ever asked me that. We use saliva a lot more than most people do. We're always licking our fingers or hands and it tastes like shit, so maybe that's why we spit. Or it's because we're hungover and our tongue is the size of a pillow.

It is back to the Marriott's RiverCafe on Monday for lunch with Mark Feinsand and a quick chat with Sweeny Murti.

Mark is a heavyset man in his thirties. He has the tough-talking, raspy voice of the born-and-raised New Yorker he is. I love reading his articles in the *Daily News,* as well as his blog, because he has a no-frills, just-the-facts style, and you never worry you might be missing something.

"I hope you got some sleep after that marathon on Friday night," I say after we sit down and order lunch. "Were the players pissed off that they had to be out there until 3:30 in the morning?"

"They hate doubleheaders, so they were just as happy to get that game out of the way."

"They'll never make the play-offs with this pitching."

He laughs. "I was a Yankee fan for most of my life, so I understand all your craziness. But I can't cover the team objectively and be a fan. You can't cheer in the press box."

"Why do some players resent the media?"

"Some of them think our job is to create as much controversy as we can, to stir the shit, to sell papers, to get our names on TV. But most of us got into this because we love baseball and we love writing."

"How about A-Rod? Do you think he'll stay in New York?"

"I change my mind every day."

"Tell me about Jeter."

Mark sits back and glances out the window.

"I went to cover Jeter at Columbia-Presbyterian. Every year he does this charity where he goes with one of his buddies, dressed up as Santa Claus. He visits the sick kids on the children's ward and gives them the thrill of their life. So I was the only reporter at the hospital that year—my first at MLB.com. This PR woman was whisking Jeter around, and I was standing in the back. I was told, 'Just stay there and we'll get him for you.' The PR woman started to take Jeter away, and he said, 'When do I talk to the media?' She said, 'There's no media.' Jeter stopped, looked at me, and said, 'What about him?' The PR woman said, 'Oh, yeah. I forgot.' Jeter told her, 'Give me 5 minutes.' He walked toward me, and we ducked into a stairwell. I asked him a couple of questions about the day and the charity and then asked him a couple of baseball questions. He said, 'Thanks a lot. Merry Christmas.' He not only took the time to realize I was there, but he made sure I was taken care of. Did he break any big news that day? No. But it was classy on his part."

"Very," I say. The story makes me like Jeter more. "Did you have anyone to show you the ropes when you started out?"

"I had Sweeny. I interned at the FAN, and he was there then. He helped me a lot. Now when I see somebody new, I try to be nice. Of course there are limits to being nice when someone's a foof."

"A foof?"

"A guy who asks stupid questions. Last year on Father's Day, some guy showed up and asked Joe Torre what he remembered about his father. Well, do a little homework, guy. Know that Joe Torre grew up with domestic violence and started a foundation because of it."

"Was everybody cringing?"

"It was the most uncomfortable thing I've ever seen. Joe said, 'I don't know if you're aware of my history, but my father abused my mother and you might not want to ask me that.' The guy said, 'No, I do!' We were all just sitting there going, 'Please go away.'"

"Sounds like Joe handled it well."

"Joe handles everything well. He makes this job a thousand times easier."

"My only issue with Joe is his bullpen management."

Mark rolls his eyes. I am clearly a foof. "The Torre bashing brings me back to the subject of Yankee fans. They're spoiled. That's all there is to it—ridiculous, spoiled brats. Having been one, I know."

"Do you think they're spoiled from winning or from having an owner who'll buy them anybody?"

"Both. Yankee fans have to appreciate how hard it is to win."

Sweeny Murti walks over to the table. It is his turn with me, and Mark vacates his chair.

Sweeny is a handsome 37-year-old—as thin and wiry as Edwar Ramirez. He is friendly and easygoing, and it is not a stretch to picture him helping Mark during his first season with the Yankees. He needs to get to the ballpark soon, so our conversation is brief.

It is interesting to hear what it is like to cover the Yankees for a radio station as opposed to a newspaper. And, of course, we talk about the team's pitching woes and chances to make the play-offs. But what sticks with me—gnaws at me—is his assessment of Yankee fans, which echoes Mark's.

"Teams will have ups and downs, but Yankee fans don't want anything but ups," he says. "The fact is you don't win every year—you can't win every year—and the fans will have to deal with that."

Have all the championships completely warped me? Have I lost all sense of perspective? Do I really not know how hard it is to win? I remember all too vividly how hard it was to win on the tennis court. I could never shut down my opponent when it counted, never close the deal. Have I become a killer through the Yankees? Have I turned into the baseball-fan version of one of those spoiled, selfish, entitled women who used to beat me in the finals of tournament after tournament? The ones who threw their rackets when they missed a shot and disputed every call that went against them and were so competitive they even had to "win" the warm-ups?

It is off to Comerica Park for the series finale and the Yankees' last trip to Detroit this season. Our seats are in section 344, row 1—at the left-field foul pole. A woman throws peanuts at the people in the row below and thinks it is hysterically funny. Once again, the Comerica employees sit on their butts and do nothing.

Mussina is on the mound. I can't picture him getting another start if he gets shelled tonight.

He gives up a run in the first, two more in the second, and three more in the third. The guy has nothing, as opposed to Verlander, who is handcuffing the Yankees. Edwar and Henn don't help us from the pen, and the Tigers pound out 20 hits.

The final score is 16–0.

"I can't believe that in three starts I've forgotten how to pitch after 17 years," Mussina tells the media afterward.

❧

While we wait to board our flight to LaGuardia on Tuesday morning, I hop on my laptop and read what the beat writers are saying about Yankeeville. They are reporting that Mussina will be meeting with Torre and Guidry to discuss his future—whether he should work out his problems on the mound during Sunday's game against Tampa Bay or take some time off.

Our flight lands in New York. I didn't drink putrid plane wine or even miss it.

We check back into the Marmara, our home away from home. It feels wonderfully familiar. Since this is a slow week in New York with everybody fleeing to the Hamptons for the Labor Day holiday, we are given the same extra-large apartment we had last time at a special, lower rate.

Tonight begins yet another episode in the drama that is Yankees–Red Sox, as we open the first of a three-game set tonight. The Stadium is bulging with men, women, and children in Yankees gear, many of them looking a little lost. We, on the other hand, feel like regulars. We take shortcuts. We maneuver through and around people. We get an elbow in the ribs and give an elbow right back. We are no longer intimidated.

We go right up to the Tier level. We have not eaten since breakfast, so we buy food. Michael, who has rated the Yankee Stadium hot dog to be the worst of any he has sampled so far, nevertheless tries again. He looks at it, turns up his nose, and sends it back.

"Whassup?" says the girl behind the counter.

"It's not cooked," he says. "I want another one. And I want it hot."

Our seats are in Tier 32, row B—in the outfield just to the left of the foul pole. There are lots of Red Sox fans in our section. I can't understand why anyone would scream "Yankees suck" for nine straight innings.

Tiger Woods is in the house. So is Cameron Diaz.

Pettitte is going against Dice-K tonight. Joe announced before the game that Mussina will skip his next start against the Devil Rays and that another kid, Ian Kennedy, will be called up from Scranton to take his place.

Dice-K pitches to Damon in the top of the first. I cannot stand him. Dice-K, I mean. Same with Beckett, Schilling, and Pap Smear. Same with Manny and Big Sloppy. They are so arrogant. I hate them.

We are tied at 2–2 until the fifth, when Jeter's solo shot puts us ahead.

Varitek's own solo shot—I *really* hate Varitek—knots things up again in the seventh.

Damon's two-run homer in the bottom of the frame warrants a long curtain call. The crowd continues to cheer him not only for breaking the tie but also for sticking it to his old team.

In the top of the eighth, Joba trots in from the bullpen to chants of his name. I pray this is not the game when he finally screws up. It is not.

"Enter Sandman" heralds Mo's entrance in the top of the ninth. Varitek strikes out. Crisp strikes out. Lugo lines out. Three up, three down. Game over. What is it Boston fans are always saying about Mo? That the Red Sox have figured him out? No way.

Wednesday is a gorgeous day—sunny and hot but without the usual summer humidity, and Michael and I take advantage of it by walking all over the city.

Our seats for tonight's contest are in Tier 35, row B—in the upper reaches of right field. I am next to a Red Sox couple. They are in their late twenties and are wearing the blue caps with the stupid red "B" on them. I can't stand sitting next to them, but I try to be on good behavior.

The guy is from Connecticut. His girlfriend is from Boston. She is the noisy one. She is blond and effervescent and says that she loves the Red Sox more than she loves members of her own family.

"How do your parents feel about that?" I ask.

"They love the Red Sox more than they love me," she says.

The scoreboard is showing a "Yankeeography" of Andy Pettitte.

"He really sucks," says the blonde.

I do a double take. What sort of person would say Pettitte sucks at Yankee Stadium and for what reason? I am going to smash her face.

"By the way," I say, "how come the Red Sox get a new shortstop every year?"

Michael gives me a look.

"Because we're not the Evil Empire," she says. "We can't go out and buy the best players."

She is not just a Red Sox fan. She is a moronic Red Sox fan. Does she not know that her team has the second-highest payroll in baseball?

"You did spend a hefty chunk of change on Dice-K," I say. "And how about that $70 million contract for J. D. Drew?"

"There should be a limit on the number of trades teams can make so that fans in, like, Baltimore can finally know what it's like to win."

There should be a limit on Red Sox fans allowed into Yankee Stadium. "The fans in Baltimore know what it's like to win. Ever hear of Frank Robinson? Brooks Robinson? Jim Palmer?"

"And Boog Powell," Michael adds. "Best food in the American League."

Bob Sheppard gives us the lineups.

"Jeter is so overrated," the blonde pipes up again.

You do not trash the Captain. "I see Manny is out of the lineup," I counter. "Did he pull a hamstring tying his shoelaces?"

She turns away in a snit.

Clemens takes the mound. He was Beckett's idol growing up, and this is the first time they have faced each other. The Rocket hits Pedroia with a heater. There are no warnings issued, but the pitch must be retaliation either for Dice-K hitting A-Rod last night or for Pedroia's comment after the game that A-Rod's hard slide into Lugo was "a cheap shot."

In the bottom of the seventh, with the Yankees up 3–1, A-Rod belts one of Beckett's pitches for a line-drive homer, his 44th on the season and 508th overall, tying Frank Thomas. Josh is history.

Farnsworth comes in for the top of the eighth. He gets Ortiz to fly out, and there are huge cheers. But he gives up a two-run homer to Youkilis for 4–3 and sucks all the air out of the Stadium. Well, except for the blonde and her boyfriend, who are bouncing up and down with joy. After Farnsworth walks Varitek, Kyle gets the hook from Joe, who brings in Mo for four outs—again. Crisp grounds out. Hinske grounds out. Lugo grounds out. Pedroia grounds out. Game over. Yeah, the Red Sox have figured Mo out all right.

"Great meeting you guys," I say to the blonde and her boyfriend as Frank Sinatra croons in the background. "Hope you had a good time."

Thursday is a day game after a night game. I know the routine by now. Get up. Get dressed. Get some work done. Get to the ballpark.

I check e-mail. There is nothing from anybody who can help me meet my Yankee. What will I do? How will I make the interview happen? Will I have to give the publisher their money back if I fail?

Our seats for today's game are in Tier 28, row T, which means we are in for one of those steep climbs that make me breathless. We are along the left field line in fair territory, and we are surrounded—really surrounded—by Red Sox fans. The guy behind me yells "Yankees suck" even before the lineups are announced.

I turn around. "Go fuck yourself."

"Hey, come on," Michael scolds me. "There's a kid here."

A boy of about 7 is sitting below us. He is wearing a Red Sox cap.

"He can go fuck himself, too."

Wang takes the mound, and his band of rooters wave their Taiwanese flags. The Red Sox fan behind me yells, "Wang sucks!" I want to kill him.

The Yankees get on the board in the bottom of the third with Cano's solo shot off Schilling. The Red Sox fan yells, "Jeter wears lipstick!" It is bizarre, because Jeter is not even up. The same moron shouts, "Hip, hip, Jor-*gay*!" I turn around to say something, but Michael clamps his hand down on my arm.

Cano goes deep for the second time in the bottom of the fifth. The Red Sox fan yells, "Jeter blows A-Rod!" I guess that in Boston being gay must be the worst thing you can possibly be.

In the bottom of the seventh, after Melky gets some chin music from Schilling, the Red Sox fan shouts, "Hit him in the head next time!"

That does it. I get up from my seat, turn around and yell, "Shut your fucking piehole or I'll shut it for you!"

"What the hell are you thinking?" Michael says as he pulls me back into my seat. "The only reason you're not getting your skull cracked open is because you're a girl. I'm the one he'll hit."

I smile. I have not been called a girl since, well, I was a girl.

Wang has pitched a gem through seven, and Joba keeps Boston scoreless in the eighth. Okajima comes in for Schilling in the bottom half and allows two more runs for 5–0. We are all on our feet, cheering and clapping and gearing up for the sweep, as Joba reappears in the ninth. He lets go of a fastball that sails over the head of Youkilis, who glares toward the mound. The next pitch? Same place. The home plate umpire ejects Joba. Joe comes out to argue that both pitches slipped out of the kid's hand, but the ump is not buying it. Joba takes a seat to a standing ovation. Edwar replaces him and retires Lowell and Drew. Game over.

"Great stuff," says Michael as we file out.

"As good as it gets."

❧

On Friday I go for a power walk. It is hot and sticky, but I need the exercise. Watching ballgames is very sedentary.

I am marching past clothing stores and electronics stores and drugstores. And then I put on the brakes when I get to a Korean market. I spot the ripest, reddest, most luscious-looking tomatoes and suddenly feel a pang of sadness— that the tomatoes we were growing at home in California have died, that the tomato season is almost over, that the summer is almost over.

Summer has always meant swimming and riding around in my convertible and hanging out at the beach. But it is the start of the Labor Day weekend, and I have not done any of those things. And while this trip is a dream come true in that I get to follow the Yankees, it has also afflicted me with tunnel vision. All I think about is baseball, even more than before. There is a war in Iraq and a crisis in health care and a raging debate about global warming, but I am in a baseball bubble. This morning, for instance, there was an article in the *Times* with the headline "For Struggling Tribe, Dark Side to a Windfall." I assumed they were talking about the Cleveland Indians instead of a Native American tribe out west!

Later, Michael and I meet my mother for lunch at an Italian restaurant.

"Are the Yankees being nicer to you?" Mom asks.

"Not yet."

"So many nuts out there." She shakes her head. "I guess they think you're one of them."

She goes on to say how much she loves Melky and Jeter and Jorge.

"I wish I could warm to A-Rod, though. There's something about him that turns me off."

"Is it the spitting?" My mother has a thing about that.

"He doesn't look like he's enjoying himself. He should be more like Canoe."

"Cano."

"And I like the right fielder. You know who I mean."

"Abreu."

She smiles shyly. "I have a little crush on him."

"How is it that you can be in love with them without getting all upset when they lose?"

She pats my hand. "The wisdom of old age, dearie."

Since it is the Friday night of a holiday weekend and we are playing Tampa Bay, not Boston, the #4 subway is not that crowded. The baby boomer woman standing next to me admires my Yankees hat, which is black and has rhinestones adorning the N and Y.

"We're going to the game tonight," she says, nodding at her husband. "We go to practically every game."

"My wife's writing a book about the Yankees!" Michael blurts out. "It all started after she said in the *New York Times* she was divorcing them!"

The woman squeals. "*You're* the one who wrote that article?"

"We read it," says the husband. "That was really *you*?"

"Yes," I say.

The woman reaches into her purse and pulls out a piece of paper. It is her grocery list. She hands it to me and asks me to sign it. I am actually giving an autograph on a subway.

At the Stadium we waltz up to Ticket Window #74, where Cass Halpin, the Devil Rays' head of VIP relations, instructed us to pick up our complimentary tickets.

Since we are VIPs, we are on the main level, in box 212, row F, instead of up in the Tier. It is the section reserved for the friends and family of the visiting team, according to the pretty young woman who oversees security for the section. Michael tells her she is the first nice security person we have met, and she laughs.

Hughes is on the mound and gives up a run in the top of the first. The people around us are cheering, because they are all relatives of the Devil Rays players. I smile at them to let them know that I like the Rays, too. I also like the fact that these men and women are rooting for their team, not trashing the Yankees. They are not bitter and angry and using the word *suck*. They are a positive group.

The Yankees look flat at the plate, like they always do after they play Boston.

Hughes is at 81 pitches by the top of the fifth—not exactly an efficient outing. After he serves up a homer to Pena, he leaves for Chris Britton, the latest call-up, who comes back out in the sixth and gives up Pena's second homer of the day. Bruney is responsible for another three runs.

The Yankees lose 9–1. This is our 2007 season right here.

As Michael and I leave the Stadium, I tell him I was touched by the way the relatives of the Devil Rays supported their boys. "I hardly ever think about the players as real people having real flesh-and-blood families."

"They're not the products of immaculate conception."

"I realize that. There was just something refreshing about the family members cheering for their kids tonight. It was like a high school game where all the parents show up. I really enjoyed myself."

He looks dumbstruck. "The Yankees lost and you enjoyed yourself?"

I nod. "I liked the way people rooted for their team even though that team is in last place."

"It's called loyalty."

September 1 feels like fall. A cold front blew in late last night; and today is cooler, less humid, with brilliant sunshine. The city is very quiet—well, except for the construction on Second Avenue—and it almost feels as if Michael and I are the only ones here.

Today is a day game after a night game—the second in the series against Tampa Bay. We are in the same box, 212, as last night, but in row B, which is even closer to the field.

I introduce myself to some of the Devil Rays families. Behind me are the parents and aunt and uncle of Dan Wheeler, a relief pitcher. They travel from Rhode Island to see their boy whenever he is playing in New York or Boston. Dan's father, Norman, is a friendly, down-to-earth man—the opposite of the stereotypically pushy sports parent.

The big Yankees news today is that our starter is Ian Kennedy. The 22-year-old has been promoted from Scranton to take Mussina's spot in the rotation. He is short and slight and looks about 14. From what I can tell during the warm-up, his pitching style resembles Moose's.

He goes seven innings, allowing three runs. He shows a lot of poise and, best of all, throws strikes.

The Yankees are cruising to a 9–3 victory until Viz comes in for the top of the eighth. He gives up a couple of runs, and the crowd boos him, fearing this game might slip away. Joe must be having the same fear, because he brings in Mo for four quick outs and gets them.

Back at the hotel, I check e-mail. There is one from Kim Jones. I had followed up and asked if she would be available for lunch on either Friday or Saturday of next week, when we are in KC.

"No, sorry, neither will work. Kim."

That is her entire response. For a communicator, she is not very communicative.

I send her another e-mail. "Is there any time that would be convenient for you?"

It does not take long for her reply to land in my inbox.

"Jane: As I mentioned previously, I'm going to try to get back to you at some point."

A smackdown! I am tempted to tell her not to bother *trying,* but if she is way busier than, say, John Sterling or Tyler Kepner, so be it.

Sunday is a day game—the last in the Tampa Bay series—and once again we are in box 212, row F, with Dan Wheeler's family. We also have Delmon Young's father, who has graying hair and a distinguished air.

Pettitte is pitching against Hammel.

Tampa Bay gets on the board in the top of the third with a solo shot by Navarro. I chat with Norman Wheeler, Dan's father. He says his son used to play for Houston before being traded to the Rays for Ty Wigginton.

"Did he like playing for the Astros?" I ask.

"Yeah," says Norman. "He's still friends with Andy Pettitte. They had a nice hug when they saw each other on Friday."

"How about Clemens?"

Norman smiles. "No hug."

"Did you always know Dan would be a professional ballplayer?"

He shakes his head. "Just like you never think you'll win the lottery."

"You're really proud of him."

"I am." He grins. "He's a great kid. And this team is better than you think. Just wait and see."

Andy Phillips is hit by a pitch on his right hand and is sent to the hospital for an MRI. He is replaced at first by Betemit, which surprises me since Mientkiewicz is back with the team.

Pettitte works in and out of trouble all day. He is at 102 pitches in the bottom of the sixth, and I figure he is done. But he comes back out for the seventh and gives up three runs.

Edwar takes a beating in the top of the eighth, allowing two homers that put the Rays ahead 8–2.

In the bottom of the eighth, the Rays make a pitching change: Dan Wheeler. I am so excited! His parents are my new friends! Let's go, Dan!

His mother and aunt are too nervous to watch and hide their eyes, but Norman cups his hands around his mouth and yells, "Come on, Wheels!" Michael and I cheer for Wheels, too. He gets Giambi and Melky to fly out. There are congratulations all around.

The Yankees lose two of three to the last-place Devil Rays but cling to their two-game lead over Seattle for the wild card.

Back at the hotel, Michael says he is getting another cold. I pray this one goes away quickly, like the one he caught in Detroit.

AL EAST STANDINGS/SEPTEMBER 2

TEAM	W	L	PCT	GB
BOSTON	82	55	.599	—
NEW YORK	76	61	.555	6.0
TORONTO	70	66	.515	11.5
BALTIMORE	59	76	.437	22.0
TAMPA BAY	56	81	.409	26.0

Week 23
September 3, 2007

I think the world of Brian Cashman. There aren't enough guys like him in the big leagues. Before I came here, people told him I was an arrogant prick—that if things didn't go well I would burn you. I was in a bad state of mind last year. But he was open and honest with me, and I explained myself, and he let me prove I'm a good guy in the clubhouse. Guys like me? We give everything we have.

It is Labor Day and Michael doesn't feel like celebrating. He is sneezing and hacking. I say he should skip today's game and rest so his cold doesn't blossom into anything worse. He protests at first—"This is the beginning of an important series against the Mariners!"—but caves after another sneezing attack.

My sister is happy to be his surrogate. We meet at the 86th Street subway station about noon and ride to the Bronx together. We make an unlikely pair. She has short dark hair and a normal woman's figure. I have long blond hair and am shaped like a pencil.

When we arrive at the Stadium, I point skyward. "We'll be sitting up there." She doesn't go to many games, so I want to prepare her.

"These aren't *that* bad," she says, once we have settled into our seats in Tier 13, row H.

For me, the seats are great. Sure, they are insanely high up, but they are also between home plate and first base—prime viewing.

During the "Yankeeography" about Catfish Hunter, I spot a sixtysomething woman sitting alone a couple of rows below us. She has short gray hair under her Yankees cap, is wearing earphones that are plugged into a Sony radio with a Yankees sticker on it, and is filling in names on a scorecard. I am curious about her—I have become curious about fans in general and She-Fans in particular—and hop down to speak to her.

"Are you a longtime fan?" I ask.

"Since I was a little girl," she says with a wistful smile. "My father introduced me to the game. It was the greatest gift he ever gave me."

I think about other She-Fans I have met. Their fathers introduced them to the game, too. "Do you think we'll make it into the postseason?"

"The pitching is inconsistent, but if we get quality innings out of the young kids, we could do it. And once we're in, anything can happen."

"I'd hate to see us climb back from where we were, only to get knocked out in the first round."

"We all have such high expectations—it goes with the territory—but sometimes things don't work out, and we just have to accept it."

I study this woman as if she were a science project. She is a She-Fan like me, and yet she approaches the Yankees with such balance.

"Have you been a Yankee fan for a long time?" she asks me.

I nod. "I'm writing a book about my relationship with them."

I expect her to laugh or roll her eyes, but she asks for my name. "I'll be on the lookout for the book."

The Yankees jump out to a 1–0 lead in the bottom of the first, but Clemens, who is said to have foot blisters, has nothing. Ichiro's homer in the third is just the beginning, and the Mariners are up 5–1 when Mussina comes in to relieve in the fifth.

"Sorry for inviting you to this pathetic display," I tell my sister. In addition to Clemens's miserable outing, the Yankees are stifled by Hernandez, the Mariners' hard-throwing starter. He is hurling 98 mph fastballs with 80 mph sliders thrown in.

"What do you mean?" she says. "I'm having a great time."

Mussina does not exactly shut the Mariners down, but he is not as horrendous as he has been. He allows two runs over four innings, and the score is 7–1 as he departs for Chris Britton in the top of the eighth.

The woman I spoke to earlier gets up to go. I didn't figure her for someone who would leave before a game is over.

"Seen enough?" I call out to her.

"Some days they don't have it," she says with a chuckle. "There's always tomorrow."

Amazing. The Yankees are about to lose to a team they need to beat, and yet she doesn't act even a little miffed.

When I get back to the hotel, I check on Michael, who is still sneezing. I also check e-mail. There is one from Larry Brooks, who says he may be covering the Kansas City and Toronto road trips and hopes we can get together in one place or the other. He passes along the contact info of a friend of his named Jen Royle. He says she interviews all the Yankees for the YES Web site and knows them really well. "She's a great girl," he says.

On Tuesday morning George King has an article in the *Post* about the party A-Rod hosted last night at the waterfront mansion he is renting in Westchester. I am furious that I was not invited. Of course, I am not even allowed in the press box, but I can picture myself all dressed up, sipping Dom Pérignon, munching on those miniature hamburgers that are so popular at cocktail parties these days and chatting with various players and their wives. I would surely have scored an interview with a Yankee.

Michael is still feeling rotten, so I leave him to sleep and rest. It is another beautiful sunny day, and I enjoy my walk down First Avenue to Luca, the restaurant where I meet Kat O'Brien for lunch. She is an adorable 27-year-old from Davenport, Iowa, who covered the Texas Rangers for the *Fort Worth Star-Telegram* before joining *Newsday*. This is her first season as the Yankees' beat writer.

While we eat, I ask Kat about the team and their chances of winning a championship and their chemistry in the clubhouse, and she is very knowledgeable about all of it. But mostly I am curious what it is like to be the Yankees' only female beat writer.

"Was the idea of moving to New York daunting?" I ask.

"It was exciting," she says. "I'm not really afraid of new experiences."

"Was it hard to make friends with the other beat writers?"

"Not really. I had heard that they were cliquish, but I knew most of them from covering the Rangers. Being female can be a negative in some ways, but it's also helpful because people remember you."

"How is it a negative?"

"Older people who've been around the game for a long time don't really think women would know anything about sports. And you hear sexual comments."

"How do you deal with that?"

"I pretty much ignore it. But I speak Spanish, and that makes it kind of interesting. One time I overheard something along those lines. I turned around and said something back in Spanish. One of the players said to the others, 'Be careful. She understands.'"

Back at the hotel, I check on Michael. He is still feeling awful, so I enlist my friend Marty to be my date for tonight's game.

Marty is a Mets fan and, therefore, hates the Yankees, and when we get to the Stadium, he is not as diplomatic as my sister was about the seat he is stuck with. We are in Tier 11, row H, above home plate.

"How the hell are you supposed to focus on the game from all the way up here?" he says.

"You'll get used to it," I say. "By the fifth inning, you won't feel like barfing."

As Wang takes the mound, Marty asks me how the book is coming. I say I have not met a Yankee yet.

"This Jason Zillo guy is still stonewalling you?"

"I even asked him if I could interview him, and he never let me."

He says I should try going through the players' agents. He pulls out a piece of paper and writes down the names of the agents he knows. He has been producing Broadway musicals for years and has no fear when it comes to picking up the phone and calling people. "One way or another, you'll have your Yankee."

Wang's sinker is really impressive tonight. He holds the Mariners scoreless through six. In the bottom of the inning, A-Rod hits a towering blast into the upper deck in left. The Yankees are up 4–0 in the seventh when Joe finally puts Mientkiewicz in at first base. It bothers me that we have a Gold Glove infielder and don't use him.

The Yankees break the game wide open in the bottom of the seventh, scoring seven runs, but Seattle scores two off Vizcaino in the top of the eighth for 11–3. Viz is showered with boos as he trudges to the dugout.

"Yankee fans are merciless," Marty remarks. "You're ahead by eight fucking runs."

"No lead is safe with this bullpen."

The final score is 12–3, and the Yankees are now two up on the Mariners for the wild card.

I wake up on Wednesday with Michael's cold. I figured it was only a matter of time before I caught it. I can't afford to be out of it today—not for my reunion with "the girls"—Barb, Diane, and Patty. I am counting on them to tell me how to meet my Yankee.

I pull myself together and hurry over to Sarabeth's, the appointed restaurant on Madison and 92nd Street. Standing near the entrance are three middle-aged women who can only be Barb, Diane, and Patty. I have not seen them in 40 years, and yet I recognize them immediately.

Barb is "the tall one." She has light blond hair that curls under her chin and is dressed in a chic black outfit. She looks prosperous and put together. Diane has light brown hair, full lips, and eyes that widen when she is excited and demonstrative, which is often. And Patty has flaming red hair with bangs that fall into her eyes. She is the most soft-spoken of the three but giggles frequently—the happy-go-lucky, free spirit. They are just as funny and approachable as I remember.

We go inside, get a corner table for four, and order lunch. I explain how I came to write a book about divorcing the Yankees and ask permission to turn on the tape recorder.

"My relationship with Sparky brought me such pleasure and pain!" Diane blurts out.

"Sparky Lyle?"

"It's such a long saga, and I don't even know if I should get into it," she says, dying to get into it. "What I do know is that my story with Barb and Patty would be a great movie. I would write it myself, but—"

"Let's stay on point," Barb cuts her off. You can tell they have been through this before. "What happened was, my dad actually played minor league baseball and my brothers were interested in baseball, so I became interested in base-ball *players*."

Patty laughs. "All three of us grew up in Philly. Barb and I were childhood friends."

"When we were 14," Barb continues, "we used to go to games at Connie Mack Stadium. My poor father would have to park outside and wait until all the ballplayers came out so I could shake their hands and say hello. We were all crazy about Richie Ashburn, and I knew what car he drove."

"It was a different time," Patty says wistfully. "The players parked their own cars and didn't lock them."

"So Patty and I got in Richie's car one day during a game," says Barb. "We laid down in the backseat and stayed very quiet. They brought his car up to him, and he got in and started driving. All of a sudden, I went, 'Richie!' He turned around and said, 'What the hell?' I said, 'I love you.'"

We all laugh. "You were definitely the nervy one," I say to her.

"I was," she acknowledges. "But that started our relationship with Richie. From then on, we were the 14-year-old girls who would open his car door for him when he came out. He would say thank you and pat us on the head and muss our hair. All the guys treated us like their little pets."

"When did you become more than the Phillies' little pets?" I ask.

"We started going to spring training," Barb says.

Patty laughs and points at Diane. "We told our parents we were staying at your house."

"We got friendly with Clay Dalrymple, for example," says Barb. "He was a catcher with the Phillies. We used to babysit for him. But after we went to spring training the first time, we started looking at them all differently. We would check out the new players and say, 'Oh, we like this one or that one.' By that time we were well known at the ballpark. We were allowed to wait outside the clubhouse and say hi to the players."

"Were there other girls hanging out at the ballpark, too?" I ask.

"They were slutty girls," says Diane. "We were still virgins."

"Which is why the ballplayers called us the Cherry Sisters," Barb says. "We would make out with them, but that was it."

"We were groupies," says Patty.

"We were *not* groupies!" Barb insists.

"How do you all define *groupie*?" I ask them.

"Groupies are those women who want to take half the team," says Diane. "I think we were just looking for love in the wrong way."

"And we were very selective," says Barb. "That's the difference."

"So you're just virgins who hang out at the ballpark," I confirm.

"We would even go there in the off-season," says Barb, "or when the team was on the road. We'd be let inside the clubhouse. We'd steal their jockstraps."

Everybody laughs. "When did you start dating the players?"

"It was Frank Torre who got us started," says Diane. "His nickname in Philly was 'Toast' for 'Toast of the Town.' I remember seeing him leaving the games with a stogie hanging from his lips and a bevy of tall Playboy Bunny types on each arm. One night Barb, Patty, and I were waiting for a taxi to take us home from the stadium after a rainout. Frank saw us and asked if we'd like to go to a party. That was the beginning of our social life with the players—a step up from being their little mascots."

"After that we'd go to bars where we knew they hung out, and we'd make out with them," Barb says.

"We were so young we weren't scared of anything," adds Patty.

"When I think back now," Barb says, "I don't know how I got out of some of the situations I put myself in. I was once in a car accident with Jack Hamilton at 2 o'clock in the morning. I ran because I was afraid Jack would get in trouble. There was actually an article in the paper the next day saying they suspected a female was in the car."

"We all put ourselves in bad situations," Diane agrees. "One time in spring training we were making out with the players and their wives showed up. We had to jump in the shower and hide."

"Eventually you moved to New York and shared an apartment," I say. "How did you meet players in your new town?"

"You get to know them, and they get traded to different teams," says Patty. "They come into town and introduce you to their new teammates."

"I remember one night in New York," says Diane. "Jack Hamilton, who had been traded to the Mets, came over with Tug McGraw. We all went out for drinks. We lived right around the corner from Mr. Laffs." Mr. Laffs was a hot spot on the Upper East Side owned by Yankee Phil Linz and frequented by ballplayers.

"When I met you three, you were hanging out with Red Sox players," I say.

"The first one I met was Yastrzemski," says Diane. "One night we were in Mr. Laffs, and I ended up talking to Carl for hours. He was very intelligent, which separated him from the herd. He came to the apartment a few times."

"I was dating a Red Sox pitcher named Billy Landis," says Barb.

"And Tony Conigliaro," Diane reminds her.

Barb nods. "I was probably the only one who went out with both Jack Hamilton and Tony Conigliaro."

"We didn't always have sex," Diane wants me to know.

"It was more innocent in those days," says Patty.

"I once spent the night with a player who just wanted to cuddle," Barb says with a laugh. "He missed his fiancée."

More laughs all around. I turn to Diane. "What was it about Sparky that appealed to you?"

"There was a certain love of life that I never found in another man." She looks forlorn. "He was hard to forget. During the first year, we were more like friends—definitely not lovers. The relationship intensified the next year."

"How?" I say.

"He gave me the diamond tie tack he got when the Red Sox won the pennant in 1967. I had it made into a charm with his name on the back and put it on my charm bracelet. And he used the 'M' word."

"What 'M' word?" Barb asks.

"Marriage," Diane says.

"But if you'd married him, you could have become the wife he'd cheat on next." The minute I say the words, I wish I could take them back.

"It wouldn't matter," Diane says. "I'm married to someone else, but if Sparky came up on the white horse to rescue me, I would go with him in a second. I'm only capable of loving one person. And it's him."

There is a moment of silence.

"What made you all give up the life?" I ask.

"It was Joe Torre who banged our heads together and told us to stop," says Barb. "I thought he was one of the nicest people I ever met in baseball."

We all look at Diane, knowing she is stuck on Sparky.

I turn to Barb. "You have three daughters. Do they know about this part of your life?"

"I raised my kids in a very structured way with the right schools and the right this and that," she says. "When my oldest daughter began having her first experiences with men, I thought I was going to have a nervous breakdown. Part of it was that I had buried my past so deep that I never wanted to see it again. I had reinvented myself. In therapy I realized that my experiences in the past were the fun aspect of me, the exciting aspect of me, and I shouldn't bury them. It helped to be open about all this and laugh with my daughter about it. I can look back and say, 'God, that was fun.'"

Patty nods. "It was a whimsical, magical time."

We finish lunch and say good-bye. I walk to the hotel feeling envious. I am not wishing I had been a groupie. The longing I am experiencing now has more to do with that playfulness. When did I lose my playfulness when it comes to the Yankees?

By late afternoon I am sneezing and hacking along with Michael, and there is no way I can go to tonight's finale against Seattle. We watch on TV.

Hughes goes six innings in one of his best outings yet, and Joba retires the side in order in the top of the seventh. The Yankees are down 2–1 with only two hits—until A-Rod belts his 511th homer in the bottom of the inning, tying Mel Ott and the score. The Yankees score five more runs before A-Rod steps to the plate for the second time in the inning. And for the second time, he homers—this time tying Eddie Mathews and Ernie Banks. The Yanks are up 9–2, and Michael and I chant "MVP!" Abreu scores on a wild pitch in the bottom of the eighth, and Mo works a scoreless ninth.

The Yankees win 10–2. I down a little plastic cup full of NyQuil to celebrate.

The NyQuil makes me high. As I slip into sleep, I have this fuzzy vision of myself leaping into the air with joy that the Yankees beat the Red Sox at Fenway Park in their last matchup of the season.

Thursday is getaway day, and all I feel like doing is getting more sleep. My head is pounding and my body aches, and I am flushed and chilled at the same time. But my cold is merely a nuisance. Michael's is threatening to turn into something worse, given his compromised immune system. We take a cab to Newark airport for our 12:20 ExpressJet flight to Kansas City.

At the airport I ask the man at the ticket counter about our flight's equipment. He tells me it is a 50-seater—a "baby jet."

The Embraer 125 baby jet lands in KC, where our hotel, the Inter-Continental at the Country Club Plaza, is where the Yankees will be staying.

I remember it is Suzyn Waldman's birthday. I call room service and order a dessert with a candle in it and a card from me and ask that it all be delivered to her room as soon as she checks in.

Michael and I are bundled up in bed slurping chicken soup when she calls to say thanks for the birthday dessert, which the hotel initially sent to the wrong room. We laugh about how lame the InterContinental is.

Our colds are a little better when we wake up on Friday. We head down to the lobby. Yankee fans have gathered to see the players board the team bus for Kauffman Stadium. I see Wilson Betemit standing near the entrance. Maybe he is my Yankee.

"Wilson?" I say.

"Hey," he says with a big smile.

"Hey." I am not sure how much English he understands. "It . . . is . . . great . . . to . . . meet . . . you."

He laughs. "Have a nice day." And off he goes.

We leave the hotel and walk to George Brett's restaurant. George Brett is the Cal Ripken of Kansas City. Everything here is named after him.

We sit at a table by the window and survey all the baseball memorabilia on the walls. Two women in Yankees shirts are at the next table.

"Have you flown in from New York for the series?" I ask them.

"We drove in from Nebraska," one of them says. "It's only 3 hours away."

"We came to see Joba, our local hero," says the other. "His father, Harlan, and a whole gang of family and friends have come, too."

I look in the other direction and spot a father and his freckle-faced son sitting at a table in the back of the restaurant.

"They're the same father and son we saw at Spuntini in Toronto," I tell Michael.

"They are *not*."

"Jorge came over to talk to them and we were trying to figure out how they were associated with the Yankees, remember?"

He is still not convinced, so I get up and go over to their table.

"Excuse me," I say. "Were you two eating dinner at Spuntini when the Yankees were in Toronto?"

"We were there," the father says. He smiles but is a little stunned.

"My husband and I were at the restaurant that night." I point at Michael, who is hiding his face, pretending not to know me. "You were talking to Posada, and we were wondering how you knew him."

"I'm Tom Goodman," he introduces himself. "My company, Goodman Media International, handles the PR for Joe Torre's Safe at Home Foundation."

"Tom Goodman? Did you by any chance grow up on Oak Lane in Scarsdale?"

"I did!"

"We were practically next-door neighbors!"

Tom invites me to sit down with him and his son Matthew. I wave Michael over to join us. Yankeeville is a small world.

While the four of us eat lunch together, I give Tom a little background on the book and my unsuccessful dealings with Jason Zillo.

"Why don't you try Rick Cerrone, who ran the Yankees' media relations department until the end of last season," he suggests. "He might be an interesting person to talk to. I'll e-mail you his contact info."

There is a city bus called the Royals Express that stops at the different hotels in the Country Club Plaza and takes everybody straight to Kauffman Stadium for each home game. About 40 of us pile onto the 5:25 p.m. bus to tonight's series opener, and most are dressed in Yankees gear. I stand in the aisle, sandwiched between strangers, just like on the subway. I find myself body to body with a barrel-chested man with bleached platinum hair. He is wearing a Yankees T-shirt, a Yankees cap with a blue interlocking "N" and "Y" that light up when he flicks a switch, Yankees sneakers, a Yankees wristwatch, a Yankees necklace, and a Yankees earring.

"What's up with all the Yankees stuff?" I say.

"I'm from Bayonne, New Jersey," he says.

"And you traveled to Kansas City to see them play?"

"Been a Yankee fan my whole life."

"I can see that." He is a vision of Yankee-ness.

"You haven't seen this." He lifts the sleeve of his T-shirt to show me the Yankees tattoo on his bicep. "It's permanent."

"What if they keep losing and you realize they aren't the team you thought they were?"

He gives me a look. "It's permanent. I go down with the ship."

A fiftysomething woman next to us chimes in. "I hate tattoos. But if I were ever going to get one, it would be a Yankees tattoo. And it would be a permanent one, because the way I feel about them will never change."

I am struck by the unconditional love they feel, by their *loyalty*—the word Michael keeps using. It would not occur to them not to be Yankee fans. Their devotion has nothing to do with winning. They are faithful to their team, year in and year out.

Kauffman Stadium is bad '70s architecture—something between a flying saucer and a concrete donut. The centerfield scoreboard wears the Royals' crown. And fireworks erupt from the fountains out there after the last note of the national anthem is sung. And there are billboards advertising a George Brett MasterCard.

We ride the escalator up to section 316, row F—way up behind home plate on the first base side. Ian Kennedy is making his second start.

The Yankees jump on top 2–0, and the Royals tie it up in the bottom of the second. Kennedy goes five innings, and Farnsworth retires the side in order in the sixth.

With the Yankees up 3–2 in the seventh, Joba takes the mound. You would think we were in Nebraska with all the cheering. The woman behind us says she is from Lincoln.

"Do you know Joba personally?" I ask.

She beams. "We all came to see him. He's a fine boy."

He throws a scoreless seventh and eighth.

Mo shuts the Royals down in the ninth for his 24th save. The Yankees win their third straight game and now have a three-game lead in the wild-card race over Detroit, who has knocked Seattle out of it.

On Saturday, I meet Larry Brooks for an early lunch in the hotel's Oak Room. His once sandy brown hair has flecks of gray in it now, but that is the only sign that he has aged. He is fit with broad shoulders and a boyish smile. We laugh as we try to remember how long it has been since we have seen each other. Ten years? Fifteen? Too long, we decide.

We exchange updates on our lives and discuss hockey, Larry's primary beat at the *Post*. Eventually, we get around to the Yankees. His column about last night's game focused on Joba and his special relationship with his father.

John Sterling walks in. Years ago he was an usher at Larry's wedding, so they spend a few minutes catching up. Yankeeville *is* a small world.

"How do you think the Yankees will do if they get into the play-offs?" I ask Larry.

"They don't have much chance to win the World Series," he says. "And that would mean failure for them."

"Yankee fans have to appreciate how hard it is to win," I say.

Larry looks at me like I have had a brain transplant. "Where did that come from?"

Since tonight's game has a 6:05 start, Michael and I head to the bus stop at

4:45. There is a large group waiting for the Royals Express, most of them Yankee fans. But I also notice a man wearing a Royals cap and T-shirt, and I am delighted. I have been eager to ask KC fans how they root for a team with a perennially losing record.

The man is standing off by himself. I walk over to him and nearly faint; his face is covered with tumors. His features are so distorted and disfigured that I think he must be wearing a Halloween mask. If you have seen *The Elephant Man,* you get the idea. His arms and neck are similarly lumpy. He wears his cap very low on his head. I cannot imagine what it is like to live inside his skin.

"Hey," I say in my most chipper voice. "Are you going to the game tonight?"

"Yup." He keeps his head down, not meeting my eyes.

"You a big Royals fan?"

This elicits a smile. "Been watching 'em a long time."

"Have any favorite players?"

"Alex Gordon, our third baseman. Real good-looking kid. Played college ball in Nebraska like the Yankees' kid, Chamberlain."

"You don't mind that the Royals lose so much?"

He bristles. "We won the World Series in '85. I go to see 'em for better or worse."

When the bus comes along, I wish him and his team luck and walk away counting my blessings, the way you do whenever it dawns on you how lucky you are. I am sure there are people with his disease who confine themselves to their house, never risking ridicule. And yet this guy not only ventures out in public, but goes to a baseball stadium, just so he can see his team play in person—and probably lose. If he is not a true fan, I do not know who is.

For tonight's game we are in section 140, row EE, which is on the main level in right field, at the foul pole.

Pettitte gets the start versus Bannister.

The Yankees play home run derby. Damon and Betemit go deep. So does A-Rod—twice. In the bottom of the sixth, with the Yanks up 11–2, you would think the Royals fans would lose interest and leave. They don't. In fact, they cheer loudly when their team scores a run off Chris Britton in the eighth.

We beat Kansas City 11–5, but the fans here are not the least bit upset. They have spent a sunny day at the ballpark, and life is good.

We take the bus back to the Plaza, where it is not just any Saturday night.

Tonight is the special WaterFire—an annual event where fires are set in the man-made canals that weave in and around the shopping area.

"All this and the Yankees won," says Michael as he snaps pictures of the flames reflecting on the water.

I don't answer. I am studying my own reflection. I am thinking about the Royals fan on the bus. And I am wondering who the hell I am these days.

Sunday is getaway day for the Yankees, but not for Michael and me. The team is flying to Toronto after this afternoon's game, but our flight doesn't leave until tomorrow night at 6:00. I watch their minions load luggage onto their bus. It will be awfully quiet at the hotel without them. No autograph seekers. No groupies. No beat writers. No nutty hangers-on. No members of the traveling carnival, period. I will miss everybody.

Our own bus, the Royals Express, leaves at 12:25 for the 1:10 start. It is not crowded today, so we get seats. In back of us is a guy in his forties wearing a Red Sox cap. I ask him—nicely—what he is doing here. He says he is from Vermont and came to KC on business. When he found out the Yankees were in town, he got tickets for the game to boo them in person.

"Why are Red Sox fans so angry?" I ask. "You won the World Series in '04 and beat the Yankees to get there. What's your problem?"

"You beat us over and over and in the most horrible ways," he says. "And besides that, Red Sox fans never let go of anything."

He is still fuming about Boston's loss to Baltimore yesterday.

"Dice-K walked three batters in an inning, and Francona didn't take him out. The next batter hit a grand slam. That loss was totally preventable!"

I laugh at how much he reminds me of myself. "You have a very comfortable lead in the division."

He shakes his head. "There is no such thing for a Red Sox fan. The Yankees can always come back and beat us. The fear never goes away."

I pat him on the shoulder to console him.

Michael can't believe I am being friendly to someone with that "B" on his cap. "What have you done with my wife?" he whispers in my ear.

As we start to get off the bus, I pass two elderly, silver-haired women sitting together in Royals T-shirts.

"Need any help?" I ask.

"With what?" one of them replies.

"Walking up the aisle or making it down the steps."

"We're fine, honey. Just catching our breath."

"Do you come to the games very often?"

"Every Sunday, like clockwork," the other woman pipes up. "First we go to church. Then we come see our boys. We never miss a game when they're home."

I wish them a good day and follow Michael out of the bus. "Talk about She-Fans. Those two are hardcore," I say. "I love that their doubleheader is religion and baseball."

We settle into our seats just in time for the national anthem. We are in section 307, row H—back in the upper deck but behind home plate instead of in the right-field boonies.

Wang is going for his 18th victory. He has Taiwanese fans here in KC. They are waving their little flags.

A-Rod hits his 52nd home run in the top of the first, and even Royals fans applaud. The guy has now homered in his fifth straight game.

The Royals tie the score at 3–3 in the bottom of the fourth on a bases-loaded double by Alex Gordon, the favorite of the fan on the bus. But the Yanks take a 6–3 lead on RBIs by Posada and Cano.

Farnsworth pitches a scoreless eighth. Mo is lights out in the ninth. And we sweep a team we needed to sweep. We have won five straight and are now four over the Tigers for the wild card.

AL EAST STANDINGS/SEPTEMBER 9

TEAM	W	L	PCT	GB
BOSTON	87	57	.604	—
NEW YORK	81	62	.566	5.5
TORONTO	72	70	.507	14.0
BALTIMORE	61	81	.430	25.0
TAMPA BAY	60	83	.420	26.5

Week 24
September 10, 2007

All any player wishes for is to know they're in the lineup every day—no matter who's pitching or how you're swinging the bat. As the Boston series was coming up, Bowa kept saying, "Be ready to play. Your time is coming." I said, "Bowa, I'm always ready to play."

"I had another Yankee dream," I tell Michael on Monday morning. "It was Damon this time. He needed to get in touch with his mother and asked me to help him find her."

"You must really think you're indispensable to the Yankees," he says.

After breakfast I check e-mail. And—shock of all shocks—there is one from Jason Zillo!

"Sorry for the delay," he writes. "If you are still interested, I may have a bit of time over the next few days while in Toronto."

I scream with excitement.

I immediately reply that I am flying to Toronto tonight and will be available during the series anytime he is. I give him my cell phone number.

At 5:30 we board the Bombardier CRJ/100 at the KC airport. We land in Toronto without incident and move through Customs. Our officer is a tough guy, like the last one.

"What is the nature of your business in Canada?"

"I'm writing a book about the Yankees and am here to see them play the Blue Jays."

"Too bad for you," he growls. "The Yankees suck, eh?"

On Tuesday morning, I read in the Toronto *Globe and Mail* that it's September 11—the anniversary of 9/11. I have been so out of touch with the real world that I forgot what the date signified.

Fortunately, they have not forgotten at the Rogers Centre, where tonight we open a three-game series against the Blue Jays. We are in section 113A, row 4—right on the field behind first base—and have a great view of the pregame ceremony commemorating 9/11 and New York City firefighters. As the Yankees stand next to each other along the first-base line, caps across their hearts, Canadian firefighters play "Amazing Grace" on the bagpipes. It is a beautiful and tasteful observance.

Hughes gets the start. He is not dominant, but he keeps the Yankees in the game. Posada hits his 20th homer to put the Yanks up 4–2, and they break the game open on Giambi's grand slam. Edwar is brilliant in relief and Ohlendorf, the latest call-up, retires the Jays in order to end the game.

The Yankees win 9–2—their sixth straight victory.

There is medical news on Wednesday. Apparently, Clemens has a sore elbow. His MRI shows ligament damage, but he is penciled in to start Sunday's big game in Boston. Michael doesn't feel so great, either. He is still sneezing, and the weather here doesn't help. It is cold and blustery. Where did summer go?

I don't hear from Jason Zillo about getting together, so I e-mail him again.

Frustrated, I contact Rick Cerrone, the Yankees' former media relations director. He is senior vice president at Dan Klores Communications, a PR firm in New York. He is as friendly as can be when I say that Tom Goodman suggested I get in touch.

"I should tell you right away I can't talk about the Yankees," he says. "It's still too painful. When they didn't renew my contract at the end of last year, it was like coming home and finding a note from my wife saying she left me for another man. I don't have a team anymore. I just don't have a team."

"Can you tell me what happened?"

"I'll just say that after 11 years on the job, making three times what I made when I started, they wanted to promote Jason, who had been my assistant. I was devastated. I was living my dream."

"I'm sorry things ended that way for you."

"Me, too."

"Tell me something. Why is it so hard getting access to the Yankees?"

"Let me explain the job and maybe it'll put Jason's position in perspective for you," he says. "My biggest challenge was that there were hundreds of people requesting this and that. Every single one of them knew who I was, but I didn't know who every single one of them was. So whenever a request would come across my desk my motto was: 'Nothing good can come of this.' When someone asks for access, you just never know what will come of it."

"I'm not trying to bring the organization down," I say. "I'm just writing a book about my relationship with them."

"If I were in charge, you would have access. I'll put in a good word with Jason."

Our seats at the Rogers Centre tonight are in section 130A—along the third base line and *in the front row*. We have finally made it to the railing. There is no one between A-Rod and me except a Mountie.

Mussina is making his first start since August 27, and I have no idea what to expect from him.

Damon is the DH tonight, and when he strikes out in the top of the first, the cretin next to me yells, "Hey, Jesus. Why'd you cut off your hair?"

The cretin is a 30-year-old Yankee fan from New Jersey, now living in Toronto. He hates Damon for being a former Red Sock, but he reserves his deepest venom for A-Rod.

"He's a pretty boy who's as gay as Mike Piazza."

I was too harsh by singling out the idiots in Detroit who harassed the Mariners fan for being a Jap-loving gay Jew. This guy from New Jersey is no higher on the food chain. When the speakers blast the "Mexican Hat Dance," he says, "It's a stupid Chico song, but it's better than the Jew song they play at Yankee Stadium." I assume he is referring to "Hava Nagila."

Mussina is brilliant, holding the Jays scoreless through seven-plus innings, allowing the batters to do their jobs. The Yanks are up 4–0 when Joba pitches the bottom of the eighth and gives up the first run of his major league career, albeit unearned, for 4–1. Mo notches his 26th save.

The Yankees win their seventh straight game. This is the streak I have been waiting for.

On Thursday there is still no response from Jason Zillo.

Our seats for tonight's finale at the Rogers Centre are in section 113A, row 3—back on the first-base side. Ian Kennedy goes against A. J. Burnett—a tough matchup for the kid. Betemit is at first, which makes me wonder yet again why the Yankees bothered to sign Mientkiewicz.

After the Jays score on a double by the Big Hurt in the first, both pitchers really settle in. Burnett is nasty, but Kennedy is not giving anything away, either. He has a one-hitter through seven innings. With the score tied at 1–1, Joe pulls him for Viz. The Yankees don't get to Burnett in the top of the ninth, even though he is at 120 pitches. Joe sends Britton out for the bottom half and I scratch my head. Is he saving everyone for Boston? Britton gives up singles to Rios and the Big Hurt, and we lose 2–1—a game we could and should have won.

The Yankees are coming down the stretch now, with less than three more weeks to go in the season. The series in Boston this weekend will mean something—well, it always means something between the Yankees and Red Sox—and could determine whether there will be October baseball for both teams.

As for me, I am really looking forward to this weekend. I will see my old Scarsdale friend Susan, whom I have not seen since Michael and I got married. I will see Michael's brother Geoff, whom I have not seen since we moved to California. And I will see Boston, which I have not seen since the '60s, when I sat on the floor of some hippie-folkie place and listened to Richie Havens sing Dylan songs. It is not only that the clock is ticking on my quest to meet a Yankee. It is also ticking on Michael's health; his cold has moved into his chest. We are coming down a stretch of our own.

Friday is both getaway day and game day.

The Hyatt in downtown Boston is around the corner from Boston Common, which means it is around the corner from the Ritz-Carlton, which means it is around the corner from where the Yankees are staying.

"May we have a quiet room?" I ask the man at the front desk when we check in.

"Certainly." He hands me our keys.

After a short nap, we walk to the Boylston Street Station. The early evening weather is clear and cold. I am thankful Michael and I packed our winter jackets, and we bundle up. By the way, mine is red.

"Everyone will assume I'm a Red Sox fan," I say as we ride the C train on the green line to Kenmore station. "No one will throw anything at me."

"Pussy," says Michael.

We get off the subway and wind our way down the narrow streets toward Fenway. Crowds are lined up outside various pubs and restaurants, which are already bulging with people. More crowds congregate around the street vendors—the "Sausage King" seems to be a big favorite. It is as if they are all attending a giant block party.

We enter through Gate C and head to the Big Concourse, where a food court offers several concessions. I end up with the dreaded chicken tenders. Michael gets a double order of hot dogs since each one is so small. He says they are limp and cold and nestled in a mushy bun. The food here is beyond disgusting.

"But we aren't here for the food," he says cheerfully as we go looking for our seats. He loves Fenway. He thinks it is the coolest of all the ballparks, because it is historic and quirky and reminds him of Little League.

We find the bleachers. Actually, it is not the bleachers that are hard to find. It is our seats. They are way up in section 43, row 40—the two seats at the very end of the row, in right field. One of the people we have to step over is an obese woman who is chain-smoking. There are no ushers or security guards around, and I am not about to lecture her about her lung cancer stick. She is way bigger than I am.

Within minutes the chain-smoker is joined by three other people who seem—how can I put this delicately?—mentally challenged in a just-out-of-the-asylum sort of way. They move down the row and fill in the empty seats between the chain-smoker and us. One of them is a man with a gigantic scar that runs down the middle of his forehead. As soon as he lands in his seat, he slumps over and shuts his eyes. Another is a tall, creepy, heavyset man—we are talking 6'5" and 280 pounds minimum—with pockmarked skin and a long, brown braid. He is wearing baggy gray sweatpants, along with a beat-up leather jacket. He takes the seat next to Michael. Well, he takes part of Michael's seat, too, because he is too large to fit into his own seat.

"Hello. My name is Barry," he says to us, speaking in a very slow, slurred speech. "What's your name?"

"Michael," says my husband.

"Jane," I say.

Barry stares off into space.

The other member of their group is a woman who sits between Barry and Scarface. She is wearing a white uniform under her wool coat. She reaches into her purse for a vial of pills and dispenses them to Barry, Scarface, and the chain-smoker.

There are small pockets of Yankee fans in the bleachers, and they are barraged with "Yankees suck" chants. I, on the other hand, am warm and safe in my red jacket. I even pretend to be a Boston fan. Every few minutes I shout, "Let's go, Red Sox!" and nobody bothers me.

I take a long look around the ballpark. It is certainly unusual with its Green Monster. But the fans are right on top of the field. What is so awe-inspiring about that? Yankee Stadium is regal, imposing. This place is puny—like a toy park.

The lineups are announced, and I am surprised to hear Giambi is playing first. Jason is a nice guy, by all the beat writers' accounts. But Mientkiewicz is the one who can catch the ball at first base, so why not use him in an important series like this?

The pitching match up is Pettitte versus Dice-K.

Here we go.

After Damon beats out an infield single, Dice-K throws high and tight to Jeter. A-Rod gets plunked on the first pitch he sees. No warnings are issued.

In the bottom of the first, Lugo reaches on an error by Giambi, who really does have lobster claws for hands. But it is in the bottom of the second that Boston gets on the board. Ellsbury, the rookie who is playing center instead of Crisp, singles home Youkilis for 1–0.

Andy is at 58 pitches in the bottom of the third. He is laboring. Drew reaches on Giambi's second error, scoring Lowell. Boston goes ahead 2–0.

The Yankees score their first run in the top of the fourth when Matsui's triple scores Posada.

The Red Sox come right back in the bottom of the inning against Pettitte, who allows three more runs for 5–1.

Barry, our new friend from the asylum, has been relatively comatose during the game, but he wakes up to cheer for Pedroia.

"Dustin got off to a slow start, but he's gonna be great for many years," he tells us.

"You're a big Red Sox fan, huh?" I say.

"I love the Red Sox," he says with a child's adoration. "Do you?"

"Yes," I say.

"Of course we do," says Michael.

"Are you having a good time tonight?" he asks, his eyes hopeful.

It is such a sweet question and it is said with such earnestness that it takes me aback, and I reexamine my impression of Barry. He is very probably institutionalized, his life a complete mess, and yet he wants to know if we are having a good time. He is anything but creepy.

"We're having a very good time," I say. "Fenway is quite a place."

He nods. "I've never been here before."

"Really?" I say. He loves the team so much but has never been able to attend a game. How sad is that?

He nods again. "This is the best night of my whole, whole life."

His words are heartbreaking. Maybe I am nobody's number one fan. Maybe Barry is the real thing. He shames me with his lack of pretense. I am deeply moved by him, the way I was deeply moved by the man on the Royals Express. It is no small feat for either of them to get to the ballpark. And yet they not only show up but also don't boast about their team or disparage the opposition. Baseball is still magical for them.

I stop being cynical with my "Let's go, Red Sox!" chants. I keep quiet and let everybody boo the Yankees, who deserve booing tonight. The Red Sox are on course to win in humiliating fashion.

Veras relieves Pettitte in the bottom of the fifth. Two beach balls are batted around in our section. So much for my belief that Red Sox fans are purists when it comes to this sort of thing. Are rally monkeys next?

Dice-K departs in the top of the sixth, having thrown 120 pitches. Damon bloops a single off Timlin, scoring Posada for 5–2, but it feels like too little too late.

The bottom of the sixth brings more mediocrity for the Yankees. After Lugo singles off Veras, Ortiz is intentionally walked. Lowell flies to right, and Abreu nearly nails Big Sloppy wandering off first, but "lobster claws" can't handle the ball. Youkilis singles, scoring Lugo.

Joe replaces Veras with Sean Henn. Drew singles, scoring Ortiz for 7–2. The Red Sox are piling on. It is grotesque.

After Lopez and Okajima shut the Yanks down in the top of the seventh, I tell Michael I think we should leave. He has been coughing and blowing his nose and looks pale. I am worried about him.

"Leave?" he says, shocked that I would even make the suggestion.

"I don't want you getting any sicker."

"I'll be fine."

"I've heard that before."

"This is Yankees–Red Sox!"

I feel his forehead. It is hot. He should be inside, not sitting out here where the temperature is dropping by the minute.

"Our bullpen is about to give up a hundred runs," I say. "What's the point of sitting here and watching that? I need to get you to the hotel."

"What if the Yankees make a comeback?"

"Right. And pigs can fly. Let's go."

He is gripped by a sneezing jag and starts to shiver. He concedes that he feels like shit. But leaving is not easy; we have to forge a path over Barry.

Michael taps him on the shoulder. "Would you mind getting up for a second so we can pass?"

Barry obliges. He is wobbly and it takes him a while, but he stands. He asks if we remember his name.

"Sure," Michael says. "Barry, right?"

He grins. "Sorry, but I don't remember yours. Is it Joe?"

"It's Michael, but don't worry about it. It was a pleasure to meet you."

Barry smiles at me. "Good-bye, Kathy."

Once we escape the ballpark, it is a quick subway ride to our stop at Boylston Street. From there we only have to walk past the Ritz-Carlton—

"Wait," I say, stopping in my tracks in front of the Ritz's restaurant and bar. Through the large window I can see a flat-screen television showing what I assume are highlights. ESPN broadcasted the game, so they are probably doing a wrap-up. "Let's check out the final score."

Michael and I move closer to the window and peer inside.

"Oh my God!" I say.

"Are you fucking kidding me?" says Michael.

It is not a highlights reel. The game is still in progress! It is the eighth inning and the score in 8–7 in favor of the Yankees!

"How is this possible?" I say. "We left in the bottom of the seventh, and that was almost an hour ago."

"I'm gonna kill you for making me leave."

We stand there in the street with our noses pressed against the glass.

"What's going on?" asks a passerby.

"Yankees–Red Sox!" Michael says. "The Yankees are winning 8–7!"

"No way!" the guy says. "When I left Fenway they were losing."

"*We know*," Michael and I say.

More and more people gather at the window to watch. The maître d' of the restaurant flicks his wrist to shoo us away. We are annoying the patrons.

"Let's make a run for it," says Michael.

"Right," I say. "Go."

When we get to the Hyatt's bar, we are not alone. Everyone has heard about the turn of events in the game, and now we are all glued to the TV. A waiter brings everybody up to date: the back-to-back homers by Giambi and Cano against Okajima in the top of the eighth; the walk to Melky and the double by Damon; Jeter's single and Abreu's double against Pap Smear to tie the game at 7–7; the single by A-Rod that put the Yankees on top 8–7.

We are now watching Pap Smear stalk off the mound in the top of the eighth and curse furiously into his glove.

Viz pitches a scoreless eighth, and Mo comes in for the ninth. When he gives up a leadoff single to Drew, I squeeze Michael's hand so tightly I nearly cut off his circulation.

"It'll be okay," he says. "Have a little faith."

Mo strikes out Varitek, gets Kielty to fly out, and strikes out Ellsbury for his 27th save.

It is an improbable game. A game that lasts 4 hours and 43 minutes. A game that brings the Yankees to within 4½ of Boston. A game that could change the course of the season.

Upstairs in our room, I help Michael into bed and take his temperature. It is 101. After I bring him some Tylenol, I sit on the bed next to him. I take a deep breath and feel tears prick at my eyes.

"It's over," I say. "We're going home."

"What are you talking about?"

"The Yankees just had the most miraculous comeback—the best game of the year. I've had my fun. I've seen them turn their season around. I've been part of the traveling carnival. But none of that is worth winding up in the ER at Mass General."

"It's just a cold!" Michael coughs for one solid minute.

"With you, there is no 'just.' Remember that fever you had last year? It started off as no big deal. The next thing I know you're being carted away in an ambulance. And don't give me the Roger Maris story."

He glares at me. "If you want to go back to Santa Barbara, be my guest. I'm staying."

"Oh, yeah?" I get up and glare back at him, the tears rolling down my cheeks now. "You're putting me in an impossible situation and you do it all the time and it's not fair!"

"Poor baby."

"You don't take care of yourself, and I'm the one who suffers! I give up my dreams to clean up your messes!"

He sits up in bed, his face flushed with fever and fury. "Don't suffer on my account. Nobody asked you to do a goddamn thing. You treat me like a fucking child!"

"You act like one. I'm supposed to be researching a book. Instead, I'm standing here worrying about you!"

"Listen, I'm having the time of my life. These games are *my* joy, *my* passion. Do what you want, but I'm not leaving. I'm finishing what we started."

"MAYBE YOU DIDN'T HEAR ME," I yell, because I hate him and love him at the same stupid second. "I said I was willing to give all this up for you."

He applauds mockingly. "I've been looking forward to this Boston series forever—the great seats for Sunday night, seeing my brother, all of it."

"But you're sick!"

"I'll patch myself up the way I always do." He sinks back against the pillows and coughs/wheezes/chokes. "You need to stop trying to control everything, especially me."

"Fine. So what do you want me to do?"

"Whatever you want. I'm staying. There are risks in life."

It is raining on Saturday morning. My first thought is whether Michael is feeling any better, but I don't give him the satisfaction of asking. Instead, I muse out loud whether there will be baseball and whether I will find any takers for tomorrow night's tickets.

"Actually, why don't I just give them to Jake and his girlfriend?" I say. Jake is his brother Geoff's son and an avid Sox fan. I am proving what a saintly individual I am.

"They'll be very appreciative," Michael says with a trace of a smile and calls his brother with the news. After he hangs up, he volunteers that he still feels crummy, but the fever is gone. "So. We're good?" This is his way of apologizing.

"We're good." This is my way of apologizing.

Today's game is on Fox, so it has a 3:55 start. Our bleachers seats are better than last night's—section 37, row 25, in dead center field. The sun has emerged and it is a glorious, if chilly, afternoon. Michael zips up my red jacket and tucks my hair inside the hood.

It is Beckett versus Wang, who can't be thrilled about Giambi playing first base again—not with all the ground balls his sinkers induce.

In the top of the first, Jeter cracks a homer and the Yankees draw first blood. The Red Sox get the run back in the bottom of the inning on a Lowell single that scores Pedroia.

Wang is not sharp at all. He hits Youkilis on the right wrist in the bottom of the fifth, and "Yook" comes out of the game. Ellsbury, who goes in to run for him, moves to third on Ortiz's single. Drew's base hit scores Ellsbury for 2–1.

The Yankees bats are stone cold today. Beckett is at 93 pitches in the top of the sixth, and yet all they can manage are three straight groundouts.

In the bottom of the sixth, Hinske tries to score on Pedroia's grounder to Cano and barrels into Posada at the plate. Jorge is dazed but somehow holds on to the ball for the out. Ellsbury singles, scoring Crisp, and Ortiz doubles, scoring Pedroia and Ellsbury. It is 5–1. Joe comes out to lift Wang, who looks disconsolate.

Beckett hits Giambi with a pitch on the right elbow in the top of the seventh—obvious retaliation for the Youkilis thing—and the umpire warns both benches. Otherwise, the Yankees don't do much. It is absurd how feeble they are tonight. I would say they are headed for certain defeat, but I said the same thing last night and look how that turned out.

In the bottom of the seventh, our bullpen is an abomination. Does anyone know how to throw strikes? After Edwar walks Drew and retires Varitek, Joe replaces him with Villone, who promptly walks Hinske. Joe comes back out looking really pissed and calls for Bruney, last night's winning pitcher. Crisp doubles, scoring Drew. Lugo walks. Joe makes another trip to the mound, this time to summon Sean Henn. Ellsbury singles, scoring Crisp and Lugo. Big Sloppy walks, loading the bases for Lowell. Out pops Joe. He signals for Ohlendorf, who walks Lowell on four pitches, scoring Ellsbury for 9–1.

In the eighth, the crowd sings along to "Sweet Caroline," complete with the "So good, so good, so good" routine that makes me want to stick needles in my eyes. Ohlendorf gives up a solo homer to Hinske for 10–1, which is the final score.

As I listen to the "Yankees suck" chants that rain down from every corner of Fenway, I can only shake my head. I should have followed my instincts and gone back to Santa Barbara. God is such a kidder.

"I'm hungry," says Michael, as we head for the exits. "Where should we go to eat?"

"Back to the hotel," I say, entwining my arm through his. "We'll order up some chicken soup for you."

"No room service," he says. "We're going out."

I do not protest.

We decide on the Ritz-Carlton, since it looked appealing last night and is right around the corner from the Hyatt. We snag the last table for two.

"Good evening, young lady." The waiter appears and greets me with a bow at the waist, reminding me of Mussina.

"I'd love a glass of wine."

He brings me a glass of Syrah, which is delicious, but the salmon he brings later is so raw it is still flopping around on the plate. I send it back.

Michael's spaghetti Bolognese is perfectly cooked. He is eating with gusto when he looks toward the entrance to the restaurant.

"Brian Cashman just walked in," he whispers.

I spin around to see if the person he thinks is Cashman is Cashman, but the wall of people waiting to get in blocks my view.

"He looks pissed off that there's a line," Michael says, proud that he is the one to recognize somebody for a change.

"If we want to hold on to this table we'll have to keep ordering food, like we did at Spuntini. Are you feeling well enough for that?"

"I'm fine."

Just then, the nearby table for four opens up. I fix my eyes on it, expecting to see Cashman sit there. The waiter comes back with my salmon and a speech about how busy the kitchen is. When he leaves, I see that there are now three men sitting at the table. None of them is Cashman, but one of them is a Yankee! Oh my God!

"The guy with his back to us is Doug Mientkiewicz," I whisper to Michael.

He takes a look. "It is *not*."

"It is *so*."

"Mientkiewicz is bigger than that."

I roll my eyes—How can he doubt me after all this time?—and then zero in on Doug, who looks cute with his still-wet hair, black T-shirt, and blue jeans. He lifts his bottle of beer and I see that he is wearing his World Series ring from when he won the championship with Boston.

"This is my chance!"

"You can't just go over and interrupt his meal. That's tacky."

We spend the next 20 minutes debating exactly how I should approach Mientkiewicz. The maître d' walks past our table a thousand times. I can feel how badly he wants to shove our food down our throats so we will pay up and let someone far more important take our place.

"I've got it," I say finally.

I signal for the waiter. He must have been advised to hurry us out of there, because he swipes our plates and asks if we want the check.

"We want dessert and coffee," I say.

Michael orders something chocolate and I order a Jamaican coffee with extra whipped cream. I hate Jamaican coffee.

"Before you go," I say to the waiter, nodding at Mientkiewicz, "I'd like you to send that man another bottle of whatever he's having and put it on my tab."

"I can't do that, young lady," says the waiter. "I must get the gentleman's permission first."

I have never heard of needing permission to buy someone a drink, but I hold my breath as I watch him lean down to talk to Mientkiewicz.

"What if he doesn't want another beer?" I whisper to Michael.

"Not possible," he says.

Mientkiewicz turns around to look at me, hops up from his chair, and bounds over to our table. My heart explodes.

"Hey," he says with a big smile. "You don't have to do this."

"Sure I do," I hear myself say. He has dark, liquid eyes and is much more attractive with his cap off. He looks uncannily like a former boyfriend of mine, and I have this grotesque urge to throw my arms around him. "I'm a fan of yours. We both are."

"Old fans or new ones?" Doug asks.

"Yankee fans." I introduce myself and Michael. "I'm writing a book about the 2007 season and have been following the team since the All-Star break."

He listens attentively as I talk about the book. Or maybe he is just being polite because I am supplying the Miller Lite. Who cares? I figured my Yankee would either be some dumb farm boy or an arrogant prick, but Doug is articulate and charming and very, very nice. He kneels down beside me—at my feet—and we continue to chat.

"I really admire your play at first base," I tell him. "The Yankees need your glove."

"I appreciate that," he says.

"And Peter Abraham and George King say you treat the media with respect."

"You know, people told me to be wary of the New York media when I first went there with the Mets. But when my son was born, I got notes from New York writers to congratulate me, whereas I got none from the writers in Minnesota—and I was a Twin for a long time."

Okay, maybe he didn't use the word *whereas*. I was freaking out while he was talking. I do know that he asked again if I was sure about the beer, and I said absolutely.

"Thanks very much." He stands up out of his crouch and shakes my hand. "Can I return the favor?"

I look at Michael. If there was ever an opening, this is it. I should say, "Yes, Doug. You can let me interview you for my book." But I don't want our first conversation to be all agenda driven and based on me wanting something from him. It is more appropriate—less tacky—to simply establish a connection tonight and follow up about the book another time. Well, and there is the

fact that I am too scared to ask him for an interview. Michael is right: I am
a pussy.

"You can return the favor," I say. "You can find a way to play first base
tomorrow night. We don't need any more errors over there."

He smiles, getting my drift about Giambi. "I hope I play," he says and gives
me a little salute as he sits back down at his table.

I take a very long sip of the Jamaican coffee.

"That stuff will keep you up all night," Michael warns, knowing I am caf-
feinated without caffeine.

I reach across the table and squeeze his hand. "You need to stop trying to
control everything. There are risks in life."

Sunday is bright and sunny but cold. I turn up the heat in our room. Michael
is popping Coricidins like M&M's.

I call Marty with the news that I have finally met my Yankee.

"You told me there's always one, and you were right," I say.

"So you set up an interview with Mientkiewicz?"

"No."

"You explained that you want to interview him."

"No."

"You gave him your card and asked him to call you."

"No!"

"What were you thinking?"

"That I was finally having a real conversation with somebody on the team,"
I say. "I'm a pussy, okay?"

Marty tells me to contact Jason Zillo and tell him that I want to interview
Mientkiewicz.

"Right," I say. "I will."

But I don't. What is the point? I e-mail Peter Abraham and ask if he would
pass along Doug's cell phone number.

Susan Tofias meets us in the lobby of the Hyatt around 2:00. I love this
woman. I spent almost as much time at her house growing up as I did at my
own. We have not seen each other in 15 years, and yet the minute we start talking, it is as if no time has passed, and we spend 3 hours in the hotel's lounge
sharing reminiscences. I am thrilled my book is allowing us to have a long-
overdue reunion.

Michael's brother Geoff arrives from Concord around 5:00 with his son Jake and Jake's bubbly girlfriend, Brenna. Geoff is 7 years younger than Michael, but they seem like contemporaries. They are both professional photographers. They have the same beard and mustache and the same sweet nature.

We all pile into Susan's car, and she drives us to Fenway. The game, which is being televised on ESPN, has an 8:05 start, so we have time for an early dinner. The only hitch is that the restaurants are jammed. Jake and Brenna duck into a place on Lansdowne Street called Tequila Rain. The plan is for them to hold a table while Susan, Geoff, Michael, and I take a quick walk to Yawkey Way so Michael can shoot my photo. I am very Red Sox fan-ish in my red jacket, so none of the passersby abuse me. It is not until I don my Yankees cap for the picture that I start hearing it.

"Hey, your team's gonna lose tonight," one Sox fan snipes.

"Let's go, *wild card*," another mocks.

"Jeter sucks A-Rod's dick," yells a third.

I bury the cap in my bag once the photo shoot is over.

At 7:30 Jake and Brenna head to the bleachers, and Geoff, Michael, and I follow Susan to the amazing seats her friends are letting us use. We are in a field box to the third base side of home plate. Since there is not much foul territory at Fenway, it feels as if we are *on* the field.

Geoff is in a state of bliss. "These seats are the best I've ever had in my life."

He and Michael immediately call their sister Lawsie in Florida to tell her to look for them on ESPN. I see the same familiar Boston faces I always see when I watch games at Fenway on TV. They belong to captains of industry, corporate titans.

A-Rod is warming up in front of our eyes.

"I have to admit he's gorgeous," Susan says, in spite of the fact that she is a Red Sox fan. She went over to the dark side after marrying a Bostonian and raising her kids here.

I am about to return the favor and say Lowell is handsome except for the Groucho Marx eyebrows, but I am interrupted by the announcement of the lineups. My heart races when I hear that Mientkiewicz is playing first base tonight! Did Joe finally figure out that the Yankees need some defense at first, or is Dougie in the lineup because of that magic beer I bought him at the Ritz last night?

Schilling lumbers to the mound in the top of the first. He is facing Clemens, who is taking his turn in the rotation in spite of his sore elbow. The nearly 37,000 people in the stands are already on their feet. This is more than the rubber match of a Yankees–Red Sox series, more than a battle between two power pitchers in the twilight of their careers, more than the teams' final contest of the 2007 season. It is the Yankees' last shot at proving that Boston is not a lock for the division. If they ever needed to win a ball game, this is the one.

Damon steps to the plate. He pops the ball up, causing a minor collision between Pedroia and Drew. Jeter singles. Abreu strikes out. A-Rod grounds out. I am very aware that the TV camera is on me whenever a right-handed batter is up; I can see the red light go on. But my hosts have no cause for concern. I will not embarrass them. I am staying quiet in my red jacket.

In the bottom of the inning, Ellsbury flies to left—an easy out—but the ball pops out of Damon's glove for an error. Pedroia flies out. Ellsbury steals second on Clemens. Ortiz walks. Lowell's single brings Ellsbury home. The crowd jeers, "Ro-ger! Ro-ger!" After Drew flies out, Varitek hits a liner that Mientkiewicz spears, saving the Yankees two runs. The magic Miller Lite is coursing through his veins, giving him superhuman powers. He makes another great play that saves a run in the bottom of the second. And in the top of the third, he actually gets a hit.

Schilling and Clemens are dealing, neither willing to fold. But the Yankees tie the score in the top of the fifth on a solo shot by Cano.

In the bottom of the fifth, Mientkiewicz makes two more dazzling plays. One is on a line drive by Lugo, and the other is on a feed to Clemens on an Ellsbury ground out.

The score is still tied at 1–1 in the bottom of the seventh, but Clemens is done. Joba walks onto the mound to a cascade of boos. He has to be a little nervous, despite his bravado. He goes to 3-and-2 on Hinske before allowing a double. As Crisp comes to the plate, a Sox fan jumps onto the field from the first-base side, sprints over to Hinske, and tries to high-five him. When Hinske turns his back, the fan steals Cano's cap right off his head and races with it into left field, where he is chased and ultimately tackled by a couple of security guys. The incident provides a brief respite from the tension that has been building, but the intensity is back as soon as the fan is dragged off. Joba retires Crisp, Lugo, and Ellsbury.

As we head into the top of the eighth, the temperature has really dipped, and it is *cold*. Vendors from Legal Sea Foods come around selling "hot chowdah," and I consider buying some for Michael to warm him up. But he is having a blast, jawing back and forth with Geoff after every pitch. I am the one who is anxious. I have kept my promise and not even whispered a "Let's go, Yankees." I have maintained the neutrality of Switzerland. But I am squirming in my fancy seat. I pull the hood tighter over my head.

In the top of the eighth with the score still knotted at 1 apiece, Mientkiewicz doubles down the left field line. Giambi bats for Molina and doubles off the centerfield wall, sending Dougie to third. Bronson Sardinha, a call-up from Scranton, pinch runs for Giambi. Damon grounds out, breaking his bat and spraying splinters everywhere. And then something momentous happens: Jeter homers, scoring Dougie and Sardinha. The Yankee fans in the ballpark go wild, unafraid of getting booed or punched out. Susan glares at me, as if to check that I am behaving. She need not worry. But I would have to be dead not to feel something.

With the Yankees up 4–1, Francona pulls Schilling and brings in Lopez and Delcarmen to quell the insurgency.

Joba is back for the bottom of the eighth. He strikes out Pedroia and gets Ortiz to fly out but gives up a homer to Lowell for 4–2.

In the top of the ninth, I sit here thinking the Yankees can't be content with a two-run lead. Not at Fenway. But I figure they can hit Gagne, who has been a disappointment in his short stay with the Red Sox. I am wrong. Gagne strikes out Posada and gets Cano and Melky to fly out. No insurance runs. No cushion. Nothing but a much-too-quick inning.

Everybody is standing as Mo comes on for the bottom of the ninth. How many times has this scene played out before my eyes? Forever. Just never with me in attendance in the midst of what is now sheer bedlam. The Sox fans clap, chant, stomp. The noise is deafening. As I watch Mo turn his back to home plate to pray, I pray, too.

"Dear God. Please watch over Mo and give his cutter location and movement. Amen."

Mo walks Varitek. The crowd goes berserk, smelling a comeback. The atmosphere is so frenzied and the moment so charged with electricity that I cover my hands over my eyes and peek out through my fingers. That is not showing partisanship, is it?

Hinske grounds out, moving Varitek to second. One out.

Crisp grounds out, sending Varitek to third. Two outs.

Lugo doubles into the gap in centerfield, scoring Varitek for 4–3. The place is a madhouse, and the insanity only heightens after Mo hits Ellsbury on the left kneecap and walks Pedroia, loading the bases for Big Sloppy.

"Is this great theater or what?" Geoff says.

Michael high-fives him. "As good as it gets."

I say nothing. I am literally holding myself in, sucking in my breath, standing absolutely still. I am remembering the woman in the Bronx who told me she comes back tomorrow no matter what. I am remembering the man on the Royals Express who told me he goes down with the ship. I am remembering the man with the lumps all over his body and the two old ladies with their church-and-baseball Sunday ritual. And I am remembering Barry, who wanted us to share in the best night of his life. I am remembering how they each inspired me in different ways to be a baseball fan—to believe in a team unconditionally and without reservation, to experience the magic of the game without vitriol or a sense of entitlement, to be gracious in both victory and defeat.

Ortiz steps in. Before Mo throws a single pitch, Joe walks out to talk to him. No, he is not pulling his closer; he is settling him down and probably settling himself down while he is at it.

But Mo doesn't settle down. He goes to a full count on Ortiz, who fouls off pitch after pitch after pitch. This at bat is killing me.

Come on, Mo. You have faced this guy a million times. You know how to get him out. You can do this. The Yankees can do this. We can do this.

I take my hands away from my eyes. I could care less that Jason Zillo has refused me press credentials, that Derek Jeter will never know my name, that the relationship between fan and team is not reciprocal. I just want to watch my boys and cheer for them.

"Let's go, Yankees!" I scream at the top of my lungs. I throw off the hood of my jacket and unzip it, revealing my navy blue Yankee sweatshirt underneath. I turn directly to the TV camera and point to the interlocking N-Y on my chest: "LET'S GO YANKEEEEES!!!!!"

Susan is stunned, as are all the corporate titans in our VIP section. Michael bursts out laughing.

Ortiz hits a high pop-up to short left-center. Jeter backpedals. Back, back,

back he goes. He makes the catch and pumps his fist. The second that ball is in his glove I leap into the air with unbridled joy, just like I did in my fuzzy NyQuil-induced dream. I hug Susan, my friend, the Red Sox fan. The other Sox fans in our section are shooting me daggers, but she is happy for me. She knows true love never dies.

AL EAST STANDINGS/SEPTEMBER 16

TEAM	W	L	PCT	GB
BOSTON	90	60	.600	—
NEW YORK	85	64	.570	4.5
TORONTO	74	75	.497	15.5
BALTIMORE	64	84	.432	25.5
TAMPA BAY	63	87	.420	27.0

Book Three

for
better
or
worse

Week 25
September 17, 2007

I was getting ready to play in Boston Sunday night with the series tied 1–1. Rocket came up to me, punched my chest, and said, "Be my rock tonight. It's you and me, kid. You and me." It gave me goose bumps. That whole day was in slow motion for me. I'm not the most Christian person on the planet, but I talked to Him before that game. I said, "If you can give me one more night, make it be tonight. I've put too much into this game to flop now."

I wake up on Monday without a voice. My cheering last night gave me a mean case of laryngitis. Michael, who is so congested that his chest rattles, says I sound sexy.

Our flight into Newark leaves at 9:30 a.m., but we don't have it in us to rush for it. We avoid the airport hassles and rent a car to New York. It is a crystal-clear sunny day, and the 3-hour drive is peaceful. I am happy, radiant. There is one tiny problem. My publisher will probably dump the book when they find out I haven't interviewed a single Yankee. But it is okay. Time to let all that go.

We check back into the Marmara. This will be our last stay here unless the Yankees make it into the play-offs. Never mind their dismal first half of the season. Never mind their spotty pitching. Never mind that Matsui's knee is bad or that Giambi's body has broken down or that Joba has not been battle tested. There are positives: A-Rod's homers, Posada's career year, Jeter's consistency, Cano's patience at the plate, Abreu's hot streak, Melky's arm, Damon's play in left, Shelley's power off the bench, and, of course, Mientkiewicz's defense at first. The situation is not perfect, but I like our chances.

By midafternoon, Michael and I are both exhausted. There is no way we can go to tonight's game—the first of three against Baltimore. We watch it on TV, hoping a good night's sleep will fix us up.

Hughes is facing Daniel Cabrera. And Mientkiewicz is starting at first base for the second game in a row.

Hughes allows two runs in the top of the first, but Mientkiewicz smacks a bases-loaded single that scores Posada and Giambi in the bottom of the second.

"That bottle of Miller Lite was definitely a magic beer," I say to Michael.

"You should e-mail Jason Zillo to set up the interview."

"It's okay. I'm just glad he's playing well."

The Yankees pad their lead, and Hughes shuts down the O's. In the top of the ninth, we are ahead 8–3 and Joe calls for Farnsworth. Kyle issues a walk, uncorks a wild pitch, and gives up a couple of singles. Joe comes back out to remove him for Mo, who is probably sick of being his own setup man. With the score at 8–5, he strikes out Mora to end the game. He notches his 29th save, and the Yankees move to within 3½ games of Boston, who lost to Toronto thanks to three home runs by the Big Hurt.

Michael and I both feel better on Tuesday. He is not rattling and I am not rasping, and we are ready for baseball.

At 6 o'clock we take the subway to the Bronx for tonight's game against Baltimore. We arrive at the Stadium just in time for the lineups, only it is not Bob Sheppard who is announcing them. It is not until after the game that I hear he is out with laryngitis. I hope he is okay. Meanwhile, whoever is pinch-hitting for him does an amazing job of imitating his cadences.

Mientkiewicz is starting at first—again. Mussina is on the mound, trying to win his 10th game of the season.

Our seats are better than usual—one level down from our regular haunt in the Tier in section 628, row F, between home plate and third base.

"It's great to be back," I tell Michael as we watch the Yankees take their final warm-up tosses. "What a difference a month makes."

"You hated it in the beginning."

"And now I don't—not the security guards or the pushy, obnoxious people or even these hard, uncomfortable seats."

"You fit right in." Michael appraises me. I have traded in the red jacket for a

Yankees jacket, the one Joe Torre wears on chilly nights like this. It is a relief that I am free to love my team in plain view of others, after having to hide my true feelings in Boston. I am in the Yankees' house now, my house. For so long I have wondered where "home" is. Tonight I know.

Mussina throws a shutout through seven. He walks off the mound to "Moooose" calls and a standing ovation. I am happy for him. His season mirrors the Yankees' season—lots of ups and downs. Like the team, he has fought his way back.

The Yankees turn the game into a laugher in the bottom of the seventh, pounding out hit after hit, including a single by Mientkiewicz. The guy has four RBIs on the night, including a homer!

As the Yanks wrap up their 12–0 victory, the scoreboard lets us know that Boston has lost to Toronto again. Gagne gave it up, and now the Yankees trail the Red Sox by a mere 2½ games.

It is Wednesday, and I am having lunch with Larry's friend Jen Royle at the Time Warner Center. I snag a table at the busy Landmarc restaurant, and Jen comes along soon after. She is as perky as I expected from watching her videos on the YES Web site. She is 33, has long, wavy brown hair falling around her face, and wears a little white tank top of the type I have not worn since I was her age.

"You grew up in Boston," I say. "How did you end up covering the enemy?"

She laughs. "It wasn't something I ever thought would happen. My father took me to Red Sox games with my two brothers and my grandfather. I hated the Yankees. *Hated them!* Even when they got into the World Series after 9/11, I didn't say, 'Come on, Yankees. Do it for the city!' I was taught to hate them. I was that asshole who wore my 'Yankees Suck' T-shirt to Fenway Park."

"Sounds like you're not a Yankee hater anymore. When did that change for you?"

"A few months after I got the job with YES. I started to care about people in that clubhouse. I remember having a couple of conversations with Jorge about his son being sick. I remember talking to Sheffield about his uncle, Doc Gooden, being a drug addict. Somebody once told me, 'Hey, Jen. Snap out of it. They're not your friends.' Maybe they're not my friends, but they're people. They're not a uniform or a number."

"You mentioned on the phone that the Yankees helped your father when he was sick."

She inhales deeply and her eyes well up. "In December of '05, my mother called to say my father had stage four lung cancer that had metastasized."

"How did the Yankees figure into this?"

"There was a 3-week wait to get my father into Mass General or Dana-Farber. I called Larry and asked what I should do. He said, 'Call Terry Francona. Call Theo Epstein. Call Brian Cashman. Get yourself a good doctor for him.' I said, 'Brian Cashman?' And then I remembered that Dr. Hershon, the team doctor, went to Harvard Medical School. 'Call Cash,' Larry said. I called Cash, who called Dr. Hershon, who got my father into Mass General in a matter of days."

The tears are running down her cheeks.

"The Yankees were amazing," she continues. "During this whole experience, Mo was teaching me about death; that if it's God's plan it will happen. One day after my dad was out of the hospital, he said, 'Why don't you bring your parents to Fenway Park when we're there in May.' I brought them to Fenway. The game was rained out, but I got my parents field passes. I went into the locker room, and Mo was sitting on the couch watching TV. I said, 'Mo, they're here.' He shuffled into his flip-flops and came outside. He saw my parents and greeted them by their first names. He gave my mother a hug and a kiss, and then he said he wanted to talk to my dad alone. Right before they went off together, he looked at my parents and said, 'I want you to know that we love your daughter. You did such a good job of growing her up.'"

The Yankees are not the Mafia. I am almost moved to tears myself at this point. It is impossible not to be moved by acts of kindness, especially acts of kindness from people you have been led to believe are cold and unfeeling.

"Mo took my father aside, and they had a discussion about something," Jen recalls. "I never asked what they talked about. The next time I went home, my father gave me a letter in a manila envelope. He said, 'Don't open it until you get on the train.' I read it on the train back to New York. It said, 'Dear Jen, I don't think you'll ever know how proud you make me. Thank you for being my daughter. Please be careful.'"

Jen breaks down.

"At the bottom of the letter it said, 'P.S. Please give the enclosed letter to Mr. Rivera.' Inside the envelope was a separate letter to Mo. I don't know what it said, but I gave it to Mo, who told me everything would be okay. I said, 'What do you mean? My father's dying.' Mo said, 'Yes, but he's okay with it and God's okay with it. Everything's going to be fine.'"

I am quiet, silenced by Jen's apparent reverence for the team she was raised to despise.

"Did you hear from the Yankees after your father died?" I ask.

"Individual players sent flowers, but there was a humungous bouquet of red roses with a card that said 'New York Yankees.'"

Our seats for the finale of this last home stand against the Orioles are in section 631, row E tonight—in the level just below the upper Tier and above first base. Pettitte is going for his 200th career win against the Orioles' Brian Burres. Earlier in the day Detroit was swept by Cleveland, so the Yankees have a chance to go up by 5½ games in the wild card race.

Matsui's solo shot, his 25th of the season, puts the Yankees on the board in the bottom of the second. They score another run in the fifth, thanks to a single by Mientkiewicz. The guy is on fire!

The Orioles get a run back in the top of the sixth for 2–1, but that is the only scoring they will do off Pettitte, who is really sharp tonight. He leaves in the eighth and gets a big hand. Joba strikes out Mora to end the inning, getting an even bigger hand.

I stand when Mo trots in from the bullpen to "Enter Sandman." I think about his kindness toward Jen and her parents, and I love him even more. He is not lights out, however. His location is off, and you can feel the anxiety in the stands. Will he bear down and get this game over with?

Have a little faith, I tell myself. It occurs to me that having faith in a baseball team and having faith in God both require believing in something we can't always understand. What are the words "Maybe next year" if not an expression of faith?

Just then, the scoreboard reports that the Red Sox have been swept by Toronto—Pap Smear gave up a grand slam to Russ Adams!—and if the Yankees hold on, they will have pulled to within 1½ games of Boston!

Okay, Mo. Let's get this done.

He doesn't hear me. He walks Hernandez, loading the bases. It is not his night, and yet everyone is cheering him on. I am blowing out my vocal cords. "Let's go, Mo!"

He strikes out Moore, gets his 30th save, and preserves Pettitte's 200th win.

❧

Thursday is an off day, and it is a good thing for the Red Sox. The Boston media are using words like *collapse* to describe the sweep at the hands of the Jays. The team has shut down Okajima for several days with a tired arm, and they have no idea when Manny will return to the lineup.

Today is lunch with Ellen, my literary agent. I not only trust her in all professional matters but also value our close friendship.

We meet at a restaurant called A Voce near the Trident Media Group offices on East 26th Street. She is petite, almost fragile looking, but she is fearsome on behalf of her authors.

"I've started to read the sports section," she says proudly. "I know who Alex Rodriguez is now. Have you met him?"

"Not yet."

At 6:30 I hop into a cab for tonight's activity: dinner with Leigh Haber, my editor, at Cafe Luxembourg on 70th and Amsterdam. We crossed paths years ago when we were both book publicists, and now I am one of her authors. Publishing, like baseball, is a small world.

Leigh tells me she is a Yankee fan even though she grew up in Connecticut with a Red Sox–worshipping father. "You picked a great season to write about," she says.

I regale her with stories about the cities I have been to and the fans I have encountered and the games I have watched.

"Now tell me all the juicy, insider stuff." She leans in closer. "Which players have you met? A-Rod?"

"No."

"Jeter?"

"Well, no."

"Posada?"

"Uh-uh."

"Who *have* you talked to?"
"Doug Mientkiewicz."
"Who?"

***

I wake up on Friday from another Yankee dream and wonder if other women have dreams about their favorite team.

Women are different from men in the way we are fans. Female fans view the game from a more emotional perspective. We are just as knowledgeable about the sport as men, but we are as fascinated by the interactions between the players as we are by the velocity on a pitcher's fastball. Some of us wear pink caps and jerseys, while others of us think it is maddening that we are consigned to our own color. What we all share is a passion for the game, for our team, for our guys. I see us in every city and ballpark and hotel lobby, cheering and hanging out and snapping photos. We are teenagers and twentysomethings, soccer moms and corporate executives, baby boomers and seniors. We are everywhere.

Our seats for tonight's opener against Toronto are back in the up-up-up there section—Tier 19, row J, midway between first base and the right-field foul pole. The pitching matchup is Wang against Halladay.

Halladay has a 4–0 shutout going into the bottom of the ninth and is poised to throw a complete game. But the Yankees scratch out two runs, and he heads for the showers. We are all on our feet, cheering for a comeback. Giambi, pinch-hitting for Mienkiewicz, singles on the first pitch, knotting the score at 4–4. All 54,000 of us jump up and down and shake the Stadium. We go into extra innings.

Mo appears in the top of the 10th and retires the side in order.

Joba pitches a masterful 11th and 12th.

It is after midnight when Jeter singles on the first pitch in the bottom of the 13th. This is it, we all think. We will win it here. But Abreu hits into a fielder's choice and A-Rod pops up. Matsui walks, giving us more hope. Then Molina strikes out, and everybody groans.

Zaun's homer off Bruney in the top of the 14th stuns the crowd—at least those of us who are still left—and the Yankees lose 5–4.

Saturday is not just a day game after a night game. It is the day game after a night game that lasted 4 hours and 45 minutes.

We put on our Yankees gear and head out around noon for the 1:05 start. We discover it is raining. We go back inside and turn on the YES Network for an update. Sure enough, the tarp is on the field and the start of the game will be delayed.

By 2:50 we are at the Stadium and the sun is out. Our seats are in Tier 12, row D, above home plate on the third base side. We are up 1–0 over the Jays when Hughes starts nibbling. By the end of the fifth, Toronto is ahead by 3–2 and he is done.

To my right are a group of Red Sox fans who came to root against the Yankees. I ignore them—until the middle of the seventh. They have the unmitigated gall to sing "Sweet Caroline" during "God Bless America." I give them the most withering look I can muster.

The game is another insane marathon that is tied at 11–11 in the bottom of the 10th when Melky's single scores Damon for the 12–11 final.

Sunday is technically the last game at the Stadium of the 2007 regular season; tomorrow's is a makeup game. I can't believe the trip is almost over. I can't believe I didn't get my interview with Mientkiewicz, either. It is not as if I didn't try. Still, my editor will probably hate me forever, and I will have to find another way to earn a living.

It is a gorgeous day—sunny and clear and in the 70s—as if New York is showing us its best just when we are about to leave it. Our seats for today are in Tier 14, row C—the nonalcohol section, about halfway between home and third. As the Bleachers Creatures do the roll call, I chant along with them. "Mel-ky!" "Bob-bie!" "Rob-in-son!"

"What's wrong?" Michael asks when he sees that I am crying as I shout "Der-ek Jet-er!" along with the Creatures.

"I don't want it to end."

I am now part of this place, with all its idiosyncrasies, and it is part of me.

Mussina is going for his third consecutive win since returning from his "hiatus." The crowd is jazzed, but there is also a somber quality that pervades the Stadium, as if we all know this is an ending of sorts.

Joe appears on the scoreboard before the bottom of the first to thank the fans for showing up this season—over four million strong.

"*Now* why are you crying?" Michael asks.

"He's saying good-bye," I tell him. "You know how I hate good-byes."

I really can't do good-byes, big ones and small ones and anything-in-between ones. I cried when Johnny Carson left the *Tonight Show*. I cried when *The Sopranos* left HBO. I cried when our exterminator left to become a guitarist in a rock band.

"Good-byes are inevitable," says Michael.

"Disco Stu" pops up on the scoreboard. He is a season-tickets holder who wears garish shirts and dances like a maniac for the scoreboard camera. He is among the unforgettable cast of characters at Yankee Stadium—like the Bleacher Creatures and Freddy the Pan Man and the vendor who shrieks "Ice cold water!"

Bobby Murcer is up next on the scoreboard. Like Joe, he thanks the fans for their support this season.

"I know." Michael pats my arm when he catches me crying again.

I wipe my eyes with a tissue. "I'm going to miss them so much."

I flash back to the first half of the season when I was so angry—angry at the Yankees for being flawed and angry at the *New York Times* readers for branding me a bad fan. I *was* a bad fan. I had lost the joy, the magic, the faith. But now here I am at the last real game of the last home stand, and I feel a shift in the way I love the Yankees. I still want them to win every single game, and I don't know how I will cope if they get into the play-offs and then lose in the first round. But in the meantime, I have spent 2 months watching them warm up, watching them play, watching them walk in and out of hotel lobbies, watching them eat and drink and drive cars and do normal-people things. I have read everything written about them and listened to everything the beat writers have told me about them. I know this team in a way I didn't know them before. I know they cheat on their wives and inject banned substances into their bodies and are not the role models everybody wishes they were. I know. I know. I know. And I love them still.

The Yankees go up 6–3 in the bottom of the fifth and tack on another run in the seventh. Mussina has been absolutely brilliant.

Viz starts the eighth and gives up a two-run homer to Stairs for 7–5. The crowd chants, "We want Joba!" Joe obliges, and Joba preserves the win for Mussina, his 250th, and for the Yankees.

Michael goes back to the Marmara, and I head over to a bistro called Island to meet Kathy Sulkes, one of my oldest and dearest friends. A television news producer for many years, she is moving to Mexico.

"Here's to new adventures," I say, as we clink wine glasses.

"By the way," she says, "I was at dinner over the weekend with my former CBS pal, Gary Paul Gates. He's a Yankee fan."

"Cool."

"I mentioned your book and how it started with the article in the *Times* about the divorce. Gary and the other men got all excited and said, 'We loved that article!'"

"I'm amazed so many people even saw it."

"There's more," Kathy says. "I told Gary you've been having trouble getting past the Yankees' media guy, and he has a friend who can help."

I laugh. I have heard that one before.

"No, really," she says. "He told me this friend knows Steinbrenner and can pick up the phone and open doors for you. Should I pursue it?"

"Why not?"

AL EAST STANDINGS/SEPTEMBER 23

TEAM	W	L	PCT	GB
BOSTON	92	64	.590	—
NEW YORK	90	65	.581	1.5
TORONTO	78	77	.503	13.5
BALTIMORE	66	89	.426	25.5
TAMPA BAY	64	92	.410	28.0

Week 26
September 24, 2007

If Joe wants to hit and run, he doesn't have to hesitate with me. Same with the bunt. You're not gonna ask Alex to move a guy over; you're gonna ask Alex to do his thing. But I give Joe a chance to manage the way he did when he won all the championships.

Kathy calls on Monday morning. She has spoken to Gary Gates and found out that the person he knows with connections to Steinbrenner is Gene Orza, chief operating officer of the Players Association.

"Call Gary before today's game," she advises. "He's waiting."

I reach Gary, who tells me he has known Gene Orza for years and plays poker with him twice a week. "When Gene calls the Yankees, they listen," he says. "What would you need from him?"

I give him a brief summary of my dealings with Jason Zillo. "It's probably too late, but I would love to interview Doug Mientkiewicz."

"I'll speak to Gene and see how he wants to handle this. It's a busy time for him, but I'll do my best. Any friend of Kathy's is a lifelong friend of mine."

Today is an odd day at the ballpark. The final home stand of the season officially ended yesterday, so this makeup game against the Jays has the feel of the last day of high school, when everybody has already gotten into the college of their choice and only a fraction of the class shows up.

Once we are inside, I spot the vendor we love—the woman who shouts, "Ice cold water!" I tap her on the shoulder.

"You were our favorite vendor this season," I say. "You really should be on Broadway with that voice of yours."

"Thank you so much," she says in a much softer tone than she uses in the stands. "May God bless you for being such a nice person."

She puts down her supply of bottled water and gives me a hug.

"Good-bye," I say as she goes off to work. Michael hands me a tissue.

Our seats are in Tier 14, the same section as last night, but since there is only a smattering of people, the ushers tell us to move down and sit wherever we want.

Pettitte is pitching because Clemens's hamstring is still acting up.

My cell phone rings in the top of the sixth.

"Hello?"

"It's Gary Gates. I spoke to Gene, and he's glad to help with the Yankees' media guy. Send him an e-mail with exactly what you need."

"Thanks so much," I say. "I'm very grateful."

"My pleasure. What's the score of the game?"

"Four–nothing Toronto. The Yankees stink today."

He laughs. "Just remember that the course of true love never runs smooth."

We score a measly run in the bottom of the sixth, but it is no contest. Toronto wins 4–1. We were lackadaisical.

Back at the hotel, I read Peter Abraham's blog. He writes that he and the other beat writers have made hotel and plane reservations in all the cities where the Yankees might conceivably play in the postseason. I have not thought about doing this, even though the Yanks could clinch as early as tomorrow night in Tampa.

"We don't have reservations anywhere," I tell Michael.

"Then we'd better get on it," he says.

We spend the next hour coming up with a zillion different travel scenarios. We book hotels in Anaheim, Cleveland, and New York and flights to and from the same cities. And I call Mike, the ticket broker, who confirms that he can get me play-off tickets. We are covered.

My final task before our flight tomorrow morning is to write to Gene Orza. The e-mail I compose is way too long and convoluted, but I send it and cross my fingers.

On Tuesday morning Michael and I are at Newark airport, waiting for our 10:00 flight to Tampa, when I recognize Bruce Beck, the NBC sports anchor. He is sitting with another guy, and they are talking about Jason Zillo and clubhouse passes and champagne celebrations.

"Bruce Beck is flying down to cover the clinch party," I whisper to Michael.

"Let me guess: You want to interview him on the plane."

"Not really."

We board the plane, take our seats, and strap ourselves in. After we reach our cruising altitude, I get up to use the restroom. On my way back I recognize the man sitting on the aisle in the seat directly behind mine. He is the one who was talking to Bruce Beck at the gate.

"Excuse me," I say. "I overheard you mentioning the Yankees before."

He is a nice-looking man in his early forties with dark hair, blue eyes, and a toothy grin. "I'm the chief sports photographer for the *Post*. My name's Charles Wenzelberg."

"I see your pictures every day." I sit back down and turn around so I can face him. I introduce myself and tell him about the book.

He flips up the cover of his laptop and powers up the computer. "I'd be glad to show you some of the pictures and answer any questions."

Boy, have things changed. I spent the entire trip begging people in Yankee-ville to talk to me. Now they are volunteering.

"I remember a great photo of A-Rod and Jeter that ran in the *Post* right after A-Rod joined the Yankees," I say.

Charles finds it on the computer and shows it to me. A-Rod and Jeter are standing side by side on the field, looking like buddies, even though they were hardly speaking to each other at the time.

"Everyone was trying to get a picture of them together during A-Rod's first spring training," he explains. "A-Rod didn't have a problem with it. Jeter did. But Derek agreed to it because does the right thing for the organization. I took a few pictures of them, but they looked totally uncomfortable. As Jeter was about to leave, I said, 'Derek, I need you for another minute.' He said, 'Okay. What do you want me to do?' I put him and A-Rod back together and asked Derek to lean his arm on Alex's shoulder. But once again, he looked like he was being asked to touch fire without an oven mitt on. I said, 'Okay, guys. Now I need big, goofy smiles.' The two of them gave me the smile and I made four more pictures. Jeter said, 'Thanks. Gotta go.' He ran off, and Alex shrugged his shoulders at me."

"Did you ever have to shoot Steinbrenner?"

"In 2003, the *Post* was doing this glossy magazine pullout. We had to get a portrait of George in Monument Park. He was supposed to be there at 3:30. I got there at 1 o'clock and set up my stuff. I put tape down on the ground so George would know exactly where to stand. Three thirty came. Four thirty came. Five thirty came. Someone at the Yankees called and said, 'He's just leaving the restaurant in Manhattan.' Six thirty came."

"You were standing there waiting all that time?"

"All afternoon. At one point a security guy called me and said, 'The eagle has landed.' They brought George out in a golf cart. He came in, and I took three or four pictures. He had his arms folded, and he was wearing his sunglasses. I said, 'Mr. Steinbrenner, I really need you to take your sunglasses off.' He peeled them off his face with this John Wayne swagger. I said, 'What I'd like you to do is stand on the tape.' He said, 'I see the tape! I know what to do!' We wanted him to be holding one of the magazines, so I handed him one. He said, 'You're try-ing to stir up controversy with me and Jeter, but it's not gonna happen!' I said, 'Mr. Steinbrenner, I don't know what you're talking about.' He said, 'You handed me the magazine with Jeter on the cover!' At the beginning of the year he had called Jeter out for his nightlife. I said, 'With all due respect, that's not what I'm trying to do. Would you rather hold the one with Mickey Mantle on the cover?' He said, 'Yeah. Give me that one.' Rick Cerrone, who handled PR for the Yankees then, came over and said, 'Okay. We can't do any more.' I said to Rick, 'Sorry, but I'm not done.' I gave the magazine to Mr. Steinbrenner, took a few more pictures, and that was it. After George walked away, three of the Yankees' people said, 'Wow. A lot of photographers would have folded in that situation.' To me, he was just another person."

"Do you think the Yankees will clinch a play-off spot tonight?"

He shrugs. "I'll be following them around until they do."

It is hot and sticky when our taxi pulls up to the historic—and very pink—Renaissance Vinoy Hotel in St. Petersburg, where the Yankees are also staying.

After we check in to our room, Michael's younger sister Lawsie arrives. She lives in Jacksonville but has driven down to visit with us—another bonus of this trip, since we have not seen her in a while. She is a Yankee fan and can't wait to catch a glimpse of the players as they leave the hotel for Tropicana Field. We sit on the veranda and watch taxis and limos circle around the driveway to pick them up. Lawsie jumps when she spots A-Rod.

"He looks *huge*," she says. "His arms are *massive*."

I laugh because I am remembering the first time I saw him up close. I thought he looked huge, too. Maybe I am getting used to seeing him because he is starting to look normal-size to me now.

Before we leave for the game, I hurry back to the room to check e-mail. On my way I bump into John Sterling, who is his usual dapper self in his dark suit with the handkerchief in his jacket pocket.

"Why, it's Jane Heller," he says, giving me a hug. "You know, the Yankees have been winning since you came on board."

I beam.

"I hope you'll keep going with us into the play-offs."

I am delirious with his use of the word *us*. I am a member of the Yankees traveling carnival now.

Back in the room, there is an e-mail from Gene Orza. He writes simply: "I'm on it." Things really are looking up.

Michael, Lawsie, and I hop onto the 5:30 shuttle, which takes the Vinoy's guests straight to the VIP entrance at Tropicana Field—a beige building with a dome on it.

Inside, I give my name to the attractive brunette who is presiding over the VIP table.

"Jane!" she says. "I'm so glad to meet you!"

Cass welcomes us as if we are long-lost friends and hands me an envelope with tonight's tickets. While Michael and Lawsie take a tour of the stadium, I go with Cass to a private lounge, where she tells me Matt Silverman, the Rays' president, will be in to talk to me.

The lounge is a glass-enclosed space that overlooks the stadium, which, like the Rogers Centre, has artificial turf instead of grass and feels like a very large gymnasium. As the Yankees take batting practice, I survey the place. What strikes me is how generic the atmosphere is. Nothing about the Trop says "tropical." Where is the funky Florida stuff—the palm trees, the flamingoes, the kitsch?

Matt enters and greets me warmly. He is a handsome man with dark hair and dark eyes. I thank him for the tickets, and he thanks me for the nice words about the Rays in the *Times* piece.

We discuss some of his talented players—Scott Kazmir, Carl Crawford, B. J. Upton, Carlos Pena.

"Any chance the Rays will let the Yankees clinch tonight?" I tease.

"No chance."

Our seats are in section 108, row L. They are way down on the field, to the first base side of home plate, and they are upholstered—like our green Barcaloungers.

Igawa pitches five scoreless innings, A-Rod smacks a grand slam, and the Yankees are up 5–0. I can practically taste the champagne.

But then Joe brings in Edwar for the bottom of the sixth, and he gives up a run. Bruney is worse; he walks in a run and serves up a grand slam.

In the top of the eighth, with the Rays ahead 6–5, Dan Wheeler comes in to pitch. Michael and I remember sitting with his parents during the series in the Bronx, but we can't root for him with a postseason spot on the line. The Yankees tie the score on an error by Navarro.

It is 6–6 until the bottom of the 10th. Navarro blasts Karsten's third pitch into the seats for a walk-off homer. No champagne tonight.

At Wednesday night's game, we are in our seats when Charles Wenzelberg stops by to tell us that George Steinbrenner is in his private box.

"Hopefully, he'll get to see them clinch tonight," I say.

"If they do clinch, I'll try to save you a champagne cork from the party," he offers.

It is not quite the same as being invited to the party, but it is an incredibly sweet gesture.

Wang is going for his 19th win tonight. The Yankees score seven runs in the top of the fifth. They look determined to clinch. Pena homers off Wang in the bottom of the fifth, but the Yanks keep pounding away at the Rays' bullpen. When it is 12–2, Charles and the other photographers start to cover their equipment in plastic so the cameras don't get doused with champagne. With the Yankees ahead by 12–4, Mo takes the mound in the bottom of the ninth. The Yankee fans at the Trop are on their feet, chanting, cheering, and applauding. Ruggiano: Out! Young: Out! Norton: Out!

As the players converge on each other near the mound, I stand with my hands pressed together in the prayer position, thanking God that the Yankees did it. They were eight games under .500 on May 29 and went on to become the best team in the league with the highest winning percentage.

On Thursday morning, Michael and I are reading all the accounts of last night's festivities when the Vinoy's fire alarm makes us jump. We are told to evacuate immediately.

We throw on some clothes and grab our carry-on bags and computers and stand outside in the hall looking bewildered. John Sterling pops out of his room in his T-shirt, sweatpants, and bed hair.

"It's probably a false alarm," he says, rubbing his eyes. "I'm going back to sleep."

"Did you have a good time at the celebration last night?" I ask.

"Oh, it was great. After the celebration at the ballpark—they only use cheap champagne for that—I went to dinner with Joe and everybody, and we drank Dom Pérignon."

"Sounds wonderful."

"How's everything going with the book?"

"I'm trying to interview Doug Mientkiewicz."

"Doug would be perfect," he says. "He's smart and charming. Is Jason setting it up?"

"Gene Orza is on it."

Our seats at Tropicana Field for tonight's series finale are the same—section 108, row L. Joe is resting most of the regulars. He is conceding the division title to the Red Sox and preparing the team for the postseason. I know this is the correct move, but I would have enjoyed making Boston sweat a little.

Hughes is facing Kazmir in what is the Devil Rays' last home game of the season. The season tickets holders say good-bye to each other with those magic words: "Maybe next year."

In the top of the fourth, with both pitchers throwing scoreless ball, my cell phone rings.

"It's Charles Wenzelberg," he says. "I'm at Shea working the Mets game, but I wanted you to know that I did save you a cork from last night's party."

I am so excited that I spontaneously rise to my feet.

"Sit the fuck down, lady!" the man behind me yells.

I sit back down.

"Are you going to the postseason?" Charles asks.

"You bet. It looks like we'll be starting off in Cleveland."

"I'll bring you the cork."

I am floating. I know, I know. We are talking about a cork, not the Dom Pérignon. Back in April when I was furious at the Yankees, I never dreamed they would have anything to celebrate, much less with me in attendance. And now a member of the traveling carnival thought enough of my devotion to the team to save me a souvenir from their most triumphant night of the year.

Hughes goes seven strong innings, and the Yankees win 3–1.

Back at the hotel it is dead quiet, the way it always is after the Yanks take off on their charter and fly away. We will be joining them in Baltimore, just like we did in July. It was our first stop of the regular season, and now it will be our last.

⚜

On Friday morning, Michael and I land at Dulles, rent a car, and drive an hour to the Renaissance Harborfront on East Pratt Street, where we are staying along with the Yankees. The lobby is filled with men, women, and children in Joba jerseys, the latest must-have garment for a Yankee fan.

I ask the woman at the front desk for a quiet room. She gives me one on nine, where I find a uniformed policeman sitting in a chair near the elevator. I am not only at the Yankees' hotel; I am on their floor.

Michael and I hold hands as we walk over to Camden Yards. It is a beautiful night—clear and warm with a nearly full moon. We stop at Boog's Barbecue. There is a long line, but I have been salivating for the pit turkey sandwich, baked beans, and spicy sauce for 2 months.

"You're not having any?" I ask Michael, who is not loading up.

"Better not," he says.

Our seats are in the upper deck—section 340, row DD—with a really good view over home plate.

Mussina is pitching against Leicester.

In the top of the eighth, with the Yanks up 9–6, the scoreboard tells us that the Red Sox have beaten Minnesota. If we lose this game, Boston wins the division.

Mo comes in for the bottom of the ninth to nail down the victory—and blows it. Baltimore ties the game at 9–9, and we go into extra innings.

The bats do nothing in the top of the 10th, and Joe brings in Edwar to pitch the bottom half. He loads the bases, then strikes out Millar on a wicked changeup, only to give up a bunt RBI single to Mora.

The Yanks lose 10–9, and there goes the division. I remind myself that the Red Sox were the wild-card team when they won the World Series in '04. We can do it, too.

It is a glorious afternoon on Saturday with blue skies and temperatures in the 70s. I visit the Baltimore Basilica, a local landmark reputed to be the first cathedral ever built in America after the adoption of the Constitution. It is one of the most breathtaking churches I have ever seen.

I mount the steps and peek in the open door. There is not a single other tourist or worshipper this morning. I have the place all to myself.

I enter the cathedral and give myself a tour, admiring the inspirational paintings on the white domed ceiling. And then I take a seat in one of the pews and breathe in the silence. I let my mind empty, except to appreciate the peace and serenity of my surroundings.

I lower my head.

"Dear God," I say. "Thank you for this extraordinary adventure; for my being able to watch the team I love with the husband I love by my side; for the family and friends I've reconnected with and for the new friends I've made. And thank you for getting the Yankees into the play-offs—no small miracle there, right?"

There is a mob scene in the lobby of the Renaissance by the time I get back. Yankee fans are everywhere.

Upstairs in our room, I check e-mail. There is one from Suzyn Waldman. I had e-mailed her about getting together in Cleveland, but she explains that a lot of people from the Yankees' "Tampa faction" will be there, so she will not be available. I am finally getting it that the dinner we had in Detroit was not the forging of a friendship.

Michael and I walk to Camden Yards for tonight's game. There is the usual long line for Boog's Barbecue, and Boog himself is there.

"Hey, Boog," I say. "Who do you like in the postseason?"

He smirks at my Yankees shirt. "Not your team."

Our seats are in section 316, row MM—on the right-field side. Pettitte is going against Daniel Cabrera. The "B" team is in again so the regulars can rest up for Cleveland.

It is one of those ugly games where neither side is playing well. The Yankees win 11–10.

Sunday is a quiet day, as it always is when the Yankees leave town. By the time Michael and I head out for the afternoon game at Camden Yards, the traveling carnival has checked out of the Renaissance Harborfront. They will fly back to New York after the game and arrive in Cleveland on Tuesday. I miss them already.

The afternoon is perfect for baseball—in the 70s, without a cloud in the sky. Our seats are in section 360, row BB, on the left field side. Following tradition, Joe hands over the managerial duties for the last game of the season to one of the veteran players. Today it is Jorge who will manage. Sean Henn is facing off against Brian Burres.

The Yankee fan next to me is a contractor from New Jersey.

"The Yankees were my only constant as a kid," he tells me. "I never give up on them."

"You have faith," I say.

"You got that right."

The Yankees score in the first after A-Rod singles Jeter home. The Orioles tie the score in the bottom of the second on Millar's solo homer.

It is 4–1 Yankees in the third when A-Rod comes out of the game and gets a huge ovation. Talk about a monster season—a .314 batting average, 54 homers, and 156 RBIs.

I check the scoreboard and see that the Mets are about to be bounced out of the season, losing badly to the Phillies. I call my friend Marty to offer my condolences.

"They're playing like dead people!" he rants, the sounds of a sports bar in the background. "Why should I even care about them?"

"Marty, come on. You don't mean it."

"And Willie! He's just not motivating them!"

Is this how I sounded when I wanted the divorce?

With the Yankees ahead by 10–3 in the bottom of the ninth, Farnsworth serves up a homer, then retires the O's to end the game—and the season.

"Well, that's it," I say to the Yankee fan next to me.

"On to Cleveland." He checks stats on his PDA. "They finished with 968 runs, the most for the franchise since 1937."

I worry about those 968 runs. It is always the bats that go cold in the post-season. I wish I could set aside, like, 50 of them for next week.

Michael and I have dinner at Phillips, a seafood place overlooking the harbor.

"Where are you guys from?" the waiter asks.

I almost say "New York" but catch myself. "California," I tell him.

"I've only been to California once," he says. "Someday I'll get back out there."

Someday I will, too. Just not yet. Please, not yet.

AL EAST STANDINGS/SEPTEMBER 30

TEAM	W	L	PCT	GB
BOSTON	96	66	.593	—
NEW YORK	94	68	.580	2.0
TORONTO	83	79	.512	13.0
BALTIMORE	69	93	.426	27.0
TAMPA BAY	66	96	.407	30.0

Week 27
October 1, 2007

Play-off baseball is all about breaks.

Our plane lands in Cleveland around 8:30 on Monday night. It is wet and cold—very different from the summer weather we had here in August.

We check in to another Renaissance, this one in Tower City, the same downtown complex where the Yankees will be staying at the Ritz-Carlton. The Renaissance is a beautiful old hotel, built in 1918, according to the brochure handed to me by the woman at the front desk. I ask her for a quiet room, and she puts us in a quiet suite—a "parlor suite," which consists of a living room with a wet bar and a tiny bedroom. It is dark with low ceilings, and it has the musty smell of a hotel that was built in 1918. But it will be our home for the next 5 nights, so we settle in.

On Tuesday I wake up with no clue where I am. I bang my head on the wall of our parlor-suite bedroom, mistaking it for the way to the bathroom. This is the downside of staying at one hotel after another. You are at the new place, but you think you are still at the old place.

I go off to have a shampoo and blow-dry at the Marengo Institute, which sounds as if it should be a think tank or a medical research center but is the salon the concierge recommended. I need to look my best for the play-offs.

Later, as Michael and I are enjoying our pasta dinner at Bice, an Italian restaurant next to the Ritz-Carlton, I spot Mussina walking in with a man I don't recognize. They are escorted into a back room, and I wonder if Joe has convened a team dinner, the way he did at Spuntini in Toronto. But it is just Moose and his buddy. I am thrilled to see him—and thrilled the Yankees have arrived in town.

Back in our parlor suite at the Renaissance, I write another piece for the *New York Times* sports section—one that will put a happy ending on my "trilogy" of essays about my relationship with the Yanks. When I am finished I read it to Michael.

"Is it okay?"

"It needs to be funnier."

On Wednesday it is funnier. I e-mail the piece to Tom Jolly.

By the afternoon I am restless. I take a walk. It is overcast again but up in the 70s, which everyone says is unusual for October. Tomorrow is supposed to be in the 80s and sunny—freakishly warm weather.

At the corner of Superior and 9th Street, I come upon the Catholic church I visited back in August. It is not nearly as grand as the Basilica in Baltimore, but it is beautiful just the same. I go inside and sit down in the exact spot where I sat last time. There is only one other person in the church: an elderly white-gloved woman who is sobbing and dabbing at her eyes with a lacy handkerchief. I immediately add her to my list of people to pray for.

Once I have requested blessings for all my real-life loved ones, I turn my attention to my pinstriped loved ones. "Dear God. Please let the Yankees sweep the Indians. Please let A-Rod show everyone he isn't a postseason choker. Please let our starting pitching hold up. And please don't put Farnsworth into a game.

"Oh, and please let Tom Jolly at the *New York Times* think my essay is funny. Amen."

Back at the Renaissance there is an e-mail from Tom Jolly. He says he will find a spot for my piece in Sunday's *Times*.

Michael and I celebrate by ordering room service. We watch the Red Sox beat the Angels in the first game of their series and boo both teams.

Speaking of celebrating, tomorrow is our 15th wedding anniversary. We have no plans to exchange gifts or commemorate the big day except to be in our seats for game one of Yankees–Indians.

ALDS: Game One
October 4, 2007

I texted Alex to tell him to keep his head right. I said, "I'm proud of you. You've had arguably the best year in the history of the game. You've left no questions unanswered. So just go out there and enjoy this."

Thursday is finally here. No more resorting to checking the scores and schedules of other teams. No more wondering what the atmosphere at Jacobs Field will be like. Today is the day, and I feel the excitement as soon as I step outside our room.

I run into George King of the *Post* standing by the front desk. He has just checked in.

I see Paul O'Neill talking on his cell phone. He is here for the YES Network.

The carnival has definitely come to town.

I get ready for the 6:30 game early, donning my Mo T-shirt and Yankees visor and leaving my Yankees jacket behind. Since it is unseasonably warm, I expect to be sweating, not shivering.

At the entrance to Jacobs Field, they are handing out tacky white towels so we can wave them around. No thanks. The red, white, and blue bunting draped over the railings looks festive, but there is something phony about this capacity crowd. When I was here in August, the Indians had to beg people to come to the ballpark. Now there are about 45,000 men and women walking around in red T-shirts that say "It's Tribe Time Now!" Where were they when their team was struggling?

Our seats are in section 138, row CC—on the field instead of in the bleachers this time, on the first-base side. There are a few other Yankee fans in our section, but mostly it is a home crowd and a very loud one. They are in a frenzy as they watch clips from the regular season on the scoreboard.

The ceremonial first pitch is thrown out by the fan who sits in the top row of the bleachers and bangs on his drum. An American flag the size of the entire field is carried out. And after the musicians from the Cleveland Orchestra perform the national anthem, a profusion of red, white, and blue balloons is released into the sky. It is a great spectacle and very patriotic, but I am itching to start the game already. "Let's go, Yankees!" I shout and get filthy looks from all sides. "LET'S GO, YANKEES!"

Wang versus Sabathia. CC is a Cy Young candidate and is hell on left-handed hitters, but we are the Yankees.

Damon leads off with a line drive that lands in the right-field seats. It is called foul. Joe comes out to argue. There is a little TV monitor above our heads, and I can see the replay: Damon's ball was fair. The umpires confer and reverse the call. 1–0 Yankees. Abreu and A-Rod both walk, but they are stranded when Posada and Matsui can't bring them in. At least we have made Sabathia work. He has thrown more than 25 pitches in the inning.

In the bottom of the first, Wang hits Sizemore in the foot. Not a great start. Cabrera hits into a double play, but Hafner walks. Martinez singles. Garko singles, scoring Hafner. Peralta walks, loading the bases for Kenny Fucking Lofton, who singles, scoring Martinez and Garko. It is 3–1 and Wang has no clue. "Let's go Yankees!" I chant, louder and with more urgency. I am drowned out by the Indians fans. They are not just loud; they are crazed. They are on their feet for every single pitch, and the decibel level is off the scale.

In the top of the third, CC is at 50 pitches. He is walking batters. The Yankees are forcing him to throw strikes. But they can't seem to take advantage of his wildness.

In the bottom of the third, Cabrera homers for 4–1. It is still early. The Yankees will come back. They have before, and they will again.

Cano homers in the top of the fourth for 4–2.

Shelley bats for Mientkiewicz in the top of the fifth. He singles. Damon walks. Wedge comes out to talk to Sabathia, who is at 94 pitches. CC stays in the game. Abreu lines a double, scoring Shelley. 4–3. A-Rod is intentionally walked, loading the bases for Posada with one out. Okay, Jorge. Now would be a really good time to crush one into the gap or put one in the seats. Jorge works the count to 3-and-0. "Hip, hip, Jor-hay!" I scream. Inexplicably he swings— what the fuck?—and misses. And ends up striking out. Matsui pops up, but it is Posada's at bat that has knocked the wind out of me.

Martinez homers in the bottom of the fifth with Cabrera on base for 6–3. Peralta doubles over Cano's head, and Lofton steps in to chants of "Ken-ny! Ken-ny!" He was a surly bastard when he played for the Yankees, but they love him here in Cleveland. He singles, scoring Peralta for 7–3. As chants of "Yankees suck" rain down on Wang, Joe comes to take him out. I heard that his family flew in from Taiwan for this game. They should have stayed home. Joe signals for Ross Ohlendorf, who has never pitched in this sort of pressure-cooker atmosphere. Gutierrez walks and Blake doubles to left, scoring Lofton and Gutierrez. 9–3.

The Indians have a new pitcher in the top of the sixth, and I should be relieved to be rid of Sabathia. But Perez is tough, too. He retires the side in order, with two strikeouts. The stadium speakers blare that idiotic song "Hang On Sloopy" with everybody shouting "O-H-I-O." It is worse than "Sweet Caroline."

Hafner homers in the bottom of the sixth off Ohlendorf, who then gives up a double to Martinez, hits Garko with a pitch, and gives up another double to Lofton, scoring Martinez. It is 11–3 when Joe finally comes out to get the kid, traumatizing him for life. Veras gets Gutierrez to pop up to end the inning.

Damon, Jeter, and Abreu go down in order in the top of the seventh, and Reggie Jackson, who is down in front in our section, has seen enough. He storms past my aisle seat, and I am tempted to go with him. Instead I yell, "Let's go Yankees!"

Hughes is pitching the bottom of the seventh, which I don't understand at all. He should be resting up in case he has to fill in for Clemens or Mussina. What is he doing in a blowout?

He comes back for the eighth and gives up a homer to Garko. 12–3.

We are in the top of the ninth with Betancourt on the mound. I am amazed by how many Indians fans are leaving the ballpark. If this were a play-off game in the Bronx, would there be a chance in hell I would leave? It is not raining here. There is no snowstorm. How bad could the traffic be? Giambi, batting for Shelley, singles, but Damon lines out to end this disaster.

We get booed as we make our way out of the stadium in our Yankees clothes.

I ignore it all until a fat guy with a Mohawk and a face covered in red paint plants himself in my path and yells, "Yankees suck!"

"I hope that paint gives you lead poisoning!"

Back at the hotel I tell Michael it was just one game. "We'll win tomorrow night."

He leans over to kiss me. "Happy Anniversary."

ALDS: Game Two
October 5, 2007

We had CC on the ropes. And we had the right guy at the plate twice: Jorge in the first and Jorge in the fifth. He didn't come through, but would I take that situation 162 times next year? Absolutely. Those things happen, especially in a short series. Okay. Big deal. It's just one game.

I am exhausted when I wake up on Friday. I hardly slept at all, but I did have a wonderful dream: Bud Selig ruled that the Cleveland Indians were being disqualified from the play-offs because of some financial wrongdoing by their front office, and the Yankees were the winners of the series by default. Talk about wishful thinking.

The weather is still unseasonably warm—in the high 80s—and muggier than yesterday, as if summer really has returned. I take a walk to my favorite church. I reassure God that it is okay that the Yankees lost last night. In case he is too busy to familiarize himself with the logistics of the ALDS, I explain to him that it is not essential that we sweep the Indians, only that we beat them eventually. And I ask for forgiveness for telling the fan with the painted face that I hoped he would die.

Tonight's game has a 5:00 start, and it is still hot and sticky as we walk to Jacobs Field. We pass a few Yankee fans along the route, and I fist-bump each one. We need to stick together in this time of crisis.

Our seats are the same as last night's—section 138, row CC. As I am walking up the aisle to buy bottled water, I run into Charles Wenzelberg, the photographer from the *Post*.

"Where are you sitting, so I can bring you the cork?" he asks.

The cork. He really did save it for me.

I point to our seats, and he says he will be back. Sure enough, he reappears a few minutes later with my souvenir from the champagne party. I give him a hug and thank him.

After Charles goes to work, I show the cork to Michael, handling it as if it is a rare and extremely expensive gemstone.

"Where are you planning on keeping it?" he asks. "With the rest of your Yankees stuff?"

"With my jewelry," I say.

The Jake is as loud as it was last night—maybe louder. The scoreboard is revving everybody up with clips of the players shoving pies in each other's faces (pies are known here as rally pies). What's more, the fans are incessantly waving those white dish rags that were distributed at the entrance. I can't imagine how the Yankees are supposed to concentrate in this sort of environment.

Pettitte against Fausto Carmona.

Queen Latifah throws out the ceremonial first pitch. She must be a Yankee fan, because she gives Jeter a hug as she walks off the field. A classical pianist plays the national anthem.

"Let's go Yankees!" I shout as Damon steps in to lead off the top of the first. I am really jumpy.

Damon flies out. Jeter strikes out. Abreu grounds out. I doubt Carmona even broke a sweat.

Pettitte is almost as good in his half. Sizemore singles, but Cabrera hits into a double play, and Hafner strikes out looking.

In the top of the second, A-Rod pops out on the first pitch. After Matsui walks, Posada grounds into a double play.

In the bottom of the frame, Pettitte walks Peralta, who steals second. Lofton singles, but Melky makes an incredible throw home to nail Peralta and end the threat.

"Maybe that'll give us some momentum," I say right before Melky homers to put the Yankees up 1–0.

Both pitchers are brilliant through six innings, and the tension mounts. This is the kind of game Michael loves—a tight contest where the outcome is unpredictable. I would love it more if the Yankees were ahead by 107–0.

In the bottom of the seventh, with the Yankees clinging to their one-run lead, Pettitte gets into a jam. Peralta doubles. Lofton walks on four pitches. Out comes Joe, who calls for Joba. The crowd chants "Jo-ba! Jo-ba!" in a mocking, singsong way that makes me so mad I want to decapitate the Indians fan in front of me. The next indignity is the scoreboard display, which shows a "New York sucks" sign. A "Cleveland sucks" sign would not be permitted at Yankee Stadium, much less projected onto the scoreboard with children watching. Now they are showing a picture of Senator Hillary Clinton (D–NY) with her face X-ed out. They also string up a dummy by its neck and dunk it in a vat of whipped cream for the ultimate rally pie. Meanwhile, Joba retires Gutierrez and Blake.

The Yankees go down in order in the top of the eighth. Where is the offense? How did we score 968 runs? I know we face the toughest pitchers at this time of year, but are they really that tough? I am such a nervous wreck that I am literally wiping the flop sweat off my face.

Joba comes back out for the bottom of the eighth. I try to think positively, to have *faith*. I envision that he will keep the Indians in check and turn the ball over to Mo in the ninth, and the Yankees will tie up the series on Pettitte's gutsy performance. There is nothing wrong with a 1–0 game as long as the Yankees win it.

Michael points at the infield. "What the hell . . . ?"

I look closer. Joba is swatting bugs off his face, off his neck, off his arms. I look closer still. Jeter is waving away the insects, too. So are Mientkiewicz, Cano, and A-Rod.

"This is bizarre," I say. "We don't have any bugs here in the stands. Do you think they're attracted to the lights?"

The Indians fan in front of me turns around and smirks, "They're attracted by Jeter's cologne."

I do not even bother with him. Gene Monahan hurries out of the dugout with a can of bug spray and gives Joba a thorough going-over. The others borrow it and spray themselves, too. But it becomes clear very quickly that the spray is useless. Billions of insects are swarming the players.

The Indians fan turns around again. "They're called midges," he says of the insects. "Lake Erie midges. They come out on warm fall nights."

"How do you get rid of them?"

"You don't." He laughs. "And bug spray only attracts 'em."

I need to tell the Yankees this. Lake Erie midges were obviously not in their scouting report. I need to jump over the railing and run onto the field and shout, *"Stop the madness!"*

And yet the madness does not stop. The bugs are attacking Joba, dive-bombing him, sticking to his skin. How is he supposed to pitch? They are attaching themselves to his eyeballs. I glance up at the TV monitor, and it looks as if a biblical pestilence has descended on Jacobs Field.

"Where the fuck is Joe? Why isn't he out there talking to the umpires about delaying the game?"

Michael shakes his head. It is a mystery to him, too. "Even if they refuse to delay it, the discussion itself would delay it—maybe just long enough for the bugs to let up a little."

But Joe remains in the dugout, even as his pitcher is asking for more repellant; even as his pitcher walks Sizemore, the first batter of the inning, on four pitches; even as his pitcher hurls a wild pitch past Cabrera, sending Sizemore to second; even as his pitcher allows Cabrera to sacrifice Sizemore to third; even as his pitcher throws a second wild pitch, past Martinez, sending Sizemore home with the tying run; even as his pitcher hits Martinez with a pitch and walks Garko. *Now* he comes out? And he leaves Joba in there? Does he not want to win this game?

I am trying to stay calm, but the Indians fans are going wild now that they have evened the score and reduced Joba to a head case. The inning ends with a strikeout of Peralta, but the damage is done.

The bugs are still out there when the Indians take the field for the top of the ninth, but there are fewer out there. I am sure there are people who will say that is bullshit, that I am a typical whining Yankee fan, that the bugs were equally disruptive to both teams. That is not true. Never mind what you saw on television.

It was worse for the Yankees. I was there.

Having said that, there is still a game to be played, and the Yankees have Carmona at 96 pitches. He should be vulnerable. Damon grounds out. Jeter strikes out. Abreu beats out an infield single, and there is hope. But A-Rod works the count full and then strikes out. He is having another abysmal postseason so far, but he is far from the only one. Jeter and Posada have been AWOL.

Here is Mo for the bottom of the ninth. Instead of appearing in a save situation, he is trying to preserve the tie score. He retires Lofton, Gutierrez, and Blake in order.

Perez relieves Carmona in the top of the 10th and makes the Yankees look feeble, just like he did last night.

Mo is back for the bottom of the 10th. The Jake is pure bedlam, with fans on their feet screaming with every pitch. Mo loads the bases and gives me a heart attack, but he escapes with nobody scoring.

In the top of the 11th, Perez gets three up, three down.

I grab Michael's hand for the bottom of the 11th. Vizcaino is on the mound, and Shelley has taken over at first. Viz walks Lofton on four pitches. He gives up a single to Gutierrez. Blake hits a swinging bunt, and the runners move up. Sardinha replaces Damon in left field in the middle of the inning—huh?—and Sizemore is intentionally walked to load the bases with one out. Cabrera pops out. Hafner steps in. He is a big, corn-fed North Dakotan who looks like he wants to rip the shit out of every pitch. He works the count to 3-and-2. A root canal would be more fun than this. As Jorge goes out to talk to Viz, I take off my Yankees visor, clutch it to my heart, and close my eyes. I visualize the following: The Yankees escape danger in this inning, score 20 runs in the next one, retire the Indians in order in their half, and pile on top of each other in celebration of their dramatic victory.

My visualizing doesn't work. Hafner singles home Lofton for the 2–1 win. I sit there stunned.

Eventually, we get up to avoid all the celebrating and are taunted by Indians fans as we make our way to the exit.

"Yankees suck!" yells a tub of guts in a Lofton jersey.

"SHUT YOUR FUCKING RALLY PIE HOLE!" I yell back.

In the peace and quiet of our parlor suite, Michael watches the Red Sox beat the Angels in the bottom of the ninth on Manny's homer.

I don't watch. I pack. Tomorrow we are flying back to New York, where we will turn things around. Let's go, Yankees.

Saturday is our travel day. We check out of the Renaissance and head to the airport for our 12:30 flight to Newark. There are other Yankee fans at the gate. We are all subdued but united in our determination to get back in this series and win it.

As I board the plane and pass through first class, I recognize Dusty Baker.

"That was Dusty Baker," I whisper to Michael as we are inching toward the rear of the plane. "He must be covering the series for ESPN." I love that I am still seeing members of the traveling carnival. I wonder how I will survive when I am home in Santa Barbara and don't run into baseball people every day. Not that there is a shortage of celebrities in town, but they are all boring movie stars.

During the flight I replay last night's game in my head. God knows New York has billions of cockroaches, and our cockroaches could destroy their stupid midges any day.

We land at Newark about 2:30. Dusty Baker is standing at the baggage-claim carousel with his ESPN colleague Jon Miller, whom I have always admired. I remember how intimidated I was by Michael Kay and Al Leiter at the baggage claim in Toronto nearly 3 months ago. This time I walk right over to Jon and Dusty, introduce myself, and say I am writing a book about being a Yankee fan.

We discuss the hottest topic in America: Lake Erie midges.

"Curtis Granderson, the Tigers centerfielder, was in the booth with us last night," Jon says. "He told us the bugs are called Canadian soldiers in Detroit. He also told us that bug spray makes the situation worse because it causes the bugs to stick to the skin. The Indians' trainer knew that, but the Yankees' trainer didn't."

"Joe should have tried to stop the game," I say.

"The umpires would never have allowed a delay," says Dusty, who goes looking for his bags.

"Tell me more about your book," Jon asks me.

"It all started in May with a piece in the *New York Times* about divorcing the Yankees."

"Oh, the divorce article!" He laughs. "I remember it. It was great!"

"Thanks so much." Jon Miller is a Hall of Fame broadcaster. I am very flattered.

After a long cab ride into Manhattan, we check into the good old Marmara, only to learn that there is even more construction going on.

"Is there a quiet room?" I say to the woman at the front desk.

"I give you number five-oh-four," she says in her vague foreign accent. "It's all I have left. We're sold out."

Number 504 has to be the smallest, noisiest unit in the building, but we are happy to be back.

ALDS: Game Three
October 7, 2007

In that second game, Andy Pettitte went out there like William Wallace from Braveheart. The script was written just how we wanted it. We had the guys we wanted in the situations we wanted. It just didn't work out. Were the bugs annoying? Yes. Was it miserable out there? Yes. Did they make us lose the game? No. You have to play through adversity, especially on the road.

I wake up in a cold sweat on Sunday. I had a nightmare about tonight's game—that Clemens got shelled and A-Rod went 0-for-4 and Giambi committed seven errors at first—a record that Jon Miller of ESPN said would "stand for all eternity."

I put on my Yankees clothes for the game. I want to wear them all day, to infuse myself with Yankee-ness.

I run out and buy the *New York Times* so I can see my article in the sports section. Whoever comes up with the illustrations for my pieces is very clever, and the one that accompanies today's piece—an engagement ring with an interlocking N-Y on it—is great.

While I am at the newsstand, I notice a headline about George Steinbrenner. George gave a telephone interview to the *Record* in Hackensack, New Jersey, saying that Joe Torre will no longer be the manager if the Yankees lose to the Indians.

Yikes. His timing could not be worse. What is wrong with this guy? But he has threatened to fire Joe before, and Joe is still here.

The weather today is summery but not quite as warm as yesterday—in the 70s. I take a brisk walk around the Upper East Side and try not to dwell on the obvious: This may be the last time I am here to watch the Yankees in 2007. I am positive we will win tonight, despite that stupid dream, but I have made contingency arrangements just in case. Charlie at Santa Barbara Travel Bureau has us booked on two different flights: to Cleveland if the Yankees force a game five and to Los Angeles if the Indians prevail. I get chest pains even contemplating the latter.

I come upon another beautiful church, this one right in the neighborhood of the Mamara on East 88th Street. It is the Church of the Holy Trinity, an old Episcopal church with more than a dozen stained glass windows. A sign outside its open doors beckons me: "Enter. Rest. Pray."

I go in, sit down, and get straight to the point.

"Okay, God. I know there are much more important things on your plate. But here's the situation: It's do-or-die for the Yankees, and they have their backs against the wall, and there will be no tomorrow if they don't win tonight, if you'll pardon all the sports clichés. I am begging you: *Please don't let them get swept.* See you later at the Stadium. Amen."

I feel better.

I take on a little swagger and strut down Lexington Avenue, like John Travolta in *Saturday Night Fever.* "Stayin' Alive" is the perfect soundtrack for how I am feeling. I get high-fives and fist-bumps and "Let's go Yankees!" chants from other fans as I walk. It is a beautiful thing until I pass a Red Sox fan.

"Yankees suck!" he shouts at me.

"No, you suck!" I shout back and keep walking.

Our seats are in the MVP Tier, which is a little closer to the action than where we usually sit. We are in section 9, box 619, row C—just to the first-base side of home plate.

I sit back and soak up the scene. Yankee Stadium is dressed to the nines and has never looked so gorgeous to me. The ALDS logo is stenciled on the green grass. The red, white, and blue buntings drape the railings. The fans are wearing their pinstripes. It is all too much.

"This isn't necessarily good-bye," Michael insists when he notices my expression.

"I know." I spot John Sterling in the WCBS booth.

The scoreboard has one lonely score on it: Boston is up 9–0 over the Angels. We are not getting swept like the pathetic Halos.

The Indians are announced and take their places along the third-base line. Bob Sheppard is not at the microphone because of the bronchial infection that sidelined him at the end of the regular season. I refuse to view that as a bad omen, sign, or portent.

The Yankees are announced, and the place goes wild. There are 56,000 people screaming their lungs out for each and every player, with the loudest cheers going for Joe. Everybody has heard by now what George said in the *Record,* and we are showing how much we respect our manager. A-Rod, too, gets a huge ovation. We are thanking him for helping us reach this night, not blaming him for past failures. By the time the last name is called, we are all on our feet.

The color guard marches out. A choir from West Point sings the national anthem while the flag is unfurled. Two Hornet fighter jets zoom over the Stadium. Tino throws out the first pitch. Mattingly and Eric Wedge shake hands at home plate and exchange the lineup cards with the umpires. It is all going too fast. I wish this game, this experience, this trip could last a lifetime.

I talk to the fan next to me. He is a big, tall, red-faced man who tells me he works nights for Con Ed but has called in sick to be here. He is a sweet guy, and I want us to win for his sake as well as my own.

Clemens versus Westbrook.

Over in left field hangs a sign that says "Exterminate Cleveland." Another one says "Do It for Joe."

"Let's go Yankees!" we all chant after Clemens throws strike one to Sizemore, who eventually grounds out. Cabrera reaches on Jeter's throwing error, which is soon reversed and called a hit.

"Jeter usually makes that play," says the Con Ed guy.

"He'll be okay," I say. It is way too early for concern.

But Hafner walks, moving Cabrera to second. And Garko singles Cabrera home for the first run of the game. And it is a final in Anaheim: Boston has swept the Angels.

In the bottom of the first, Damon singles and we clap until our hands are raw. Jeter hits into a double play and we are quiet.

"Jeter usually drives 'em in," says the Con Ed guy.

"He'll be okay!"

Abreu grounds out to end the inning.

Nixon homers in the top of the second for 2–0. Clemens is up to 47 pitches.

In the bottom of the second, A-Rod singles.

"His swing is back," says Michael.

"You bet." I am the little cheerleader in our group.

Jorge, who is batting behind A-Rod tonight, hits into a double play, and Giambi grounds out. It is very quiet again.

There is medical drama in the top of the third. Clemens, who has not pitched since September 16, is up 0-and-2 on Hafner when Joe and Gene Monahan trot out to the mound. They have a conference, but Clemens stays in the game and goes to 2-and-2 on Hafner.

"Throw a strike, Grandpa!" yells the huge pimply kid behind me.

People are turning on the Rocket. He is not supposed to have blisters or hamstring issues or a fatigued groin. After he walks Hafner and strikes out Martinez, there is another conference on the mound and, to everyone's horror, Clemens comes out of the game. The Con Ed guy calls his wife and asks what they are saying on TV.

"She says it's his left hamstring," he tells me.

"I can't believe this."

"Hughes is taking over," says Michael.

"I thought Joe liked to go with experience," I say. "Mussina is ready."

"Maybe Joe's saving him for tomorrow night," he says.

"There won't be a tomorrow unless we win tonight." I am descending into negativity. "Let's go, Yankees!"

Hughes throws a wild pitch to Garko, moving Hafner to second. Peralta doubles to right, scoring Hafner. 3–0.

"Bring in Pavano!" the pimply kid yells.

"How about Contreras?" shouts his friend.

"Hire Girardi already!" howls a guy way back in our section.

That one hurts the most.

I stand and clap for my team in rhythmic beats. "Let's go, Yankees!"

It is the bottom of the third. Matsui beats out an infield hit. Cano sacrifices him to second. Melky hits a swinging bunt. They throw to third to try and nail Matsui, but he is called safe in a close play. Damon singles Matsui home. 3–1. Everybody is cheering, urging them on. Jeter hits into another double play.

In the bottom of the fifth, Westbrook gives up a single to Matsui, then a double into the left-field corner by Cano, sending Matsui to third. Melky singles, scoring Hideki. 3–2. Eric Wedge visits the mound, but Westbrook stays in the game—and serves up a three-run homer to Damon. 5–3.

We all go insane, standing and clapping and hugging each other. The Con Ed guy practically crushes me, but no matter. We have taken the lead. Damon comes out for a curtain call, and 56,000 fans that used to hate him as a Red Sock pay homage.

Hughes tosses another scoreless inning in the top of the sixth. He is making a believer out of me. The Yankees pad their lead in the bottom of the frame. A-Rod beats out an infield single with great hustle down the line. The Indians gather on the mound, and Westbrook departs for Fultz. Posada singles A-Rod to second. Mientkiewicz lays down a perfect bunt, sacrificing A-Rod to third and Posada to second. Matsui is intentionally walked, loading the bases with one out for Cano, who singles to right. Nixon overruns the ball, which goes all the way to the wall for an error, scoring A-Rod, Posada, and Matsui. 8–3.

We are all delirious now.

Joba comes in for the top of the seventh. He strikes out Sizemore and Cabrera and gets Hafner to fly out on a pitch clocked at 100 mph.

Lewis is the Indians' pitcher for the bottom of the seventh, and he strikes out Jeter, Abreu, and A-Rod. I shake my head, wondering what is up with Jeter, in particular. The Captain is usually so clutch.

Joe brings Joba back for the top of the eighth, and—bugs or no bugs—Chamberlain has not been quite as effective in his second innings of back-to-back work. True to form, he gives up a single to Martinez, a walk to Peralta, a single to Lofton, and a double in the gap in left-center to Nixon. It is 8–4, and the crowd is hushed.

"Bring in Mo!" yells the pimply kid.

Joba gets Blake to fly out. There is a collective sigh of relief.

The Indians call on Borowski, their closer, for the bottom of the eighth. He walks Posada and Matsui, but the Yankees don't score.

As "Enter Sandman" blares over the speakers and Mo trots in, I watch in disgust as people leave. I apologize to Indians fans for blasting them on this subject, because there are Yankee fans who are no better. Yes, there is construction around the Stadium and yes, there is traffic on the Deegan and yes, it is

Sunday night and people have to work tomorrow. But how many times in your life do you get to watch your team in the play-offs?

Here is what those people miss: Mo retires Sizemore on a fly out and strikes out Cabrera and Hafner. It is a brilliant Mariano Rivera performance.

There are plenty of us left, and we stand and salute the Yankees. Melky dances with youthful glee as he high-fives everybody.

We do not get swept. We are not out of this series. We are stayin' alive.

I cannot remember ever being so happy.

ALDS: Game Four
October 8, 2007

When you have six different reporters coming up to you every day and going, "How do you feel about Alex's performance in the play-offs?" it gets irritating. Teams are not gonna let Alex beat them, especially in October.

The big news on Monday is that Joe is starting Wang tonight on 3 days' rest—partly because Wang has pitched well at home and partly because the other choice is Mussina. Hopefully, Wang has figured out what went wrong in game one and will be sharp for game four.

I am antsy sitting around waiting for the 7:30 start, so I take a walk. I need to get to that Holy Trinity church on 88th Street and start praying again.

I approach the church only to find that the gates around it are locked. Can they really be closed? Is it because it is Monday? Is it because it is Columbus Day?

Calm down, I tell myself. You are not that superstitious wacko anymore.

I keep walking. After an hour I go back to 88th Street, just in case the nice folks at Holy Trinity overslept and have only now gotten around to unlocking the gates. Nope. I am not gaining entry.

I call Michael at the Marmara.

"Find me a church!"

He looks for the yellow pages but can't find it.

I go back to the hotel. I close the door to the bedroom of room 504, turn off the lights, and kneel down by the bed. I cast my eyes heavenward and try to ignore the ceiling's popcorn insulation that was big in the '70s.

"Dear God. Please excuse the setting. I know the decor isn't exactly on a par with the Basilica in Baltimore. Thank you for pulling the Yankees through last night. I'm sorry to be such a pest, but could you help them win again tonight? It's a lot to ask, I know. The thing is they were beset by injuries early in the season and they played mediocre baseball, except for A-Rod. But then, after the All-Star break, they showed such heart and determination and courage. That's why they're here. That's why I'm here. Because they fought back so hard. They had faith. Maybe you feel that they and I have been rewarded enough and it's time for all of us to go home. If that's the case, I ask only that you protect me from excessive sadness."

"Are you done in there?" Michael hollers from the other side of the door.

I turn back to God. "Take care and amen."

I get up and let Michael in. We change into our Yankees clothes and head for the subway.

Our seats are the same as last night's—in the MVP Tier just to the first-base side of home plate. There are a few familiar faces but mostly new ones. Something feels off about this section tonight. Instead of the nice Con Ed guy, the man next to me is some power broker who is constantly on his cell phone.

"My friends and I shared a package of season tickets down on the field during the regular season," he tells me between phone calls. "But we got stuck up here in the nosebleed section in the postseason lottery. Sucks, huh?"

I hate this guy. There are types like him all around me tonight: people who act as if they are squeezing the game into their busy schedules. I start a "Let's go, Yankees!" chant and nobody except Michael joins in. We are facing elimination. Where is the energy? The electricity? The attitude? Maybe it's the heat. It is 87 degrees—the hottest October 8 on record for New York City. But that is no excuse.

The national anthem is performed by the Military Academy Band of West Point. No Hornet jets tonight. Just a Bob Sheppard–less announcement of the lineups. Reggie Jackson throws out the first pitch, and there is only a tepid reaction from the crowd. What the hell is going on? The good news is that the people over in left field with the "Exterminate Cleveland" sign are here again. They put up another one that says "Going Back to Cleveland." You bet we are.

"Let's get it started!" the speakers blare as the Yankees take the field.

Wang against Byrd.

Here we go.

Sizemore homers to lead off the top of the first. What the fuck? It is 1–0 just like that. Wang's sinker is not sinking. "Let's go, Yankees!" I cheer, all by myself. Cabrera grounds out. Hafner singles. Martinez hits a nubber that moves Hafner to second. Peralta singles, scoring Hafner. It is 2–0.

Jeter and Abreu hit back-to-back singles in the bottom of the first, but A-Rod strikes out and the crowd groans. They go silent after Posada flies out.

Gutierrez and Blake both single in the top of the second. People boo Wang.

"The kid won 19 games!" I say to the collective group around me. "CUT IT OUT!"

Shoppach gets hit by a pitch. Bases are loaded with nobody out. Joe wastes no time and pulls Wang. It is only the second inning.

"Mussina," says Michael as Moose comes in.

"Let's go, Yankees!"

Sizemore hits into a double play, scoring Gutierrez and allowing Blake to go to third. 3–0. Blake scores on Cabrera's single. 4–0.

This is not happening.

In the bottom of the second, after Matsui walks, a bolt of lightning flashes across the sky.

"First the bugs. Now this," says Michael. "What's next? A flood?"

It does start to rain very lightly, and I bury my head under my jacket for a few minutes until it passes.

Cano singles Matsui to second. Mientkiewicz walks, loading the bases for Damon with one out. The crowd wakes up, remembering Johnny's homer from last night. "Let's go, Yankees!" we scream. Damon fouls out, but Jeter singles, scoring Matsui. 4–1. Abreu flies out with bases loaded, but we are on the board.

Moose has an impressive third after a leadoff walk to Peralta. But the Yankees have a lousy third at the plate. A-Rod strikes out looking, and there is a smattering of boos. Posada doubles off the wall in right center. Neither Matsui nor Cano bring him home.

"This is Paul Byrd, not Johan Santana," I say to Michael.

Shoppach doubles to lead off the top of the fourth. Sizemore tries a bunt that goes foul, then walks. Cabrera bunts both runners over. The Indians are playing small ball against us. They are morphing into the hateful Angels. Hafner is intentionally walked to load the bases with one out. I start a "Let's go, Yankees!" chant. It fizzles quickly. Martinez singles, scoring Shoppach and Sizemore. 6–1.

In the bottom of the fourth, I start crying—spontaneously and without any particular provocation. It is weird. Everyone else is eating and drinking and watching the Dunkin' Donuts Subway Race, but I am despondent. The Yankees are losing, and I want more supportive company. I want us all to bond together and help each other through this shared experience and serve as a psychological buffer against impending defeat. I want us to be a mosh pit of solidarity. Kumbaya. Meanwhile, Melky singles, Mientkiewicz pops out, Damon flies out, and Jeter lines out.

Mussina retires the Indians in order in the top of the fifth. In the bottom of the inning, A-Rod singles, Posada lines to second, and Matsui pops out—and all of them get booed.

In the top of the sixth, Mussina gets two outs and is replaced by Villone, who retires Hafner to end the inning.

Cano homers in the bottom of the sixth. 6–2. That is it for Byrd. Perez is the new pitcher, and he has been killing us. Shelley, batting for Mientkiewicz, singles. Damon singles him to third.

We are coming back. Look out, Tribe.

Everybody is standing and cheering now. With Jeter coming up, this is where we turn things around.

Jeter hits into a double play. We all slump back down into our seats, stunned and deflated—except the cell phone guy next to me, who gets up.

"This crap isn't worth watching. See ya."

"Don't let the turnstiles hit you on the way out!"

Farnsworth is on the mound for the top of the seventh and is booed before he throws a pitch. He allows a single to Peralta but gets out of the inning and departs to cheers—New York in a nutshell.

After "God Bless America" comes "Take Me Out to the Ball Game." Hardly anybody sings along.

Abreu strikes out in the bottom of the seventh. And then A-Rod homers.

Finally. 6–3. Is it too late? Maybe not. Matsui walks, and the crowd gets into it. We are all chanting, "Let's go, Yankees!" It feels more like a plea than a rallying cry. Cano steps in to "Rob-bie! Rob-bie!" but he grounds out, and everybody goes silent again.

Veras is in for the top of the eighth. People are leaving in droves. I resent all these fuckers. Blake strikes out. Shoppach doubles off the wall in center. Joe comes out to talk to Veras, and the Stadium erupts with chants of "Joe-Torre! Joe-Torre!" It is unbearably sad. We are saying good-bye to our manager of the past 12 years, and he acknowledges us with a slight tip of his cap. He leaves Veras in. Sizemore is intentionally walked. Now Joe comes back out to replace Veras with Mo, who retires the two batters he faces.

Betancourt sets down the Yankees in order in the bottom of the eighth, two of them on strikeouts.

By the top of the ninth, almost everyone in our section has left.

"At least we don't have any heads blocking our view," Michael says. He has been eying me warily.

Mo is back out there, maybe for the last time if he makes good on his stated intention to test free agency. Well, you can say the same for A-Rod, Abreu, Posada, and so on. Maybe this is the last time we will see any of them in pinstripes.

Martinez singles. So does Peralta.

You can hear every word and whistle now that the crowd is so sparse. Lofton hits into a fielder's choice and goes to second on defensive indifference. Gutierrez strikes out, and Blake hits a long fly to Damon.

Bottom of the ninth. Down by three runs. We have come back from bigger deficits—like that Friday-night game in Boston last month. "Let's go, Yankees!" I chant, and my voice reverberates back at me in the now-cavernous Stadium.

Borowski is pitching. The scoreboard is encouraging people to "make some noise," but they do not. Jeter pops out. Abreu hits a majestic homer into the upper deck in right field to pull the Yankees to 6–4. What is left of the crowd comes alive as A-Rod steps in. He flies out. We are down to Posada. I want to yell, "Hip hip, Jor-hay!" but my throat has closed up. He strikes out. Game over. Series over. Season over.

I sit in my seat for a very long time. Everybody else is going or has already gone. The Stadium is creepy when it is empty like this, but I cannot leave. I am doubled over with spasms of crying. I know it is physically impossible to "sob your guts out," but I am crying so hard that it feels like it. I would say I was creating a spectacle except that there is no one but Michael to see me.

Not only is the season over, with the likelihood of an off-season filled with departures, but so is my trip. I have spent months watching the Yankees. It is the specter of missing them that is killing me. It is my love for them and now the loss of them that is making me convulse with weeping. I cannot say good-bye.

I never got to say good-bye to my father. Since I was only 6 when he died, my mother wanted to shield me from the harsh reality of his funeral. I was left to wonder why he had disappeared and when he was coming back. Before he got sick, he used to stop on his way home from work once a week and buy me a pint of Breyers vanilla ice cream—the kind with the little dark specks of vanilla beans in it. Where was he? And where was my Breyers? No matter how many afternoons I sat in the window seat near the front door, watching and waiting, he never showed. My mother withdrew into her own grief, rarely leaving the house. I had lost both my parents.

Michael lifts my arm by the elbow. "Let's go. It's time."

"Not yet!" Poor Michael. He should get combat pay for having to put up with me. "I have to feel this, to watch this."

I watch Paul O'Neill and Michael Kay doing their final stand-up in front of the YES camera; John Sterling and Suzyn Waldman wrapping up their last WCBS broadcast; the groundskeepers laying a cover over the pitcher's mound.

I bury my head in my hands and sob and sob and sob. I am a mess.

"Are you okay?" asks a woman my age in a Yankees visor.

"This is so embarrassing." I wave her away. My eyes are swollen into little slits, and I can hardly see out of them.

"I know, I know," she says, touching my knee with great tenderness.

I gaze at her, study her. She is not an angel. Just another She-Fan.

"There is nothing worse than baseball gone bad," she murmurs. "Nothing."

I nod.

She goes off into the night.

Michael cradles me in his arms. "Ready now?"

"Ready."

What was so gut-wrenching is that we felt like if we got to the play-offs, we would win the whole thing. There wasn't a doubt in anyone's mind. We were such a prepared group. Was Wanger a good matchup for that team? No. But you go with your best, and he was our best. There's nothing I would change. Sometimes you just have to tip your cap.

"Hello?" I say to the kitchen on Tuesday night. It is as if I am invading the space of a perfect stranger. Do I really live here? It is so quiet in this house.

"It's 1 o'clock in the morning," says Michael, as he wheels in the last of our suitcases. "Let's just go to bed."

"I need to unpack first." We have been on the go since early this morning. I am beyond exhausted, and my face is puffy from all the crying. Mo told the media after last night's game that we have to accept loss, just like he told Jen Royle she had to accept it, but I am still grieving.

"You can unpack tomorrow," Michael urges.

I shake my head. "You go on to bed."

Maybe when the clothes are in the hamper and the bags are put away, I will be able to let go. Or at least start to.

I'm sick to my stomach that we're done. That's the hard part of baseball in general, whether you win the World Series or you don't make it to the play-offs. You're with each other for 250 straight days, and then all of a sudden it's good-bye.

I wake up on Wednesday thinking I am at the Marmara and crash into a wall on my way to the bathroom. I am suffering from Hotel Disorientation Syndrome again, only in my own house.

Out of habit, I rush to the computer to read recaps of last night's game. There *is* no last night's game.

Still, there is plenty of activity in Yankeeville. The beat writers are speculating about Joe's future. Will he sign a new contract? Or will he be replaced by

Mattingly? Girardi? Tony La Russa? Bobby Valentine? Rumors are also rampant about A-Rod. Will he stay in New York or opt out? And if he opts out, will he sign with the Angels? Cubs? Dodgers? I don't want anybody going anywhere.

I start crying again after I check e-mail. There is one from a person called Tribe Fan who says, "Ha ha. You obnoxious Yankee fans got what you deserved."

Most of the day is about reentry. I do laundry and grocery shopping. I relearn the TV channel lineup. I call friends and make dates for dinner. I would rather talk about the Yankees than about which local restaurant changed chefs while I was away, but I am making the effort. It is not as if I have been sent back to some hellhole, after all. I live in paradise. I need to remind myself of that.

There were some years when I couldn't wait to go home after the season, because I played like shit. But I never thought about home this year. I just wanted to be with my guys.

There is some news regarding the Torre Watch on Thursday. The Yankees "brain trust" will meet in Tampa next week to discuss whether to keep him or dump him. The Boss's sons, Hank and Hal, appear to be running the show, but it is hard to tell. Some of the writers are reporting that Joe may be invited to the Tampa meetings. Others say Mattingly is the front-runner to replace Joe. I hardly notice that the Rockies beat the Diamondbacks in game one of their series.

I go on Amazon and order the DVD collection of *Sex and the City: Season Two* so I can see the episode where Carrie dates a Yankee after moping around wishing she could get over Mr. Big.

I am moping around wishing I could get over baseball. I will tell you how much I miss it. When I sit down tonight to watch *Grey's Anatomy,* I cheer, "Let's go, Yankees!"

Joe grabbed me and hugged me and said something I'll never forget: "You're a true professional. You forced yourself into the lineup, and you kept yourself in it. You handled the situation with class, and I'm very proud of you." To hear that from a guy who was one hell of a player and an even better manager meant the world to me.

My goal on Friday is to perk up. I go to the Bellezza Vita salon in Summerland to see Bruce, who does my color. After I sit down in his chair and he drapes a smock over me, he says, "Are you sick of baseball after going to all those games?"

I explain that I could never be sick of going to games any more than a lover of music could be sick of going to concerts.

"What about divorcing the Yankees?" he asks. "Is that still on?"

"I'm thinking of moving back to New York so I can be closer to them."

He laughs. I am just another eccentric client.

At home I turn on the TV. The Rockies have beaten the Diamondbacks again, and the Red Sox have destroyed Sabathia and the Indians in game one of their series. I feel a pang of regret, but it is only a pang.

To me, Joe Torre should be Manager of the Year. I know where we were mentally and physically in the first half. We weren't feeling very good about ourselves. Joe righted the ship. The guy exudes confidence and calm.

In Saturday's papers, Joe is getting an outpouring of support—players, other managers, fans, celebrities. But it is looking like the Steinbrenner boys are ready for a change. Otherwise, why not just offer him a new contract already?

Tonight Michael and I watch game two of Red Sox–Indians. It is mildly diverting. I am not invested in either team's success; I hate them both equally.

The score is 6–6 when we switch over to the movie we rented. When it is over, we switch back. Boston loses in the 11th inning after Gagne gives up an RBI single to Trot Nixon. I hate the Red Sox more.

Do I think the Red Sox are the new Yankees? No. They won one championship in 89 years. How do you compare that to 26?

I think I am getting on with my life, but I wake up crying on Sunday. I dreamed I was trying to swipe my MetroCard into the little slot at the 86th Street subway station and the turnstile wouldn't budge. I was being kept out, just like the Yankees were keeping me out during the trip. I actually hear myself saying, "Please let me in!"

"Let you in where?" Michael asks as he nudges me awake.

I explain about the dream. He shakes his head and goes to eat Rice Krispies.

This afternoon I grab my iPod and take a 5-mile walk along the beach, hoping the salt air will snap me out of my funk. I gaze at the ocean to my left and at the mountains to my right. I am lucky to be living in one of the most magnificent spots in the country. I am lucky to be supporting myself as a writer. I am lucky to be sharing this journey with a husband who loves me. It really is time to cut the crap and get on with things.

Week 29
October 15, 2007

We beat the Red Sox so many times this year. And when we didn't, early in the season, it was only because we had kids from Double A ball pitching for us.

On Monday I drive to Los Angeles for a meeting about a movie project. During the ride back, I listen to game three of Red Sox–Indians on the radio. The Indians win 4–2.

Colorado clinches the NL pennant by sweeping the Diamondbacks. Are the Rockies really that good, or is the National League just incredibly lame?

Technically, I'm a Yankee until the end of the World Series. But who knows if I'll be coming back? I hope I do. I just want a chance to earn my job. That's all a player can ask for.

On Tuesday I print out all my notes from the trip and start to figure out what structure and shape the book will take. I am having a productive work session when my cell phone rings.

"Hello?"

"Is this Jane?" asks a male voice.

"Yes."

"Doug Mientkiewicz."

I do not scream into the phone like those people who win the grand prize from Publishers Clearing House. I do not even utter a tiny gasp. I just smile. God—and Gene Orza—came through after all.

"Do you remember the magic beer at the Ritz in Boston?" I ask Doug. "You started playing regularly after that night."

He laughs. "I was thinking I should get you tickets for every game because you were my lucky charm."

Tickets for every game. Timing is everything in life.

"Would you be willing to give me some time for my book?"

"I'm pretty open, sure. I'm just home trying to recover from the season."

"Me, too."

He gives me his phone number, and we make a plan for me to call him tomorrow morning at 8:00.

I go running into Michael's office.

"My prayer was answered!"

"Which prayer are we talking about?" His head is buried in a box full of photographs.

"Doug Mientkiewicz just called!"

He looks up. "Really?"

"We're doing the interview tomorrow!"

He gets up and gives me a hug. "You got your Yankee."

Later, we watch the Indians beat the Red Sox 7–3 to go up three games to one. We wave white paper towels and yell, "It's Tribe Time now!"

I was very nostalgic with myself all year. I'd be driving to the park every day and look up and see Yankee Stadium and think: It doesn't get any better than this.

I call Mientkiewicz at 8:00 on Wednesday morning and get his voice mail. Did he forget me? I leave a message reminding him about our interview and give him my phone number.

I eat breakfast and read the newspapers. There is a rumor that Joe will be given a 1-year deal so he can pass the torch to Mattingly when the new stadium opens in 2009. There is another rumor that he will be asked to take a pay cut. There is a third that he will be kicked upstairs and offered a position in the front office. I am contemplating all this when the phone rings.

I leap off the kitchen stool and race into my office.

"Hello?"

It is not my Yankee. It is my plumber. He says he has the part for the bathroom faucet.

On my way back into the kitchen the phone rings again. This time it is Doug.

We end up talking for hours and on more than one occasion about everything from the values instilled in him by his father and his friendship with A-Rod to his years with the Twins, Red Sox, Mets, and Royals before joining the Yankees. John Sterling was right about him: He is smart and charming. He is also honest and straightforward and passionate. A-Rod may be the fantasy league Yankee, but his high school buddy is the real deal. I had promised my publisher I could reel in a big league ballplayer, and that is exactly what Doug Mientkiewicz is.

You're telling Joe that because you put a dollar value on the World Series he's gonna manage the games that much better? He knows the expectations. He knows what it means to put the jersey on. He gets it that if you don't win the last game you play in October, it's a failure.

—DOUG MIENTKIEWICZ

On Thursday there is breaking news out of Tampa. The Yankees offered Joe a 1-year contract for $5 million, with million-dollar incentives if the team makes the ALDS, the ALCS, and the World Series. Joe flew down to Florida with Cashman this morning to discuss the offer with the brain trust—and turned it down. He is out. After 12 postseasons in 12 years, he is no longer the Yankees manager. I am freaking, even though I knew this day would come, even though I have been a naysayer now and then, even though I have allowed the words "Maybe it's time for a change" to pass my lips. Joe has been a rock, a father figure, a winner. Who will replace him? And how will his departure affect the signings of Mo, Jorge, A-Rod, and Pettitte?

Jason Zillo organizes a conference call so that the Yankees can explain the situation to the beat writers. Peter Abraham posts the audio on his blog, and I am glued. Randy Levine does most of the talking, going through the details of the offer Joe left on the table. And then he, Cashman, and the Steinbrenner boys answer questions from Peter, Mark, Tyler, Sweeny, George, Kat, and the rest of the traveling carnival.

There is an e-mail from Tom Jolly at the *Times*. Apparently, the sports section has been inundated with reactions to Joe leaving. They are planning to run a full page of reflections about him, and Tom asks if I would like to contribute. I write a short piece about how bad I am at good-byes and how much I will miss Torre.

Michael and I watch Red Sox–Indians. Beckett pitches a gem, damn him, and the Sox win decisively.

"All I can think about is the Yankees," I tell Michael after the game. "I was coming out of it, but now there's so much uncertainty."

I watched Joe's press conference. I know he said he regretted not pulling us off the field in game two because of the bugs, but you can second-guess every person who ever managed a postseason game. Who's to say they would have allowed him to pull us off the field? It was just one of those unfortunate things that happen.

—DM

On Friday Joe holds a press conference at the Hilton Rye Town in Westchester, and Tom Goodman, my new friend from Spuntini in Toronto and George Brett's in Kansas City, handles the PR for the event.

I watch live coverage on ESPN. I choke up as I remember Joe's stoic look in the dugout throughout the years, all those walks to the mound, all his postgame musings. He has been the face of the Yankees—a classy face.

He says he found the 1-year aspect of the deal insulting. He was not too crazy about the incentives part, either. He answers question after question. I know how much the beat writers appreciated his accessibility. This is a sad day for them, too.

Later, Cashman reveals that the brain trust has already reached out to three candidates for the managerial job: Mattingly, Girardi, and Tony Pena. All three will fly to Tampa next week for their interviews.

Joe's body is not even cold and they are picking out his successor. On the other hand, the clock is ticking on A-Rod. Cashman repeated that the Yankees will not negotiate with him if he decides to opt out of his contract, and the opt-out date is approaching. Will hiring Mattingly increase the likelihood that A-Rod will stay in New York? What about Girardi and Pena? Or does Scott Boras simply want to sell his client to the highest bidder?

———————————————————

Look, no matter who the manager is, there's still gonna be 55,000 people ready to scream their brains out next year because they're Yankee fans.

—DM

On Saturday Scott Boras tells SI.com that A-Rod is not likely to sign with the Yankees by the deadline if the organization is in disarray. He says Alex can't possibly make a long-term commitment before knowing who the manager is going to be, not to mention whether Mo, Posada, Pettitte, and Abreu are coming back.

Michael and I turn on the TV to watch Red Sox–Indians. J. D. Drew hits a grand slam in the first inning. We turn off the TV.

———————————————————

Joe will be a tough act to follow, no doubt about it. But this is the Yankees, not Joe Blow's Trucking and Bowling Team, and Yankee fans are the most loyal fans on this earth. It takes them time to fall in love with the new guys. But when the new guys do the job, the fans love them, too.

—DM

On Sunday my "reflection" about Joe runs in the *Times*. Several of the other fans who contributed to the page say they are ashamed to be Yankee fans after the way the organization handled his dismissal.

The *Post* has an exclusive interview with Hank Steinbrenner, who calls Joe an ingrate for terming the contract offer an insult.

The *Daily News* takes a shot at Randy Levine for being the architect of Joe's departure.

It is getting ugly in Yankeeville.

Michael and I watch Red Sox–Indians. Boston wins 11–2.

Week 30
October 22, 2007

Girardi did a hell of a job when he played here, and he'd make a great manager. But you can't compare the Marlins and Yankees because they're totally different animals. With the Marlins he had 25 guys who'd never been in the big leagues before. With the Yankees you're talking about 25 guys who are weathered and battle tested.

—DM

On Monday, Joe Girardi is the first managerial candidate to be interviewed in Tampa. Mattingly will go tomorrow and Pena on Wednesday.

Peter Abraham's blog has the audio of Girardi's conference call with the beat writers. Joe talks about how much he learned from managing the Marlins and how much he wants the Yankees to win another championship. He sounds very professional and polished, but I am unmoved.

I think Donnie's ready to manage. But he's probably the most well renowned Yankee in history. He's definitely the most respected. If he comes back to manage the team and we have a bad season, does that tarnish his image?

—DM

Tuesday is Mattingly's turn to meet with the Yankees in Tampa. Afterward, he has his conference call with the beat writers. He sounds very sincere about wanting to win a championship, but he is not as articulate as Girardi. I miss Joe Torre.

I don't think Pena has a prayer in hell. I know what Tony did with Kansas City, which was arguably the biggest miracle outside of Noah's Ark. But I think it's Major League Baseball telling the Yankees they have to interview minorities.

—DM

On Wednesday I am feeling overwhelmed and conflicted by the "Who Wants to Be a Manager" reality show. Which of the three candidates is the best one to replace Joe Torre? *Can* any of them replace Joe? What will happen to my Yankees?

I call John Sterling to see how he is feeling about it all. As usual, he is cheerful and upbeat.

"Were you surprised the way things turned out with Joe?" I ask.

"I always held out hope that he would be rehired," John says.

"Have you talked to him?"

"Oh, sure. We've been friends for 25 years. We'll always be friends."

"Do you think the interviews with Girardi and Pena were just a formality and they'll give Mattingly the job?"

"You could put Larry Bowa in there. They'd all be excellent managers. But if I were the Yankees, the wrong reason to hire Mattingly would be because he's so popular. He's the most popular athlete I have ever seen in New York."

"Come on."

"You're thinking about Willis Reed or Joe Namath?"

"How about Mickey Mantle?"

"Mickey Mantle got booed. Mattingly never got booed. Never. And he gets the most applause at Old-Timers' Day."

"Why do you think that is?"

"It's something people see in him. And if they knew him, they would really applaud. He is much tougher and much baseball-brighter than people would ever think. He could give you the scouting report on every hitter and pitcher in the American League. And the players adore and respect him. He is absolutely the right choice for the Yankees in every way, shape, or form. It doesn't mean Pena or Girardi or Bowa would not be good managers. But there's only one Don Mattingly."

"What do you think will happen with A-Rod?"

"Scott Boras might be as full of crap as any human being in history. I have no idea how much the Yankees are going to offer for how many years. It's Monopoly money, Jane. If Alex doesn't want to be the Yankees' star at $30 million a year for 7 years, then let him go somewhere else. I really like Alex. He's a nice guy. But I support the Yankees 100 percent if what Boras wants is a landmark thing for Boras."

"What about Posada?"

"I think he and Mariano and Pettitte will come back. But don't forget: I'm a very optimistic human being."

"What do you make of the Steinbrenner sons?"

"Hank and Hal have very bright minds. And they have something else going for them: the brand name. How could they miss? Someone asked me the other night, 'Should the Yankees start all over?' *Start all over?* Are you kidding me? With the influx of Hughes and Chamberlain and Ian Kennedy? This might be the beginning of a great period in Yankee history."

Later, I listen to audio of Pena's conference call with the beat writers. Tony seems like a terrific guy, and I hope he stays with the Yankees—as a coach. I was leaning toward Girardi as the new manager, but after talking to John, I am rooting for Mattingly. Or not. I am still not sure.

The Red Sox destroy the Rockies in game one of the World Series.

The Yankees need to keep Larry Bowa. He was the backbone of our infield and of our young guys. He used to bury me on a nightly basis when he was on **Baseball Tonight** *and I played for the Mets. But once I started playing for him, he backed me more than anybody else.*

—DM

On Thursday Hank Steinbrenner, who is quickly emerging as the Yankees spokesman, tells the media he is impressed with all three candidates but will let Cashman and the "baseball operations people" make their recommendation before moving forward.

Does this mean they are barred from making their selection public because of the World Series? And will this whole process drag on, the way the discussion over Joe Torre's contract dragged on?

There is speculation that Grady Little is getting canned by the Dodgers and that Girardi is their first choice to replace him. More intrigue.

There is no intrigue whatsoever in game two of the World Series. Boston beats the Rockies 2–1.

The Yankees have so much more to worry about than if they're bringing me back. Like this morning, Alex said, "So have they called you?" I said, "Al. Seriously. I am piece number 179 in this equation."

—DM

There is still no word on Friday about the new Yankees manager, even though this is a World Series off day.

The only Yankees news is that they plan to pick up the option on Abreu and to give Shelley more playing time, possibly at first base.

First base? Does this mean they are not bringing back Mientkiewicz?

It doesn't take a rocket scientist to figure out that Alex doesn't need the money. But what's surprising is that he doesn't live that lavishly, he really doesn't. He's very, very conservative.

—DM

On Saturday George King's article in today's *Post* predicts that Girardi will be the Yankees' new manager. He says Girardi was Cashman's early pick and that Hank wants a "strong leader, not a father figure."

Later, there are reports that terms for a contract extension for A-Rod are being discussed in Tampa and that the figure being thrown around is about $30 million a year.

Michael and I watch the Red Sox beat the Rockies 10–5 in game three. Shitty baseball is better than no baseball.

The Yankees say they won't negotiate with Alex if he opts out, but what else are they gonna say? "We'll give you every penny you want?" That's the game

*you play. Come December, when he hasn't signed yet and they're looking
around at what they have? Show me your bluff then.*

—DM

George King's story in Sunday's *Post* claims that the Yankees are not prepared
to offer A-Rod the $30 million a year Boras is seeking. He says their offer
will be in the $27 million range. It is clear they want him to stay, but not if he
opts out, because they will lose the subsidy they got from the Rangers. The
Steinbrenner brothers want A-Rod to come in and talk to them, face-to-face,
before the actual negotiations with Boras get under way. They have left phone
messages for him, and he has not returned their calls.

Tonight Michael and I watch game four of the World Series. I am sick of
those happy-go-lucky, feel-good Red Sox—especially when they jump out to
an early lead over the pathetic Rockies. I am about to turn off the TV when
Ken Rosenthal, a Fox reporter, breaks in with a bulletin: A-Rod is opting out of
his contract with the Yankees.

I look at Michael. "What the hell is this?"

He is equally shocked. "I guess he doesn't want to be a Yankee anymore."

"We're not good enough for him?"

"He and Boras are giving baseball the finger by making the announcement
in the middle of the World Series."

We turn up the volume on the TV. In a statement, Boras referred to Hank
Steinbrenner's use of the word *transition* to describe the Yankees and said Alex
was concerned about where the franchise is headed.

"Then why didn't he go sit across the table from Hank and Hal and ask
them?" I am standing now and yelling at the TV. How dare A-Rod leave us—
and at the very moment when our archrivals are winning their second championship in 4 years!

"He made himself bigger than the World Series, bigger than Major League
Baseball," says Michael. "His reputation will take a huge hit."

I am not paying much attention as the Red Sox finish off the Rockies 4–3.
I could care less. I rush to the computer to read everything I can about the
A-Rod opt-out. Boras says he tried to reach Cashman by phone to inform him
of A-Rod's decision but was unsuccessful, so he left a voice-mail message as well
as an e-mail and a fax. How lame is that? There was plenty of time to wait for

a callback before crashing baseball's biggest night of the year and letting the Yankees hear the news along with everyone else. The nerve of these two!

I stagger out of my office and go watch *Desperate Housewives*. I am feeling pretty desperate myself. Never mind A-Rod's PR gaffe. Never mind that he blew off the Yankees and their fans. Who can we get to replace him at third base next year—someone who will hit over 50 home runs and more than 150 RBIs? Where will the run production come from? Will we sign Mike Lowell? Will A-Rod become a Red Sock?

Week 31
October 30, 2007

Maybe the franchise is in a little bit of disarray right now, but I told Al, "You can leave. Jorge can leave. Mo can leave. And they could give the manager's job to the guy on the subway. But they're still gonna draw 4½ million people. It's the Yankees, man."

—DM

On Monday Hank Steinbrenner tells the media he is incensed that A-Rod announced to a national television audience that he doesn't want to be a Yankee anymore. He reiterates that both he and his brother invited A-Rod to come to Tampa and meet with them and that Alex never had the courtesy to reply. He stands firm that he will not negotiate with him now that he has opted out.

Lost in all the A-Rod chatter is the big news that the Yankees made a formal offer to Girardi to replace Torre. Once they agree on terms, they will make it official.

And here is another bulletin: The *Post* is reporting that Torre will be the next Dodgers manager. Will Jorge and Mo move west, too? And what about A-Rod? This is all so unsettling.

I go for a beach walk. When I get home, there is more Yankee news. Boras has apologized—to the Red Sox, the Rockies, the fans, baseball—for the timing of his announcement. He says the whole thing was his fault, not his client's, and that he wishes he had handled things better. Ya think?

Later, I check Peter Abraham's blog. He not only confirms that Torre is the Dodgers' new manager but that Mattingly is about to join him as a coach.

I hurry into the living room to tell Michael, but he already knows. He is watching Keith Olbermann's show. At that very moment, Keith is saying, "These are great times for people who hate the Yankees."

The naïve sports fan will look at it like, "Oh, that's Alex being greedy." But he sets the bar for the other players in the big leagues, and it only takes one team to say, "Let's do it." Back in the day when the owners were bitching about salary caps, the two teams that bitched the most were the Texas Rangers and the Colorado Rockies. That summer one team spent $252 million on one guy, and the other team spent $290 million on two guys. That's talking out of both sides of your you-know-what.

—DM

On Tuesday it is official: Girardi has accepted the Yankees' offer and is the team's new manager.

But today's media coverage is all about A-Rod. There are rumors that Boras has a nine-figure deal in place for his client. There is a story that the Mets are A-Rod's possible next stop. And there is reaction to his defection from Johnny Damon, who says he is sad his teammate is leaving and wonders where the runs he produced will come from.

Good question, Johnny.

My anxiety over all this is not helped by the e-mails I am getting from friends here in California. "Are you going to become a Dodger fan now?" they ask.

I would never give my heart to the Dodgers just because Torre and Mattingly will be sitting in the dugout at Chavez Ravine. My love for the Yankees trumps my affection for any one person. If I learned anything over these last few months, it is that.

Mark Feinsand is reporting on his *Daily News* blog that Mo is at Legends Field right now meeting with Cashman, Levine, and the two Little Steins. Mark says the Yankees will offer him a 3-year deal worth $40 million but that he may want to test the market and see what else is out there. Another cliffhanger. And why is there no news about JoPo and his deal? Have they not made him an offer? And how about Pettitte? Is he coming back or retiring?

Peter Abraham's blog has audio of Cashman's conference call with the beat writers about A-Rod's opting out. Cashman says he regrets not having been given the opportunity to meet face-to-face with Alex and talk to him about the team's future but wishes him and C-Rod well.

As Michael and I drive to dinner with friends, I say, "It's sort of odd that Cashman was so laid back about the A-Rod thing."

"Maybe he's a laid-back guy."

"Come on. He always looks like he's on the verge of a nervous collapse."

"What's your point?"

"He might be leaving the door open for A-Rod to reconsider."

"Hank made it clear. If A-Rod doesn't want to be a Yankee, the Yankees don't want him."

"This is the Yankees we're talking about. Anything can happen."

I think the stuff that happened with Joe will weigh heavily on Pettitte's decision to come back. But the fact that he was pain free this year could make him want to play. Personally, I think Ian Kennedy is the wild card. He's more polished than both Hughes and Chamberlain.

—DM

On Wednesday the Yankees announce their coaching staff for 2008. But I want to know what they are planning to do about actual players.

Mo says he wants to remain a Yankee, but there must be an aspect of the deal he doesn't like, or he would have taken it by now.

Pettitte tells a Houston TV station that he won't make the decision about whether or not to retire until November 7.

JoPo is saying nothing.

What's the best thing about being a Yankee? It's hard to put into words. It's everything built into one: the fans, the stadium, the pride. You become a better player just by putting that jersey on.

—DM

Jason Zillo has scheduled a 1 o'clock press conference at Yankee Stadium to officially introduce Joe Girardi to the media. The event feels anticlimactic, since Girardi has done two conference calls with the writers, and everybody already knows he won the job. Moreover, the Dodgers choose today to announce the hiring of Joe Torre as their manager.

I approach the press conference with a blasé attitude and focus on other Yankee matters in the meantime. Mark Feinsand comments on how "sluggish" the organization seems in their effort to keep Posada. The same goes for Mo. What if they both sign with other teams? And how about Bobby Abreu? I thought they were picking up his option, which lapses tomorrow.

Mark also says the Yankees are talking to the White Sox about Joe Crede to fill the vacancy at third base. I do not want Joe Crede playing third base for the Yankees. He may be a stellar human being, but I want A-Rod back. There. I said it. I want those homers and those RBIs. I want that hustle on the base paths. I want that gun-of-an-arm. I even want the odd, needy personality and those overly glossed lips. Besides, he would be too cold in Chicago and too hot in Anaheim, and no one would pay any attention to him in LA because the paparazzi are too busy with Britney Spears. He belongs in New York. Maybe he is the most disingenuous man alive—a "big phony jerk" is what Michael calls him—but I want him on *our* team, not somebody else's. Love is funny. He has thrown my Yankees into the very disarray I was so worried about, and yet I am not ready to let him go.

But Cashman tells the media today that A-Rod is out of the picture. He uses the word *unequivocally*. He says the Yankees made many attempts to reach Alex but did not get a response. When he mentions the possibility of moving Cano to third, I feel the muscles in my neck tense.

He goes on to say that Jeter will not have surgery on his bad knee but Matsui will have surgery on his; that Shelley, Giambi, and Betemit will share time at first base (I will miss you, Doug); and that Joba will be in the starting rotation unless Mo leaves.

Unless Mo leaves?

I am now feeling queasy *and* tense. The Dodgers are practically throwing a parade for Torre on the other side of the country, and Cashman is talking about what remains of my team. What will we do without our old, dependable manager and our old, dependable players?

Someone needs to restore order. George is no longer the Boss, and his sons are only Bosses-in-Training. And judging by his almost daily trips to Tampa, Cashman's power has been eclipsed by the reemergence of the Florida Faction. So who, exactly, will right the ship?

It is nearly 10:00 p.m. by the time I get around to watching the video of Girardi's press conference on the YES Web site. He may be a smart man who had success managing the Marlins, and he is probably a whiz when it comes to stats and matchups and percentages. But he seems to lack gravitas. He has not been around long enough to have the wisdom to handle dramas in the clubhouse. He has not convinced me that he is the right man to lead both the veterans and the young players. He not only needs to restore order but also restore the image of the Yankees.

I lean closer to the computer screen and hit play on the video. Brian Cashman introduces the Girardis and hands Mrs. Girardi a dozen long-stemmed red roses. A blizzard of flashbulbs go off, and Mr. and Mrs. Girardi do their best to stand there and smile while getting blinded by the lights. I see Jason Zillo hovering in the background. I have never met him, of course, but he must be the guy who is directing traffic. I recognize his voice from all those conference calls. He is wearing a dark suit, is not very tall, and looks comfortable telling people what to do. He is good at being the gatekeeper. I am proof of that.

Next, Cashman presents Girardi with his brand-new Yankees jersey. Joe will be wearing number 27 this time out, to symbolize the 27th World Championship he will endeavor to bring to the franchise. He puts the jersey on over his shirt and tie, along with a Yankees cap, and stands for more photographs. And then he steps to the podium to make a statement before taking the media's questions.

"I know you didn't take this many pictures of me when I played," he says with a laugh. "I can't tell you how honored we are to put on this uniform for the third time. This is the place to be. For the Girardis, this feels like home."

Okay. He has a nice folksy manner with his Midwestern vowels—I love how he says "coach," with the elongated "O"—and he seems genuinely thrilled to have gotten the job. But if this is all the emotion he shows, it will be a long season.

"Just on a personal note," he continues, "my father hasn't spoken in a month." He pauses, choking up. "And when the lady who takes care of my father—he has Alzheimer's—showed him the picture of me as the new Yankee manager, my father said, 'Oh, *yeah*.' This means a lot to our family, our whole family."

I am moved. There is more to this man than I realized.

"How surreal of a moment is this for you?" a reporter asks. "You're just getting emotional speaking of your father. So when you think about *I am the Yankees manager* . . ."

"It's something," says Joe. "I got a call from Yogi last night. And you realize the stature of the position when Yogi calls you at your house and says, 'Do I still get to come to spring training?'"

Everybody chuckles. The new Joe makes jokes, like the old Joe.

"It just really puts it in perspective," he goes on, "because that's someone who we've all looked up to over the years. Yogi Berra called me at home on Halloween! It was really amazing!"

"Joe, you had a successful year in 2006 managing the Marlins," comes the next question. "And you voluntarily took a year off. Was there a concern to manage this year somewhere?"

"We had kind of made a commitment as a family that I was going to spend time with my father. And ultimately this is where we wanted to end up. We didn't know when it would happen, but it was a dream of ours. Was I worried? No. Because of our faith, I believe that if you're meant to manage, you're going to manage."

Our *faith*. There is that word again.

Baseball is just a game. But like religion, it has rituals. I need rituals. I need traditions. I need something to believe in, whether I worship in a church or a stadium. I believed in the Yankees and then divorced them and came all the way back to believing in them again, and what I have learned, if anything, is this: My belief—my faith—transcends individual players and is deeper than the outcome of any game, any season. It is unshakable.

"Last month hasn't been an easy one for the Yankees," says Sweeny Murti, posing the next question. "There's been a lot of upheaval."

"In every organization there is going to be change from time to time," Joe says. "That's just the nature of the business. But this is the New York Yankees.

It's not going anywhere. It's going to be here long after we're all gone. *This is the New York Yankees.*"

I sit up straighter in my chair.

I have no idea if Joe Girardi will be a great manager or even a good one. But he has me in his corner.

Epilogue
February 14, 2008

A-Rod's eyes narrow. He looks very sharp in his open-collared white shirt and dark blazer and slacks, very Master of the Universe. He is the picture of success, in fact—a man in total control of himself. And yet his mouth twitches.

"Are you worth it?" I ask again about the mammoth 10-year deal he signed with the Yankees in November. He will be paid $27.5 million per year and earn $6 million for reaching the home-run totals of Willie Mays, Babe Ruth, Hank Aaron, and Barry Bonds, plus another $6 million for breaking Bonds's record. These are not incentives; they are revenue sharing in "historic events." The deal came about after he finally had a face-to-face meeting with the Steinbrenner boys—without Scott Boras in the room. He and C-Rod persuaded Hank and Hal that his clumsy opt-out during the World Series was all a misunderstanding, that they really do love New York.

"I'm not sure," he says. "I mean, that's not my job to evaluate or appraise players. I love to play baseball."

"But if you love the game, why did you opt out of your contract on baseball's biggest night? Can you understand why so many people found that incredibly offensive?"

His mouth twitches again. We are sitting directly across from each other. I can see his every movement, even the bobbing of his Adam's apple when he swallows. "Absolutely. If I was a sportswriter, if I was a fan, I would have been very, very, very upset."

"That's a lot of *verys*."

"Well, it was very, very, very difficult. I was in my living room watching the game. I got white like a ghost."

"You got hammered by the press. A number of respected writers called you, among other things, Pay-Rod in Pinstripes. My husband, Michael, called you a big phony jerk."

"Please apologize to Michael and tell him that what happened was unacceptable. And inappropriate."

"Thank goodness Warren Buffett set you straight, billionaire to billionaire, and you ditched Boras," I say. "You did ditch him, right?"

A-Rod takes even more time answering this one, so I turn to C-Rod, who is next to him.

"Cynthia, do you think Alex has changed as a result of this?"

"He wasn't used to having to take such initiative." She is not wearing a "Fuck You" tank top. She is dressed in a chic little black sleeveless number. "He actually had to pick up the phone, make the calls, make some decisions, and stand behind them. It was a huge growing experience."

"What about your marriage, though? How did you weather the tabloid reports about an alleged extramarital affair?"

I expect the question to anger A-Rod, but he says very calmly and resolutely, "It was a challenging time. And, you know, we've learned from it. We've regrouped. We've stood up. And now I think we've become much closer because of the whole situation."

I move on to what everybody in the country is talking about: yesterday's Congressional hearings. Last month, George Mitchell released his investigation into what he termed "the steroids era" in Major League Baseball. The report named names, including those of Roger Clemens and Andy Pettitte.

"Who do you believe?" I ask. "Roger or Andy?"

"Jane, you're putting me in a tough spot. I mean, these are guys that I played with. Andy is still my teammate."

"For the record, have you ever used steroids, human growth hormone, or any other performance-enhancing substance?"

"No."

"You never felt like 'This guy's doing it. Maybe I should look into this, too? He's getting better numbers, playing better ball'?"

"I've never felt overmatched on the baseball field."

I clear my throat and look him dead in the eye. "Just one more thing before I let you go."

He wipes a bead of sweat from his glossy upper lip. "Sure."

"Are you a true Yankee?"

Another bead of sweat begins to form. His mouth does a double twitch.

"Jane! Jane! Come on. Wake up."

Someone is tugging at my arm. I open my eyes. Michael stands over me, the morning sun streaming in from the window behind him.

"Time to get up. You have a book to write."

"What?"

"You were having another Yankee dream."

I sit up and shake off my grogginess. "I got an exclusive with A-Rod."

"Don't you ever just sleep?" Michael smiles. "Do you know what today is?"

"Spring training. Pitchers and catchers report."

He wraps me in his arms. "Happy Valentine's Day."

Index

Underscored page references indicate charts.